FINANCE

Marvin E. Ray
David L. Scott
Valdosta State College

Winthrop Publishers, Inc.
Cambridge, Massachusetts

Library of Congress Cataloging in Publication Data

Ray, Marvin E
    Finance.

    Includes index.
    1.   Finance.   I.   Scott, David Logan
joint author.   II.   Title.
HG153.R38   332   78–11650
ISBN 0–87626–266–3

Cover design by Glenn Pacitto.

To Vicki, Kay, Karen, Mendi, & '57 Chevys

Contents

Preface

Finance was once defined as the art of passing money from one hand to another until it finally disappears. The accuracy of this definition will not be evaluated here; suffice it to say that finance may mean different things to different people. Some would state that finance encompasses the activities of the financial manager while others would stress the activities of the investor. The finance discipline, of course, encompasses the activities of both the financial executive and the securities analyst or portfolio manager. In addition, these individuals must be aware of the environment in which they operate. For example, they must be knowledgeable about current economic conditions, the status of the money and capital markets, Federal Reserve activities, the size of the federal deficit, and so on. In other words, financial decisions cannot be made in a vacuum. Rather, these individuals must recognize that all these factors, although beyond their control, represent a very significant input into their decision-making process. Financial vice-presidents must be aware of what the investor is looking for, while investors must be interested in the activities of the financial vice-president. In addition, both must have a knowledge of the status of the financial markets and the economy.

With these brief examples, it should be clear that the finance discipline is not made up of several segments to be considered in isolation. Rather, the functions of the various individuals (while they have their own objectives) are tied together in the web of an interrelated system. This idea is the basis upon which *Finance* is written.

Broadly speaking, our objective is to tie together the various components of finance for the reader. Academic programs in finance typically distinguish three basic areas: (1) financial markets and institutions, (2) managerial finance, and (3) investments. Recognizing the necessity of this segmentation for instructional purposes, but also recognizing the need to show how the different areas are interrelated, *Finance* consists of three basic parts. Part 1, "The Financial System and the Economy," is written to provide the reader with knowledge of the basics of financial markets and institutions. Beyond this goal, one must recognize that financial markets and institutions influence, and are influenced by, the economy in general. This relationship between the financial system and the economy represents the environment within which financial decisions are made by the financial manager and the investor. Thus, part 1 establishes the groundwork for the material to be covered in parts 2 and 3.

Part 2, "Financial Management," encompasses the basic financial decisions which, if made optimally, will lead to the attainment of the assumed objective of management to maximize the value of the firm for its owners. These basic areas, including the investment decision, the financing decision, and the dividend decision, must not be considered in isolation. Rather, as the reader covers this part of the text, he or she should view these decisions in terms of their joint impact on the value of the firm since they are interrelated. For example, as potential capital expenditures are contemplated (the investment decision), the financial manager must consider the source of funds to finance the expenditures. In addition, the manager must recognize that the financial decision influences, and is influenced by, the dividend policy decision. And all of these decisions must, of course, be made with a full appreciation of the current, and projected, status of the financial system and the economy (covered in part 1).

As the reader proceeds to part 3, "Investments," he or she should be constantly aware of the relationship among all three parts of the book. In a financing decision, the financial manager from part 2 must look at the firm as a potential creditor or owner of the firm would. The investor must view the firm from the point of view of decisions made by the financial manager since his or her objective is also related to the maximization of the value of the firm. And just as the financial manager makes decisions in light of the material from part 1, the investor must also make decisions in view of existing, and projected, conditions in the financial markets and the economy.

For readers unfamiliar with the "jargon" of finance, a glossary has been included at the end of the book. Words which appear in **boldface** type throughout the text are defined in the glossary.

It is only reasonable to expect authors to increase their level of indebtedness while writing a finance text. By accumulating a number of obligations, we have succeeded on this count. For their helpful suggestions and assistance in transforming this work from an idea to a book, we are indebted to Mike Butler of the University of North Alabama, Bob Carver of Southern Illinois University at Edwardsville, Larry Dann of the University of Oregon, and John Groth of Texas A & M University. We also express our appreciation to Frances Hattaway, Wanda Hill, Patricia Griner, and David Conine for their many hours of typing, research assistance, and general aid in helping us debug the manuscript. For whatever humor there is in this book, we would like to thank Ralph L. Woods and the McGraw-Hill Book Company for permitting us to borrow jokes from the *Modern Handbook of Humor*. Finally, but certainly not least in importance, we owe our thanks to our students who survived through the early drafts of the manuscript. All the bugs that remain are our responsibility.

1 THE FINANCIAL SYSTEM AND THE ECONOMY

1   Goals and Functioning of the Economy

*In this free-spending age, the
man who preaches economy might as well
start by saving his breath.*

Chapter 1 is the first installment in developing the environment in which the financial manager (in part 2) and the investor (in part 3) function. Specifically, the objective of this chapter is to describe our economic goals and how the economy functions to attain these goals. Although the basic theme of chapter 1 relates to the economy, certain noneconomic variables that are always lurking in the background have the potential for disturbing historical economic relationships. In addition, change is characteristic of the economy. In other words, while all the pieces may seem to fit together in an orderly fashion as they are presented in part 1, the economy cannot be approached in a cookbook manner. The financial manager and the investor must always examine economic conditions very carefully and keep in mind that history does not necessarily repeat itself.

GOALS OF THE ECONOMY

When one examines the goals of the economy, various questions may be raised. For example, what are these economic goals? What are the goals of the United States from a political point of view? Are these goals the same? If they are not the same, are they compatible with each other? Some would say the goal of the economy is to maximize real gross national product (GNP) per capita. To derive this figure, we take GNP (the total dollar amount of goods and services produced in the economy), adjust it for inflation (from GNP to real GNP), and divide this figure by the total population. The result is presumably a measure of the true living standard of the United States citizen. Others say this is a purely economic goal that relates only to the quantity of goods and services. They argue that this goal does not consider the quality of life. Arguments such as this are potentially significant to the financial manager as well as to the investor.

The typical economist, if asked about the goals of the economy, would refer to the Employment Act of 1946, a landmark in American socioeconomic legislation. This legislation and subsequent developments committed the federal government to pursue policies that directly promote the familiar economic goals of full employment, price stability, economic growth, and an acceptable balance-of-payments position.

Full Employment

A common, although perhaps narrow, definition of full employment is that everyone who is qualified for a particular job and willing to work (accept the job at the going wage rate) can find a job within a reasonable period of time. Given these conditions, if all except approximately 4% of the civilian labor force have a job, we generally conclude that we have attained the goal of full employment. The 4% figure, typically called **frictional unemployment**, represents a short-run situation in which people are either changing jobs or are seeking new ones.

While frictional unemployment (the first 4%) is considered unavoidable, anything above 4% is ordinarily related to **cyclical unemployment.** Unlike frictional unemployment, which is caused by movement on the supply side of the labor force, cyclical unemployment results from problems on the demand side. Specifically, this type of unemployment occurs when the economy is experiencing a recession and the total demand for goods and services declines. The drop in demand for labor occurs when the business firm reacts to a drop in sales by curtailing production, thus leading to an increase in unemployment. Cyclical unemployment is involuntary (the worker has no choice), whereas frictional unemployment is voluntary.

Another type of unemployment, **structural unemployment,** is long-run. Like the cyclical type, it exists due to the lack of demand for labor, but the lack of demand exists for different reasons. This type of unemployment may result from changes in technology (which decrease the demand for a particular type of labor) and changes in the demand for a particular product in a particular region. If labor is unwilling or unable to move to a new industry or a different region of the country, unemployment results.

When we talk about full employment, we typically talk in terms of the status of the labor force. But full employment in its full context should include all the factors of production including land, labor, and capital. In other words, while we want payments to labor to be maximized (in the form of wages), we also want to fully employ our other resources (land and capital) so that payments for their use are maximized (in the form of rent and interest). If we are not fully utilizing all our resources, then we are operating (as an economy) at less than our capacity.

Price Stability

If economic problems were ranked by degree of significance, inflation would be at the top of the list along with unemployment. **Inflation** is a general increase in the level of prices. Although the price of some goods (pork and beans) could be falling, the price of other goods (Cadillac Sevilles) might be increasing so that, on average, the price increases dominate any price declines and thus raise the general level of prices.

The consumer price index (CPI), probably the best-known measure of inflation, is compiled by calculating the cost of a typical market basket of goods and services purchased by urban wage earners and clerical workers, who constitute approximately half the population of the United States. (In early 1978 the CPI was revised, and a new index called the urban consumers index was created. The new index surveys data from all urban consumers, who constitute about 80% of the population.) The cost of this market basket of goods and services is then converted into a price index. For example, assume the cost of our market basket is $13,500 in 1976 and the same goods cost $15,000 in 1977 and $16,500 in 1978. If 1976 is used as the base year, the CPI is set at 100 for that year. The index for 1977 would then be 111. This figure is calculated by dividing the cost of the market basket for 1977 by the cost of the same goods in 1976, then multiplying by 100 to move the decimal two digits to the right. To construct the index for 1978, the same procedure is followed.

$$\frac{\text{Market basket cost (1978)}}{\text{Market basket cost (1976)}} \times 100 \quad \text{or} \quad \frac{\$16,500}{\$13,500} \times 100 = 122$$

Caution should be used in deciding which measure of inflation to utilize. For example, an individual using the CPI should understand that it is designed around the spending patterns of an urban wage earner. For business, a more appropriate measure might be the wholesale price index which includes hundreds of commodities from textiles to transportation equipment. Although lesser-known than either of these first two measures, the implicit GNP deflator is the most accurate indicator of general price movements because it incorporates all goods and services included in the GNP. The implicit GNP deflator, published in the monthly government

TABLE 1-1   Wholesale and Consumer Price Indexes and GNP
Implicit Price Deflator, 1957–1977 (1967 = 100)

Year	Wholesale Price Index	Consumer Price Index	GNP Implicit Price Deflator
1957	93.3	84.3	82.9
1958	94.6	86.6	85.0
1959	94.8	87.3	86.5
1960	94.9	88.7	87.8
1961	94.5	89.6	89.0
1962	94.8	90.6	90.0
1963	94.5	91.7	91.1
1964	94.7	92.9	92.6
1965	96.6	94.5	94.3
1966	99.8	97.2	96.9
1967	100.0	100.0	100.0
1968	102.5	104.2	104.5
1969	106.5	109.8	109.7
1970	110.4	116.3	115.6
1971	114.0	121.3	121.5
1972	119.1	125.3	126.7
1973	134.7	133.1	130.1
1974	160.1	147.7	146.8
1975	174.9	161.2	161.0
1976	183.0	170.5	169.4
1977	192.2	181.5	178.8

Source: *Economic Indicators, Federal Reserve Bulletin.*

publication *Economic Indicators,* is used to convert GNP to real GNP. Table 1-1 shows consumer and wholesale price movements (and for prices in general as measured by the GNP deflator) from 1957 to 1977. The figures in table 1-1 indicate that it took more than twice as many dollars to buy the same goods in 1977 as it did in 1957. Alternatively, today a dollar buys less than half as much as it did 20 years ago.

Unemployment directly affects those who are out of work and indirectly affects the entire economy. Inflation, on the other hand, affects almost all elements of society directly. When inflation exists, the consumers' purchasing power (real income) declines unless incomes increase as fast or faster than prices. Unions attempt to protect their members by bargaining for wages that increase their real income. If business cannot raise the price of its final product to offset the increase in costs (wages, new materials, equipment), profits decline. Government officials become concerned for domestic reasons as well as for our trading relationship with other nations. For example, if our prices are high relative to those in other countries, foreigners who would have purchased goods from the United States will purchase the same goods from other countries at relatively lower prices. Once inflation begins, we may get into a seemingly never-ending spiral. Since inflation affects so many people, price stability is at the top of the list of economic goals.

Economic Growth

The third goal, **economic growth**, is often defined in two ways. In its most basic form, the first definition is associated with expansion of the nation's output. However, greater output occurs both because our capacity to produce increases and because we utilize this capacity. Thus we derive our second definition of economic growth—an increase in our capacity to produce.

By the first definition of economic growth, our objective is to maximize real GNP per capita. Thus we utilize the implicit GNP deflator to convert GNP in current (today's) dollars to real GNP (GNP in constant dollars) in order to adjust for changes in the general price level. The final step, converting real GNP to a per capita basis, is taken because we are interested in the level of output produced per person over time. If the population is growing at a faster rate than real GNP, the relative welfare of each citizen declines.

This definition is a good first approximation. However, the following example demonstrates why it may be inadequate. If the economy is recovering from a recession (during which we had idle resources), we could increase real output per capita merely by utilizing more fully the capacity available before the recession. Given these conditions, most economists who support the second definition would conclude that economic growth has not occurred. In fact, it is possible (although perhaps less likely) that as we move into a recession, our capacity to produce could be increasing while our actual level of output is declining. Given these conditions, economists using the second definition would say that we have experienced some economic growth. Even though the two definitions appear incompatible, the differences between them lose much of their significance when we view economic growth as a long-run phenomenon. Over the short-run, changes in output merely reflect fluctuations in the utilization of our capacity to produce. In the long-run the growth in capacity is the dominant goal because it establishes the limit to which output can be increased.

Balance of Payments

The **balance of payments**, expressed as a goal of economic policy, was not explicitly included in the Employment Act of 1946. However, balance-of-payments problems of the late 1950s clearly demonstrated that economic policy in the United States could not be made without considering our relationship with the rest of the world. The attainment of an acceptable balance-of-payments position was first included as an economic goal in the president's 1960 economic report.

A distinction should be made between the balance of payments and the **balance of trade**. The balance of trade, which is only part (although the largest component) of the balance of payments, relates to the value of merchandise exports to and imports from all other countries. A favorable balance exists when our exports of goods and services exceed imports coming into the country (unfavorable when imports exceed exports). The balance of payments, in addition to the flow of goods and services, includes gifts, foreign aid, loans, gold, and international reserves coming in and going out of the country. To understand why trade occurs between nations (with payments returning across national borders in exchange for the goods), one might first ask why individuals specialize in what they produce. The answer is related to what economists call the theory of comparative advantage. We specialize because we are more productive in our specialty than the next person. Because we are more productive, we can sell the product at a lower price. Another person specializes for the same reason. Since each individual wants to consume both products, each can benefit from the lower prices. Trade among nations exists for the same reasons. Different nations, or regions, have a comparative advantage because they have different endowments of natural resources, population, capital, and so forth. As these nations combine their resources and produce with greater efficiency (and thus are able to sell their goods at a lower price), the basis for trade among nations is established.

This explanation of the basis for trade among nations can be utilized in explaining why the United States has experienced a chronic deficit in the balance of payments. One reason has been the inflation record in the United States. In particular, the post-1965 escalation in Vietnam resulted in inflation that created problems with our balance of trade. If the prices of our goods rise relative to the same goods produced by another country, foreigners as well as our own citizens will buy these goods from the other country, thus causing a deficit in the balance of trade for the United States. A second factor was our foreign aid and military programs. Such programs represent either a direct flow of funds out of the United States or a flow of goods out of this country with no payment in return. The result is a net outflow of capital. Another important factor was the rapid growth of productivity in Western Europe and Japan relative to the United States. Since advances in productivity enable the producing countries to turn out goods at relatively lower prices, the net result is a flow of goods out of and a flow of funds into that country.

The capital outflow problem was complicated by the flow of funds from the United States to other countries in the form of investment by

American corporations. These companies were reacting to the productivity advances abroad and, therefore, the opportunity to make profits in those countries. Other factors contributing to the balance-of-payments problem included the lack of trust in the dollar (and therefore an outflow of gold), discrimination against goods produced in the United States, and an escalation in the price of oil from oil-producing and exporting countries (OPEC). All these factors contributed to our chronic balance-of-payments deficit and further reinforced the decision to include the attainment of an acceptable balance-of-payments position among our economic goals.

Maintaining an appropriate balance-of-payments position (that is, avoiding a chronic deficit or surplus) is essential to uninterrupted trade with other countries, worldwide economic stability, and the attainment of the first three goals—full employment, price stability, and economic growth. For example, chronic deficits reduce a country's monetary reserves as capital flows out. In addition, the shift of foreigners away from consuming our goods (in favor of the same goods produced by other countries) puts recessionary pressures on the domestic economy. As this occurs, the natural reaction is to limit imports. The net result is a breakdown in trade among nations.

Attaining the Goals: Compatibility or Conflict?

The best of all worlds, in terms of our economic objectives, would be a stabilized economy—that is, an economy that is neither in a recession nor expanding too rapidly. Along with this stability, the best of all worlds would include simultaneously attaining full employment, price stability, economic growth, and an acceptable balance-of-payments position. The problem is that the best of all worlds does not exist. Although some of the goals are compatible, others may conflict with each other.

Consider the relationship between economic growth and full employment. If we define growth as greater output combined with an expansion of capacity and the full utilization of that capacity, we must have full employment to achieve economic growth. That is, if our capacity to produce has increased but we are not fully employing our resources to take advantage of that capacity, then the economy is not growing. On the other hand, if the economy is growing too rapidly, inflation may lead to a recession that would mean giving up the attainment of economic growth and full employment. Thus we need price stability to aid in our efforts to achieve economic growth.

The relationship between full employment and price stability has historically been one of conflict. That is, as economic policy was adjusted to promote expansion of the economy and reduce unemployment, prices and wages rose, and we had to give up the goal of price stability. Conversely, economists have historically thought that if price stability is to be achieved, growth in the economy must be constrained. But if the economy is constrained, unemployment may increase. Thus a trade-off may exist between the goals of full employment and price stability. In the 1970s a new relationship between full employment and price stability emerged. Because of an increase in costs (OPEC oil prices, union contracts for wages), producers raised prices. With this cost-push inflation, despite a downturn in the economy, we reached a dilemma with no apparent solution—stagflation. In other words, we experienced inflation and unemployment at the same time.

Unless we achieve our domestic goals of full employment, price stability, and economic growth, we are going to have difficulty with our balance of payments. To be competitive with other countries, we must have competitive prices. To have competitive prices, we must have advances in productivity. And to increase productivity, we must have economic growth that includes the full employment of an expanding capacity to produce. Thus, to attain our fourth objective, we must make progress in achieving the first three.

New (Noneconomic) Goals with an Economic Impact

In addition to these conventional economic goals, society has other goals that are expressed through governmental activities and regulations. Although such goals may appear noneconomic, they have economic impacts.

The economist Kenneth Boulding once wrote that one of the basic problems in our economy is "suboptimizing," or finding the best way to do something that should not be done at all. Thus economic growth has been questioned as a true indicator of well-being. In other words, if we accept Boulding's position, we could say the conventional economic goals of full employment, price stability, economic growth, and an acceptable balance of payments are not adequate; we also need to include the goal of improving the quality of life. If the establishment of the Environmental Protection Agency and existing environmental legislation is any indication of an emphasis on quality of life, it appears that we have in fact accepted this new goal. This new goal may require that firms divert funds from the purchase of ordinary plant and equipment to the purchase of pollution abatement equipment. Pollution abatement equipment, unlike ordinary machinery, produces nothing that we can sell. Thus we have an outflow of funds for the equipment but no inflow of funds in the form of revenue. The net result is generally a downward pressure on the profitability of the firm.

Other examples of noneconomic legislation with an economic impact include OSHA (Occupational Safety and Health Administration) and ERISA (Employee Retirement Income Security Act of 1974). OSHA was created to establish and enforce industrial safety rules. As with environmental legislation, OSHA in many cases requires significant expenditures by firms to comply with the new safety standards and hence exerts downward pressure on their profits. ERISA was established in 1974 to ensure that workers covered by private pension plans receive benefits when they retire. Like the first two examples, this program results in increased costs (administrative costs) with no increase in revenues.

This is not intended to be an exhaustive list of all programs in this category; such a list is beyond the scope of this text. However, as financial managers and investors we must remember that all the goals (economic as well as noneconomic) contribute to the environment in which we operate.

HOW THE ECONOMIC SYSTEM WORKS
TO ATTAIN THE GOALS

Our third economic goal, economic growth, is defined in its most basic form in terms of the expansion of **gross national product**. GNP, or total output in the economy, may be viewed in two ways. The first is in terms of expenditures for final output (the total quantity of goods and services demanded during a given period of time). This demand is typically segmented into four categories: consumer expenditures, investment expenditures by the business sector, government spending, and net spending for our exports by foreigners (exports minus imports). The second way to look at total output is to take the same aggregate figure and view it as income received in the form of wages, rent, interest, and profits. Before considering both approaches in more detail, consider this book as an example. In terms of the expenditure approach to GNP, sales of this text could be expected to be divided between acquisitions by university libraries and purchases by students for use as a text in finance courses. Additions to the holdings of state university libraries would be classified as government expenditures, while purchases by students would be classified as personal consumption expenditures. On the other hand, we could examine the book in terms of how income is distributed. Specifically, income generated from sales of the book is allocated to wages (royalties to the authors, payments for labor in the production of the book, and so on), rent (compensation paid for property resources), interest (payments by the publisher to suppliers of money for funds used to support this project), and profit (to the publisher). Since the two quantities are equal using either approach, we have simply found two ways of looking at the same thing.

The Expenditure Approach to GNP

The four categories of expenditures for final output are consumption, investment, government spending, and net exports. Consumption expenditures include expenditures by households for durable consumer items (autos, furniture), nondurable consumer goods (bread, toothpaste), and services (expenditures for haircuts, auto repairs). These expenditures are determined by disposable income, that is, income after taxes. Thus, if disposable income increases, either because of an increase in wages or a decrease in taxes, a proportion of the increase in income will be allocated to the purchase of more goods and services. The part of the increase in income that we do not spend will be saved.

The second type of expenditure for final output, investment, refers to spending for capital goods by businesses. Examples of these expenditures include construction spending, final purchases of machinery and equipment, and any changes in the level of inventories. Investment by business is partially a function of the rate of interest. As interest rates decline, investment increases; and as interest rates rise, the level of investment should decline. Consider a firm that is contemplating the purchase of a piece of equipment costing $3 million. If the rate of return on this project is 8% and the firm's cost of money is 10%, the firm will not buy this equipment because the cost of money, which must be raised to finance the investment, exceeds the rate of return on the equipment. However, if the cost of funds falls to 7%, the investment will be made. (The cost of money is not just the interest rate. This point will be clarified in chapter 9.) If this same case is extended to include all firms in the economy, it follows that the level of investment has an inverse relationship with the cost of money.

Government expenditures include all government spending—federal, state, and local levels—for goods and services. This category includes all government payrolls plus all goods purchased from the business sector. Although we can functionally relate consumption expenditures to disposable income and the level of investment to the cost of money, government spending is not so simple. Rather, federal spending is part of fiscal policy used as a tool to stabilize the economy and assist in attaining our economic goals.

So far our discussion of the expenditure approach to GNP has been confined to the domestic economy. It has been made up of consumption expenditures (C), investment (I), and government spending (G). Thus GNP equals $C + I + G$. At this point we might ask what impact exports and imports have on this equation. The purchase of goods (made in the United States) by foreigners has the same impact as the purchase of goods by Americans (GNP increases as C increases). Thus we would add exports (X) to the right-hand side of the equation $(GNP = C + I + G + X)$.

Conversely, purchases of oil from Saudi Arabia are classified as an import into the United States and stimulate the Saudi economy. Thus we would subtract imports (M) from the right-hand side of the equation so that $X - M$ represents net exports. Our final equation for gross national product becomes

$$GNP = C + I + G + (X - M) \qquad \qquad 1\text{-}1$$

The impact of our trade with other nations, in terms of the impact on GNP, depends on whether exports exceed imports or vice versa. If exports exceed imports (net exports are positive), GNP in the United States increases; if net exports are negative, GNP declines. With the addition of foreign trade to the equation, we have created a comprehensive system— one that includes all possible types of expenditures.

The Income Approach to GNP

The alternate view of GNP is to identify income received in the form of wages, rent, interest, and profits. In other words, in examining the income approach to GNP we are identifying how GNP is distributed or allocated as income. We might also ask why resources such as land, labor, capital, and entrepreneurial ability are available in the market and in what manner income is allocated to them. The answer is related to the price system. We often hear that "everything has a price." For example, in a free market the price of labor (the wage rate) fluctuates as the supply of and the demand for particular types of labor fluctuate. Thus, if a shortage of medical doctors exists, the wages paid to doctors increase. As the average income approaches $80,000, applications to medical schools should increase. Unless some group organizes to hold admissions to a given level, the supply of MDs will eventually increase and wages will fall. Likewise, if too many MDs are located in urban areas and too few in small towns, the price system operates to increase the mobility of medical doctors. Thus the price system sends out signals to all segments of the economy—including land, labor, capital, and entrepreneurial talent.

Knowledge of both the income and the expenditure approaches to GNP is necessary in understanding how the economy functions. In addition, if we understand the price system, we can see how prices send signals through the economic system and how resources can be expected to react to these signals.

We can now examine the role of government in the attainment of economic goals. Although controversy surrounds this issue, current economic policy is based on the directive embodied in the Employment Act of 1946 that the government shall promote the country's economic goals.

To carry out this directive, the government utilizes monetary and fiscal policy.

Monetary Policy

The Federal Reserve System (the Fed) is the central bank, often called the bankers' bank. Started in 1913 as a result of the Federal Reserve Act, the Fed is divided into 12 districts with headquarters in Atlanta, Boston, Chicago, Cleveland, Dallas, Kansas City, Minneapolis, New York (main headquarters), Philadelphia, Richmond, San Francisco, and St. Louis, with each having its own Federal Reserve bank. Each Federal Reserve bank is a corporation owned by the commercial banks in that region that are members of the Federal Reserve System. Although each Federal Reserve bank is owned by the member banks, the Federal Reserve is a public agency and does not exist to make a profit. The Federal Reserve System is coordinated by the Federal Reserve Board, which is a seven-member team located in Washington, D.C. Being a central bank, the Fed's primary function is to control the economy's supply of money and credit. The Fed in general alters the supply of money to counteract undesirable economic trends. If unemployment is rising and the economy is showing signs of a recession, for example, the Fed will attempt to stimulate the economy. If, on the other hand, the economy is overheating and inflation is becoming a problem, the Fed will attempt to slow the economy. The Federal Reserve has three primary tools for controlling the supply of money and credit: open-market operations, discount-rate policy, and control over member-bank reserve requirements.

Open-market operations entail the purchase and sale of government securities (Treasury bills, notes, and bonds) by the Fed in the open market to influence the size of member-bank reserves and therefore the supply of money. Each commercial bank that is a member of the Federal Reserve System must maintain a legal reserve deposit in the Federal Reserve Bank in its district. This reserve, called the reserve ratio, is an amount of cash equal to a specific percentage of its deposit liabilities. Although the original function of the reserve requirement was to make deposits safe and liquid, the primary function today is to enable the Fed to control the amount of demand deposits (checking accounts) that the member banks can create. Safety of deposits is the responsibility of the Federal Deposit Insurance Corporation (FDIC) which insures depositors up to $40,000 should a bank fail. Not all banks or savings and loans are insured by the FDIC or Federal Savings and Loan Insurance Corporation (FSLIC). Not long ago a large savings and loan bank in Norfolk encountered problems. Many depositors were shocked to learn that their deposits were not insured. To understand how open-market operations and reserve requirements work, one must understand the link between reserves and the supply of money. As a result of the legal reserve system, the banking system can create about $5 of bank deposits for each new dollar of reserves injected into the system by the Fed. For example, assume the reserve requirement is 20% and that $1 million in new reserves has come into the system as a result of the Federal Reserve's purchase of government securities. Thus the Fed (using open-market operations) has purchased $1 million in government securities from an individual. This individual deposits the $1 million in his checking account at bank 1. Bank 1 puts $200,000 (20%) in its legal reserve account since its deposits have increased by $1 million; bank 1 is now in a position to lend $800,000. After the loans are made, the funds eventually find their way into other banks through deposits and expenditures by borrowers at bank 1. Now assume the entire $800,000 is deposited in bank 2, which earmarks 20% ($160,000) to its reserve account and lends $640,000. The same process continues throughout the system until the money supply (new demand deposits via the loans) has increased by approximately $5 million. Although we have oversimplified the process, this example shows that a single bank in the system cannot create money although the banking system as a whole can create money because of the reserve system.

To determine the relationship between the reserve requirement and the money supply, simply find the reciprocal of the reserve requirement. That is, if the reserve requirement is 25%, the money supply increases (or decreases) by four times the change in reserves. If the Federal Reserve buys government securities, reserves increase by that amount and the money supply increases by an amount equal to the change in reserves times the reciprocal of the reserve ratio. To the contrary, if the Fed wants to decrease the supply of money, it sells government securities, thus decreasing reserves and, therefore, the supply of money. Government securities are bought and sold daily. This flexibility and the immediate impact of such purchases and sales on member-bank reserves makes open-market operations the most important of the Fed's three tools for controlling the supply of money.

The second tool of the Federal Reserve is its discount-rate policy. The Fed makes loans to the member banks (called discounts) and the rate charged on such loans is called the discount rate. The discount rate indicates whether the Fed is pursuing a tight or an easy monetary policy. For example, if the Fed is attempting to slow down the economy, it might sell government securities (using open-market operations) thereby reducing member-bank reserves and the supply of money. With fewer reserves, a bank is naturally inclined to borrow from the Fed. Realizing this, the Fed might be expected to raise the discount rate to discourage such borrowing. To stimulate the economy, the Fed reverses this process.

The final tool, changes in reserve requirements of member banks, is powerful but infrequently used. If the Fed increases the reserve ratio from

20% to 25% (and banks have no reserves in excess of the 20%), member banks have to borrow funds or restrict their loans and investments to meet the new requirement. If the Federal Reserve increases the discount rate at the same time to discourage borrowing from the Fed, the banks' only alternative is to restrict loans and liquidate their investments. A change in reserve requirements is thus very powerful and has an immediate impact on reserves. However, there is no reason to use it frequently because open-market operations can be used daily to achieve the same objective.

As financial managers and investors, we should be familiar with the three tools used by the federal government, but of greater importance is the process by which a change in the supply of money influences GNP. To illustrate this process, assume the Federal Reserve has concluded that the economy is entering a recession and that in its effort to counteract this trend it has decided to increase the supply of money. The initial step is for the open-market committee (which determines open-market policy) in its monthly meeting to direct the manager of the System Open Market Account (who is in charge of buying and selling government securities for the Fed) to buy government securities. As government securities are purchased in the open market, the supply of money increases and downward pressure is exerted on interest rates. As interest rates decline, it becomes more profitable for the business sector to take on more investment projects. The increase in investment (I) in the right-hand side of eq. 1–1 results in an increase in GNP. To summarize, the increase in money (m) reduces interest rates (i) which stimulates I and results in an increase in GNP, or

$$\uparrow m \rightarrow \downarrow i \rightarrow \uparrow I \rightarrow \uparrow \text{GNP} \qquad\qquad 1\text{–}2$$

Conversely, if the Federal Reserve concludes that the economy needs to be slowed, it either sells securities or increases reserve requirements in order to decrease the supply of money. As the supply of money declines, interest rates rise, the level of investment drops, and GNP declines. Thus the process is the same as in eq. 1–2, but in reverse.

$$\downarrow m \rightarrow \uparrow i \rightarrow \downarrow I \rightarrow \downarrow \text{GNP} \qquad\qquad 1\text{–}3$$

Fiscal Policy

Although the government has monetary policy at its disposal to carry out the directives of the 1946 Employment Act, it also has fiscal policy to help achieve the same objectives. **Fiscal policy** refers broadly to budgetary policy dealing with government expenditures and taxes. More specifically, we can distinguish between built-in stabilizers and discretionary fiscal policy. Although it may appear that fiscal policy, like monetary policy, entails periodic meetings by fiscal authorities to raise taxes or lower government spending, this is not completely accurate. Part of fiscal policy is structured to react automatically to changes in economic conditions. The objective of these changes, just as with monetary policy, is to lean against the prevailing winds. These built-in stabilizers include automatic changes in income taxes as well as transfers and subsidies. For example, as the economy expands, individual income increases. Since individual income tax rates are progressive, a larger percentage of personal income is collected by the government. These larger collections slow the rate of expansion. Conversely, if the economy moves into a recession, tax collections fall faster than income, thus cushioning the downturn. Like taxes, transfers and subsidies also cushion fluctuations in the economy. Transfers are government payments for which there is no direct return of goods or services. For example, during a downturn, government payments are made to individuals who are out of work, through unemployment compensation (for which no work is done). At the same time, if prices of agricultural products are falling, price-support subsidies to agriculture increase. On the other hand, payments for unemployment compensation, welfare, and subsidies decline during periods of prosperity. Although the built-in stabilizers are designed to stabilize the economy without any formal directive from the fiscal authorities, their only purpose is to cushion swings in economic activity, not to completely turn the economy around. Discretionary fiscal policy is designed to take over where built-in stabilizers become inoperative.

Discretionary fiscal policy entails the direct manipulation of government spending, transfer payments, and taxes in an attempt to attain our economic goals. The effects of discretionary fiscal policy are perhaps best understood by recalling from eq. 1-1 that $GNP = C + I + G + (X - M)$. An increase (decrease) in any of the components on the right-hand side of the equation stimulates (depresses) GNP. If the federal government initiates a new program that increases its spending (by an increase in G) for anything from Boeing 707s to paper clips, the private sector must gear up to produce those goods and GNP increases. If, on the other hand, a new program obligates the government to increase transfer payments, GNP increases but not as much as with an increase in G. Transfer payments, such as welfare payments, result in an increase in disposable income for those people receiving the payments; part of the increase is spent and part is saved. As the portion spent on consumption (C) increases, goods must be produced to satisfy this demand, and GNP (the total output of goods and services) increases. However, if the same money had been used to buy goods for use by the government, the production of those goods would have been added to the GNP (with transfer payments the initial production of goods does not occur). Thus transfer payments stimulate GNP, but the effect is not as strong as it is when the government increases its spending and receives goods in return.

Another tool of discretionary fiscal policy is the manipulation of taxes. During a recession, the increase in unemployment leads to a decline in disposable income. As disposable income declines, consumption spending declines, investment drops, and GNP falls. To offset this, the President could put together a program that would lower personal income taxes or increase the investment tax credit for the business sector. Lowering personal income taxes has the same impact as increasing transfer payments; that is, lowering taxes increases disposable income, thus stimulating consumer expenditures for goods and services (C) and causing GNP to increase. As a result of the increase in the investment tax credit, projects that were previously passed over because of the state of the economy become worthwhile ventures. Thus investment (I in our equation) increases and further stimulates GNP.

Monetary and fiscal policy share the common goals that have resulted from the Employment Act. The only apparent difference between the two approaches is that monetary policy operates by changing the money supply while fiscal policy influences the economy by initiating changes in government spending and/or taxes. But monetary and fiscal policies do not always move in the same direction, and which policy should be used has been debated for some time.

Monetary Versus Fiscal Policy

Since monetary and fiscal policies have the same objectives, it seems logical for the authorities in charge of each to coordinate their roles. But what seems logical does not always occur. One problem is that the two policies are not controlled by a single agency or governmental unit. Fiscal policy is initiated and carried out by the executive and legislative branches of government, while monetary policy is under the control of the independent Federal Reserve Board. Another factor that has a potential for putting the two policies at odds is the difference in their flexibility. Authorities of both monetary and fiscal policy must first recognize the problem, determine the appropriate action, take that action, and then wait for the economy to react. The difference emerges in the rapidity with which all this occurs. Monetary policy, particularly open-market operations, can react immediately to influence the supply of money. Once that move is made, most economists agree that the economy then reacts quickly. In the case of fiscal policy, however, once the problem in the economy is recognized, the process slows down. Although built-in stabilizers automatically go to work, it is up to Congress to pass discretionary fiscal policy, and that can consume large amounts of time. In addition, the economy reacts more slowly to changes in government spending or taxes than to actions taken by the Fed.

Monetary and fiscal policies also seem to be working at odds in what is known as the crowding-out concept. If the economy is operating fairly close to full employment but the federal government still feels that some stimulus is needed, government spending might be increased. If this increase in spending is not offset by an equal increase in tax revenues, a deficit in the budget will exist. With a deficit, the government must sell government securities in order to finance the high level of expenditures. However, if the supply of money remains constant, the greater demand by the government for funds will drive up the rate of interest and cause investment by the business sector to decline. The government borrowing thus crowds out private expenditures. To avoid this situation, the Fed could increase the money supply to keep interest rates low (such an action is called monetizing the debt). Thus government spending is increased to stimulate GNP, but without cooperation from the Fed, the result could be a decline in private investment and a smaller-than-expected change in GNP.

Although we may have a knowledge of our economic goals and how the economy functions, our job is not finished. As financial managers and investors, we must recognize that noneconomic goals might conflict with economic goals or that monetary policy might be operating at odds with fiscal policy. Monetary and fiscal authorities might not recognize the problem, or if they do, they may overreact or underreact. Our job is to remain flexible enough to react to all these possibilities.

SUMMARY

As a result of the Employment Act of 1946 and subsequent developments, the economic goals that have been established in the United States include full employment, price stability, economic growth, and an acceptable balance-of-payments position. The simultaneous attainment of all the goals is our objective, but not all the goals are compatible. In addition, new, noneconomic goals may have an economic impact. The objective of this chapter has been to describe these goals, how the economic system works, and how monetary and fiscal policies are used to attain the goals.

QUESTIONS

1. Describe the economic goals of the United States.
2. Discuss the difference between cyclical, frictional, and structural unemployment.
3. How does inflation affect practically all elements of society?

4. Why has the United States experienced a chronic deficit in the balance of payments?

5. Explain the trade-off between the goals of full employment and price stability.

6. How does the existing environmental legislation result in a downward pressure on the profitability of the firm?

7. What do expenditures of consumption, investment, government spending, and net exports include?

8. Discuss how each of the Federal Reserve's three tools may be used to influence the economy.

9. What is the result of an increase in the supply of money?

10. Explain the difference between fiscal policy and monetary policy.

11. How may manipulation of government spending and taxes stimulate the economy?

12. Since monetary and fiscal policies seem to have the same objectives, why don't the authorities always work together to achieve their goals?

SELECTED REFERENCES

BOULDING, KENNETH E. "Fundamental Games with the Gross National Product—The Role of Misleading Indicators in Social Policy." In *The Environmental Crisis*, edited by Harold W. Helfrich. New Haven, Conn.: Yale University Press, 1970.

"Government Intervention." *Business Week* (April 4, 1977), pp. 42–95.

HENNING, CHARLES N.; PIGOTT, WILLIAM; and SCOTT, ROBERT HANEY. *Financial Markets and the Economy.* Englewood Cliffs, N.J.: Prentice-Hall, 1975; part 5.

McCONNELL, CAMPBELL R. *Economics: Principles, Problems and Policies.* 6th ed. New York: McGraw-Hill, 1975; parts 2–4.

MUSGRAVE, RICHARD A., and MUSGRAVE, PEGGY B. *Public Finance in Theory and Practice.* 2nd ed. New York: McGraw-Hill, 1976; ch. 1.

SLESINGER, REUBEN E., ed. *National Economic Policy: The Presidential Reports.* Princeton, N.J.: D. Van Nostrand, 1968.

RAY, MARVIN E. *The Environmental Crisis and Corporate Debt Policy.* Lexington, Mass.: D. C. Heath and Company, 1974; chs. 2, 3.

SAMUELSON, PAUL A. *Economics.* 10th ed. New York: McGraw-Hill, 1976; parts 2, 3.

SCOTT, DAVID L. *Pollution in the Electric Power Industry,* Lexington, Mass.: D. C. Heath and Company, 1973; part 2.

SHAPIRO, EDWARD. *Macroeconomic Analysis.* 3rd ed. New York: Harcourt Brace Jovanovich, 1974; parts 1, 2.

2 Saving, Investment, and the Role of Financial Intermediaries

An old banker in a small pioneer Western town was being interviewed. He was asked, "How did you get started in banking?" "It was simple. I put out a sign reading BANK. A man came in and gave me $100. Another man came in and deposited $200. By this time my confidence was such that I put in $50 of my own money."

With an introduction to our economic goals and how the economy functions to attain the goals, we proceed now to further our understanding of the financial system and the economy. In chapter 1 we discussed the income and expenditure approaches to GNP. In this chapter we extend these approaches to explicitly include a concept that is critical to a clear understanding of the financial system and the economy—the relationship between saving and investment. In a developed nation, one group saves while another undertakes investment. With these two economic processes originating with different groups, the stage is set for a third group to bring the first two together—financial intermediaries.

SAVING AND INVESTMENT, EX ANTE AND EX POST

Caution must be exercised when using the terminology associated with saving and investment. For example, a distinction must be made between stocks and flows. To facilitate our understanding of this distinction, consider a reservoir. Rainfall causes flows into the reservoir, and the use of water for irrigation purposes along with evaporation and water lost over the spillway causes flows out of the reservoir. While additions to and subtractions from the lake represent flows, the water level in the reservoir at any point in time represents the stock of water available for irrigation. If we want to increase the lake's stock of water in order to provide for additional irrigation requirements, we must reduce the consumption of water now or else pray for rain. Like the reservoir, our economy can be viewed (in terms of the total amount of capital goods existing at a point in time) as a stock, with investment and depreciation representing flows that change the size of the stock of capital goods.

It should be noted that the stock does not increase just because the business sector invests in plant and equipment. If investment occurs at a rate that merely replaces worn-out equipment, the total stock of capital goods remains unchanged. To determine whether any change has occurred in our stock of capital goods, we must take gross investment and subtract allowances for capital consumption and depreciation. The result is **net investment**, or net additions (if the flow is positive) to our stock of capital goods. If depreciation exceeds gross investment, net investment is negative and the stock of capital goods actually declines.

A distinction should also be made between real and financial investment. One common conception of investment is associated with the purchase of stocks and bonds. This type of transaction is properly called financial investment. Real investment, on the other hand, refers to the acquisition of capital goods (such as new equipment and machinery) by the business sector. The distinction is important because only real investment can result in net additions to our stock of capital goods.

Saving is a residual, or the part of income the individual does not spend for consumption. Considered in a broader context, saving for the economy is the part of output that is not consumed and hence added to the stock of wealth. Just as additions to the water level increase the capacity of the reservoir to provide water for irrigation purposes, additions to the stock of wealth through more saving should increase the capacity to produce more goods in the future. In other words, the act of saving releases productive resources from the production of consumer goods, while the act of real investment represents the use of these resources to produce capital goods. Under these conditions, saving can be considered identical to real investment, but an additional complication must be introduced.

Saving and investment decisions are made by different groups; saving decisions are made primarily by individuals, while investment decisions take place in the business sector. Since savers and investors are different groups and are motivated by different factors, we would not expect saving and investment to be equal. But how can saving and investment be equal and unequal at the same time? This apparent contradiction can be resolved when we distinguish between planned or intended (**ex ante**) and actual (**ex post**) saving and investment. While ex ante saving and investment are not necessarily equal, ex post or actual saving and investment must be equal because the actual level of saving and investment includes both intended and unintended saving and investment. This relationship is perhaps best understood by considering investment in inventories.

Take the case of a business that predicts sales for the coming year and on the basis of these predictions determines the required level of inventory. Expenditures for these inventories represent a portion of the business's intended investment. At the same time, consumers are making decisions regarding saving and consumption primarily on the basis of expected disposable income. Because of the level of unemployment, inflation, or other uncertainties, they decide to be cautious and save a larger-than-usual portion of their disposable income. As a result, the business has lower sales and greater ending inventories than anticipated. In the end, actual (ex post) saving and investment are equal because of the business's unplanned investment in inventory. The equality exists even though planned (ex ante) saving by consumers was unequal to investment planned by the business. This relationship is significant because it affects the business's investment plans for the next period. Since its inventories are higher than expected, this business will probably decide to reduce the level of investment during the next period. Extended to the entire economy, this analysis of the relationship between ex ante savings and investment is useful in explaining why fluctuations occur in economic activity and in examining the role of financial intermediaries.

THE ROLE OF FINANCIAL INTERMEDIARIES

Recall from chapter 1 the two ways to consider GNP. The expenditure approach views GNP in terms of expenditures for final output, while the income approach considers GNP in terms of income received. Figure 2–1 utilizes these two concepts, together with saving and investment, to set the stage for financial intermediaries. The upper part of fig. 2–1 indicates that GNP can either be considered in terms of income (received in the form of wages, rent, interest, and profits) or in terms of expenditures for final output (by consumers, the business sector, government, and foreigners). The lower part of fig. 2–1 illustrates that wage income is either saved or spent by consumers for goods and services. In this figure the part of income spent for consumption is included directly in expenditures for final output, but the process of getting funds from savers to investors is more complicated.

One way to examine the link between savers and investors is to make the distinction between direct and indirect finance. **Direct finance** entails

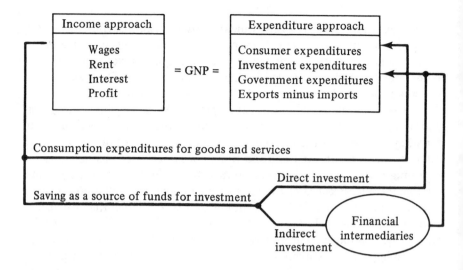

FIGURE 2–1   Saving, Investment, and the Role of Financial Intermediaries

the purchase of primary securities by surplus spending units (savers) from deficit spending units (investors). An example would be the purchase of newly issued stocks and bonds through a stockbroker. This type of transaction involves only primary issues of these securities (where a corporation is floating a new issue of securities) as opposed to the purchase of securities in the secondary market. The funds from the purchase of a primary issue go directly to the issuing corporation, but a transaction in the secondary market only transfers funds from one individual to another. This difference is significant because the purchase of securities in the secondary market does not have a direct impact on the level of real investment (the upper right-hand portion of fig. 2–1).

Indirect finance typically entails the channeling of funds from savers to investors. With indirect financing, financial intermediaries are positioned between the ultimate lenders (savers) and the ultimate borrowers (investors). In this process the intermediaries purchase primary securities from the ultimate borrowers. At the same time, the intermediaries issue indirect securities, which are claims against themselves, to the ultimate lenders. As an illustration, assume we use part of our current saving to purchase a whole life policy with a life insurance company. The insurance policy we hold is an indirect security (a claim against the insurance company). Now suppose that the managers of the company use our money to purchase part of a new issue of IBM common stock (although they are more likely to purchase stock that has already been issued). IBM uses the net proceeds of its new issue of common (primary securities held by the insurance company) to build an assembly line for a new generation of computers (real investment). Thus the process (from saver to investor) is complete. Life insurance companies are only one of many intermediaries. Others include savings and loan associations, commercial banks, finance companies, credit unions, mutual savings banks, investment companies, pension funds, and fire and casualty insurance companies. As we will see, all these intermediaries perform the same basic function as the insurance company in our example. We might ask why such institutions are needed. All these institutions charge fees for the services they provide. Why not avoid this fee and, as in our example, let the individual purchase the shares of IBM common stock himself? In other words, why not let the investor find the saver or vice versa? To answer this question, let us consider the situation of a barter economy, an underdeveloped nation, and a developed nation.

A barter economy is just what the name implies—a nation in which trade occurs only when one individual exchanges his or her goods for those of another individual. In such a system neither money nor financial institutions exist. Saving and investment (ex ante and ex post) are equal because the people who save are the same individuals who invest. Thus, if real investment is to occur in a barter economy, an individual must abstain from consumption (save) since no mechanism exists for borrowing from another saver. No deficit or surplus spending units exist; all budgets are balanced budgets. Because of such conditions, it is not difficult to see why inefficiencies and slow rates of economic growth exist in such systems.

An underdeveloped nation is commonly characterized by a large, unskilled labor force tied to agriculture. Very little industrial activity exists. Per capita income is typically low, and therefore very little saving occurs. The low rate of saving restricts real investment. The nation may be very rich in natural resources, but it is not benefiting from its natural endowments because of the low level of saving and the lack of incentive to invest. The problems of the less-developed country extend beyond the absence of an efficient system of financial intermediaries. The educational system must be upgraded, and the people must acquire skills. Productivity must be increased in the agricultural sector so that fewer can produce more in order to enable a larger part of the labor force to move to the industrial sector. To make progress in the industrial sector, real investment must increase. For saving to increase, income must increase so that funds can be obtained from within the country. Otherwise, funds must be attracted from other nations. Wherever the funds originate, a system of financial intermediaries must be developed to channel the funds to investors. Although ex post saving is equal to investment, this equality exists at low levels of GNP. Thus the primary job of financial intermediaries, once funds become available through increased saving within the country or from abroad, is to channel the funds to the most productive uses so that a higher level of GNP is attained.

Unlike the less-developed country, a developed nation is highly industrialized, the agricultural sector is typically very productive, the labor force is highly skilled, per capita income (and therefore saving) is high, and the financial system is complex and sophisticated. While the role of financial intermediaries is basically the same for both less-developed and developed countries, the primary difference between them is the range of options available to both savers and investors. With this background, we will examine the types of intermediaries in the United States and their contribution toward attaining the economic goals.

TYPES OF FINANCIAL INTERMEDIARIES

Financial intermediaries have numerous ways of performing the same basic function of bringing savers and investors together. In this section our purpose is to provide an overview of the types of financial intermediaries that exist in the United States. While there are several ways these institutions can be categorized, we will classify them as deposit-type institutions, contractual savings institutions, and others.

Deposit-Type Institutions

COMMERCIAL BANKS   As the most important intermediary participating in the financial markets, the commercial banking system ranks first in savings deposits and is the largest lender to consumers, business, and government. Financial reform may alter the degree of competition among financial intermediaries in the future, but commercial banks have historically been the only institutions permitted to accept demand deposits (checking accounts). Like other institutions, they attempt to maximize profits by lending and investing, but commercial banks are unique in their need for **liquidity.**

The assets of commercial banks represent the use of funds; their liabilities and capital accounts are their source of funds. Although banks maintain cash balances, over 80% of their assets are earning assets which include loans and investments. A typical commercial bank lends to businesses (75% of all their loans), to farmers, to consumers, and to other financial institutions. Commercial banks make long-term real estate loans, but to maintain liquidity most of their lending activity is in short- and intermediate-term loans. In addition to their primary activity of lending, banks also invest in securities: United States government securities, municipal bonds (obligations of state and local governments), and high-grade corporate bonds. The nature of commercial bank liabilities, which include primarily demand and time deposits, explains why the banks must place so much emphasis on safety and liquidity.

Member banks of the Federal Reserve System must meet reserve requirements set by the Fed. This entails retaining a specified percentage of bank deposits in vault cash or on deposit with a district Federal Reserve bank. Thus member banks must structure their portfolios to ensure that they always meet this requirement. In addition, the management of commercial banks must constantly be aware of the potential for rapid change in the level of deposits. Deposits in checking accounts are subject to withdrawal on demand. Time deposits include savings deposits and certificates of deposit (CDs). Savings deposits are the common passbook accounts, while CDs are negotiable and nonnegotiable accounts of larger denominations in which the depositor has agreed to keep the funds on deposit for a longer period of time. One might conclude that time deposits would eliminate many of the liquidity problems of the banks, but Regulation Q, in which the Fed sets maximum interest rates that can be paid on time deposits, has made these liabilities a rather undependable source of funds. To maximize their rate of return, commercial banks like to lend funds when interest rates are high. However, when interest rates prevailing in the market exceed the rate that can be paid by banks on time deposits, savers pull their funds out of commercial banks and either buy securities directly (called disintermediation) or place them in other financial institutions. The result is that the banks face a net withdrawal of time deposits when they most need the funds. In essence, because of the nature of their deposits, commercial banks must constantly attempt to maintain an optimal, but delicate, balance among safety, return, and liquidity in their portfolio of loans and investments.

SAVINGS AND LOAN ASSOCIATIONS   The function of savings and loan associations (S&L's) is specialized: to accumulate savings from the public and utilize these funds in home financing. Like commercial banks, whose depositors are insured by the Federal Deposit Insurance Corporation (FDIC), almost all S&L's have their deposits insured through the FDIC's counterpart for S&L's, the Federal Savings and Loan Insurance Corporation (FSLIC). S&L's can be either federally chartered or state chartered. Unlike commercial banks, which are typically incorporated and therefore owned by shareholders, S&L's are usually owned by their depositors. Thus the payments to savings depositors in commercial banks are called interest, while the payments to S&L depositors are called dividends. S&L's are regulated by the Federal Home Loan Bank System (FHLBS), which like the Federal Reserve is an independent federal agency.

The assets of S&L's consist of cash and securities, both relatively insignificant, and home mortgages. There are three types of home mortgages: VA (loans guaranteed by the Veterans Administration), FHA (loans insured by the Federal Housing Administration), and conventional loans. The first two types of loans are characterized by restrictions on the maximum interest rate that can be charged, how much the institution can lend, and physical characteristics of the homes on which loans are made. Although conventional mortgages are riskier for the institutions since they are without government backing, S&L's prefer this type of loan because of its higher return. In addition, conventional loans can be insured through private mortgage insurance companies. On the liability side, the deposits of S&L's are dominated by individual savings in either passbook or certificate accounts. Prior to the mid 1960s, management of S&L's believed that individual savings were not subject to volatile swings. Therefore they concluded that they were operating rationally in utilizing relatively short-term deposits as a source of funds to make long-term mortgage loans. Subsequent developments, however, have demonstrated that this imbalance in the maturity of assets and liabilities has contributed to the instability of S&L's.

MUTUAL SAVINGS BANKS   Mutual savings banks and more than 85% of S&L's are similar in their mutual form of organization. One of the primary reasons for this type of organization (as opposed to the stock form that is common in commercial banking) is that the savings banks were originally started to benefit the working class. Consistent with this purpose is the practice of distributing the earnings of savings banks to the depositors. Although a movement has existed in recent years to gain permission for savings banks and S&L's to change from mutual to stock organizations, the original idea of benefiting depositors continues to prevail.

In excess of 60% of the assets of mutual savings banks are held in the form of mortgage loans. Like S&L's, savings banks hold FHA, VA, and conventional mortgage loans. Unlike S&L's, they also hold a fairly substantial quantity of bonds. In August 1976, 25% of total assets were corporate bonds, securities of foreign governments and international organizations, and nonguaranteed issues of United States government agencies. Over 60% of the liabilities of mutual savings banks are in the form of regular savings accounts, followed by time and other deposits. Commercial banks have historically been the only institution permitted to accept demand deposits. A departure from this precedent was the introduction of NOW (negotiable order of withdrawal) accounts by savings banks in Massachusetts. These accounts are similar to checking accounts with one important distinction—the payment of interest is permitted. The introduction of NOW accounts has changed the traditional sharp distinction between demand and time deposits. This move, however, is only one in a series designed to increase the competition between commercial banks and nonbank financial intermediaries.

CREDIT UNIONS   The final deposit-type institution, the credit union, is a state or federally chartered nonprofit cooperative organization. The function of the credit union is to promote thrift and serve as a source of credit for members. Credit unions differ from the other deposit-type institutions on two counts: their members must have a common bond, and nearly all their lending is in the form of consumer loans. Thus a credit union can be organized to service the credit needs of the employees of a corporation, a profession common to all members, or the members of an association. Credit unions are typically small and simple operations compared to other institutions. Their assets are primarily consumer loans, and their liabilities are almost totally made up of members' savings shares and deposits. Because of their small size, they often have very little overhead. They may occupy office space provided free by the employer, and much of the work may be performed by volunteers. The factors that attract members to credit unions are understandable and straightforward. Because of their nonprofit objectives and low costs, credit unions pay high interest rates on deposits and charge relatively low interest rates on loans.

Contractual Savings Institutions

LIFE INSURANCE COMPANIES   Life insurance, with the exception of term insurance, is purchased for two reasons: protection and savings. To satisfy individuals who prefer protection and savings at the same time, two types of policies are available. Whole life insurance assures the policyholder that the face value of the policy will be paid at the time of death. In addition, the insured accumulates a cash value as premiums are paid on the policy. The typical whole life policy gives the insured the option of borrowing up to the amount of the cash value of the policy. Endowment policies also enable an individual to obtain both protection and savings; however, these policies emphasize savings more than whole life policies do. With an endowment policy, the insured makes payments for a specified period of time. If the insured dies before the end of the specified period, the full amount of the policy is paid. However, if death does not occur during this period, the face amount of the policy is paid to the insured. Term insurance differs from whole life and endowment policies by providing life insurance, at a lower cost, for a specified period of time with no provision for savings. Presumably, the individual may take the differential in the cost of the policies and put it into another form of saving or investment.

Life insurance companies differ from the other institutions covered thus far in their liquidity requirements. It is not difficult to see that a steady inflow of funds is a characteristic of this institution. The insured has entered into a contract with the life insurance company; if he does not make the premium payments, the insurance is simply cancelled. By utilizing mortality tables life insurance companies can predict the annual outflow of funds with considerable accuracy. The high degree of accuracy in predicting inflows and outflows of funds allows life insurance companies to structure their portfolio of assets accordingly. In matching the maturities of their assets and liabilities, life insurance companies construct portfolios consisting of (in order of importance) corporate securities, mortgages, and government securities.

PENSION FUNDS   Pension funds, which are classified as either government-administered or private, are typically initiated and administered by an employer to provide for the payment of benefits to employees (and sometimes their dependents) from the time of retirement until death. Within these two categories are the social security system, federally supervised funds, state and local government plans, and corporate pension plans. As with life insurance, a contractual arrangement specifies that participants in the pension plan make regular payments over a specified period of time. Since failure to make the payments is rare, the inflow of funds is predictable. And since the number of employees expected to retire each year is known, the outflow of funds can also be predicted with great accuracy. Liquidity is thus not a problem for the pension funds; like life insurance companies, they can accurately match the maturities of their assets and liabilities. To accomplish this, their portfolios primarily consist of stocks and bonds.

Other Financial Institutions

MUTUAL FUNDS   Mutual funds are the largest in a category of institutions called investment companies. Unlike closed-end investment companies, which issue a fixed number of shares to investors, mutual funds (open-end investment companies) are always attempting to expand via the sale of new shares. Mutual funds channel funds from savings to investment by pooling the savings of a large number of people and using this pool to purchase a large portfolio of stocks and/or bonds. The portfolio can be considered relatively diversified since investment companies must invest at least 75% of their assets in cash or securities and no more than 5% in the securities of any one company. Small savers are attracted to mutual funds for several reasons. Since the funds are typically large, they permit diversification that would not be possible if the saver invested directly in securities. Mutual funds also (presumably) offer expert management that the small investor does not possess.

To attract as many investors as possible, the investment objectives of mutual funds vary. Growth funds hold only common stocks to attract investors who do not mind being exposed to more risk in order to obtain the possibility of higher returns. For more conservative investors, income funds are available. These funds invest primarily in stocks of blue-chip companies and consistently pay high cash dividends. Balanced funds hold portfolios of fixed-income securities and low-risk common stocks. Consequently, as would be expected, they have low rates of return. In an attempt to earn relatively high rates of return while holding a relatively low-risk (liquid) portfolio, liquid asset funds hold portfolios of money market (short-term) instruments such as Treasury bills and short-term CDs in denominations of over $100,000. Finally, to attract investors in a high-income tax bracket, municipal bond funds hold portfolios consisting entirely of municipal bonds to take advantage of their tax-exempt income. Thus, while some funds attempt to attract investors in high-income tax brackets, the typical fund is designed for small savers who lack the expertise or time to manage their own portfolios. These funds give investors diversification they could not otherwise obtain and recognize that different individuals have different investment objectives.

PROPERTY AND CASUALTY INSURANCE COMPANIES Unlike life insurance companies, property and casualty insurers face considerable uncertainties with respect to the outflow of funds. They are unable to predict natural catastrophes, and they are adversely affected during periods of inflation. Thus they must tailor their asset structures to provide both high return and a considerable degree of liquidity. They invest in stocks to earn a high return and in government securities to provide for the necessary liquidity. In other words, part of the portfolio consists of common stocks to offset the possibility of a negative net underwriting income resulting from natural disasters and inflation. An additional portion of the portfolio is made up of government securities (which are very marketable) to provide funds to pay potential claims on very short notice.

RECENT ISSUES AFFECTING FINANCIAL INSTITUTIONS

Textbooks on financial institutions always seem to be out of date by the time they reach the market. Without doubt, some of the material in this section will be dated as well. Since the preceding sections have been presented to provide an overview of the functions and basic types of financial institutions, some institutions have been omitted. A more careful examination of all the institutions, including a close look at the most current developments, is the objective of texts devoted entirely to the topic of financial institutions. At the same time, an overview of the basic trends affecting financial institutions is within the scope of this book.

Some of the trends have been touched on at least briefly in earlier sections. While life insurance companies have generally remained financially stable over the years, property and casualty insurance companies periodically have been confronted with numerous problems. For several reasons (the most basic being that premiums have been outpaced by expenses, dividends, and total claims paid), some of the most common risks may be uninsurable in the future. The professional management offered by mutual funds implies that these institutions can outperform the return the investor could obtain elsewhere. But this has not been true in many cases. Mutual funds have recently faced net redemptions (more sales than purchases of mutual fund shares). If this trend is to be reversed, new ways must be found to bring the small saver back into the market for mutual funds. The most logical method of achieving this result is to develop new approaches that will actually provide the small saver with the supposed advantages of mutual funds. As a result of the Pension Reform Act of 1974 (called ERISA for the Employee Retirement Income Security Act), private pension funds have also undergone change in recent years. The benefit of this legislation seems clear: workers are assured of receiving the pension benefits they have been promised. But there is also a cost to the program. The objectives of ERISA include providing earlier pension coverage for new employees, earlier vesting of benefit rights (workers get an earlier guarantee of future benefits), and a stricter requirement for the funding of pensions (in the past, some pension plans had been financing benefits on a cash basis). One impact of this legislation has been to increase the costs, particularly administrative costs, of providing this benefit to employees.

Perhaps the most significant developments in recent years concern deposit-type institutions. Questions are being raised about the degree of competition that should (or should not) be allowed to exist among deposit-type financial institutions. The issues in this area were stimulated largely by the Hunt commission which, in late 1971, made 89 recommendations regarding commercial banks, mutual savings banks, savings and loans, credit unions, life insurance companies, and pension funds. Although the Hunt commission was designed primarily to examine the problems that S&L's of the late 1960s faced in competing in the financial markets, some additional issues have emerged since the earlier recommendations. Some of the issues raised by Congress in recent years include the following:

1. Should the banking system be subjected to multiple regulation? (One proposed bill would consolidate the Federal Reserve, the FDIC, and the Comptroller of the Currency into one agency.)

2. Should interest payments be allowed on checking accounts?

3. Should S&L's, credit unions, and mutual savings banks be allowed to offer checking account service?

4. Should interest rate ceilings be abolished on FHA and VA mortgages?

5. Should Regulation Q be abolished?

This list is not intended to be complete, but it does indicate that the appropriate role of deposit-type institutions is being questioned. Although these issues have not been resolved, it seems certain that changes are forthcoming.

FINANCIAL INTERMEDIARIES AND ATTAINING OUR ECONOMIC GOALS

In this chapter we have examined the relationship between saving and investment, the function of financial intermediaries in countries in various stages of development, and the basic types of financial institutions in the United States, along with an overview of some of the current issues facing them. Now we can see how financial institutions can assist in attaining our economic goals.

The level of saving and investment is important because of its relationship to economic growth. Equal but low-level ex post saving and investment could indicate an inefficient and slow-growth economy. Thus the amount of capital formation (the level of saving and investment) is crucial to the attainment of economic growth. At the same time, capital formation must be efficient. Not only is the amount of income devoted to real investment important; also critical is the efficiency with which saving is allocated among existing investment opportunities. It is in the allocation that financial intermediaries become a critical element. With an efficient system of financial intermediaries, a variety of financial assets are available to satisfy the desires of as many savers as possible. Thus the level of saving should be higher. With more funds available and with financial intermediaries channeling the funds to projects with the highest rate of expected return (and thus the highest productivities), capital formation will be greater and more effective, and the goal of economic growth will be more readily attained. Economic growth permits the goal of full employment to be more easily achieved. If productivity in the system is higher, as it should be, the economic system should be able to produce more goods and services without inflationary pressures, thus satisfying the goal of price stability. And with the gains in productivity along with price stability, our competitive position in world trade should be enhanced, thus facilitating the attainment of an acceptable balance-of-payments position.

SUMMARY

In a developed nation such as the United States, one group saves while another invests. Bridging the gap between these two groups are the financial intermediaries: commercial banks, savings and loan associations, mutual savings banks, credit unions, life insurance companies, pension funds, mutual funds, and property and casualty insurance companies. We have examined the characteristics of these institutions and the relationship among savings, investing, and financial intermediaries, as well as the role of this relationship in attaining our economic goals.

QUESTIONS

1. Why must allowances for capital consumption and depreciation be subtracted from gross investment to determine whether any change has occurred in the stock of capital goods?

2. Why are ex ante saving and investment not necessarily equal while ex post saving and investment must be equal?

3. Distinguish between direct and indirect financing.

4. Identify each type of deposit institution, and explain the function of each intermediary in the financial markets.

5. Why are life insurance companies and pension funds able to match the maturities of their assets and liabilities with such a high degree of accuracy?

6. How do the investment objectives of mutual funds vary?

7. Why must property and casualty insurance companies tailor their asset structure to provide a high rate of return and a considerable degree of liquidity? How do they meet this need?

8. Why is the amount of capital formation crucial to the attainment of economic growth?

SELECTED REFERENCES

Brown, Marilyn V. "The Prospects for Banking Reform." *Financial Analysts Journal* (March-April 1976), pp. 14–24.

Dougall, Herbert E., and Gaumnitz, Jack E. *Capital Markets and Institutions*. 3rd ed. Englewood Cliffs, N.J.: Prentice-Hall, 1975.

Gup, Benton E. *Financial Intermediaries: An Introduction*. Boston: Houghton Mifflin, 1976.

Hempel, George H., and Yawitz, Jess B. *Financial Management of Financial Institutions*, Englewood Cliffs, N.J.: Prentice-Hall, 1977.

Henning, Charles N.; Pigott, William; and Scott, Robert Haney. *Financial Markets and the Economy*. Englewood Cliffs, N.J.: Prentice-Hall, 1975; parts 1, 2.

Polakoff, Murray et al. *Financial Institutions and Markets*. New York: Houghton Mifflin, 1970; chs. 1, 3.

Robinson, Roland I., and Wrightsman, Dwayne. *Financial Markets: The Accumulation and Allocation of Wealth*. New York: McGraw-Hill, 1974; parts 2, 3.

3   The Determination of Interest Rates

*The black sheep of the family
had applied to his wealthy brothers for a loan, which
they agreed to grant him at an interest rate of 9 percent.
The ne'er-do-well complained
about the interest rate. "What will our poor father say
when he looks down from his eternal home and sees two
of his sons charging the other 9 percent on the loan?"
"From where he is," said one of
the brothers, "it'll look like 6 percent."*

Few concepts in the fields of economics and finance parallel the importance of the rate of interest. In general terms, the rate of interest sends out signals to the economy and, in so doing, plays a critical role in the allocation of economic and financial resources. For example, just as a high price for orange juice might be the result of a bad year for oranges in Florida, an increase in interest rates indicates a shortage of (or an excess demand for) money. And just as the market reacts to an increase in the price of bread, borrowers and lenders react to changes in interest rates.

A thorough understanding of the rate of interest is critical for success in a number of occupations, from bankers to stockbrokers to business managers in general. For purposes of this text, a knowledge of interest rates is important to understanding the relationship between the financial system and the economy. For example, the relationship between monetary policy and the economy in general (through changes in the money supply) is expressed through the interest rate. As another example, the management of financial institutions must watch interest rates closely in order to maximize the return on their loans and investments. Thus the rate of interest is critical in our development of the environment in which the financial manager and the investor make decisions. To perform optimally, financial managers and investors must not only be constantly aware of current trends in interest rates; they must also understand the factors that determine interest rates. Knowledge of trends can contribute to rational financial decisions made in reaction to current interest rates. But more important than reacting to existing conditions, a knowledge of the factors that determine interest rates (and those that explain differentials among rates) helps managers and investors predict trends in interest rates so that they can act prior to the projected changes.

When people refer to the rate of interest, the misinformed can easily conclude that a single rate of interest exists. In reality, there are many different interest rates, and these rates reflect the diverse characteristics of the various instruments that exist in these markets. Despite the multiplicity of interest rates, we approach the next part of this chapter as if there were a single rate. Our objective is to examine the forces that play a part in determining all interest rates. Then the relationship between the maturity of securities and their yield will be covered through a discussion of the term structure of interest rates. The chapter will conclude with an examination of factors other than maturity that influence yield.

DETERMINATION OF THE RATE OF INTEREST

Simply stated, the rate of interest is the price of money. As with any commodity, the price is determined by (among other factors) the interaction of supply and demand. The exact process that determines the price of money can become fairly complicated. Two approaches, the liquidity preference theory and the loanable funds theory, are generally utilized to explain the process. According to the liquidity preference theory, the rate of interest is determined by the supply of and demand for money, while the loanable funds theory turns to the supply of and demand for loanable funds. While differing in methodology, both approaches yield essentially the same result. Which approach one should utilize is debatable. Persons with a background in macroeconomics will probably feel more comfortable with the liquidity preference framework. Financial analysts (as well as texts in the area of financial institutions) commonly emphasize the loanable funds framework. Since both approaches are used and each yields essentially the same result, both are presented here, and readers can make their own judgment.

Liquidity Preference Framework

Somewhat more difficult to understand than the loanable funds approach, the liquidity preference framework originates from the work of John Maynard Keynes in the 1930s. As noted above, the rate of interest is determined by the interaction between the supply of and demand for money. In this approach, the supply of money is assumed to be a given quantity. Demand indicates the preference for liquidity. Since money is the most liquid of all assets, an increase in the demand for money is the equivalent of an increase in the demand for liquidity (in the literature, liquidity preference denotes a demand for money). Keynes identified three motives for having a preference for liquidity—in other words, three components of the demand for money.

The first, the transactions motive, refers to the demand for money to support the day-to-day transactions in the economy. According to Keynes, the transactions demand for money is functionally related to GNP. Thus, as economic activity increases and more trade occurs, more money is needed to support the larger number of transactions that accompany expanded economic activity. It is reasonable to expect the transactions demand for money to be a function of the rate of interest as well. Higher interest rates tend to minimize the amount of money held (because it earns the holder no income) to support a given level of transactions. For example, as interest rates increase, businesses minimize average checking account balances so more funds can be placed in interest-paying deposits or investments. Such economizing results in an inverse relationship between the rate of interest and the transactions demand for money.

The second motive, the precautionary demand, arises because of the uncertainty of future receipts and expenditures. Receipts may be delayed or expenditures increased without notice. Thus individuals and firms maintain balances to meet unforeseen contingencies. Like the transactions demand, the precautionary demand for money is considered directly related to the level of income; individuals with higher levels of income feel they should have larger contingency balances and the capacity to allocate funds for such purposes. Like the transactions motive, this motive for holding money is influenced to some degree by the rate of interest. As interest rates rise, individuals may feel less need for balances for precautionary purposes and therefore move the funds into interest-paying assets. Although both the transactions and precautionary demands for money are considered to be influenced by the rate of interest, it is common practice to ignore this relationship, group the two under the title transactions demand, and relate them to the level of income. The transactions demand for money is illustrated in fig. 3-1 where M_t is the transactions demand and Y is the level of income. If income is zero, balances needed for transactions purposes are

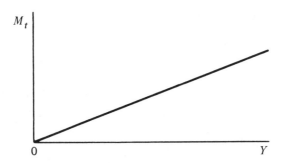

<figure>FIGURE 3–1   Transactions Demand for Money</figure>

nominal. Thus if Y is zero, M_t is zero; and as income increases, the balances needed to support the higher level of income also increase (the relationship is assumed to be linear).

The third motive for holding money, called the speculative demand, relates to balances held for purposes of speculating on future market movements. For example, an individual who believes that security prices are high and are going to decline would sell (or postpone purchasing) the securities and hold the money in idle balances. Under these conditions, the speculative demand for money would be high. If, on the other hand, security prices are relatively low and the individual expects them to rise, he would move out of his liquid position and buy securities. In addition to the expected gain from an increase in the price of the security, the investor would receive a relatively high return from interest income. Thus the speculative demand for money would be low. The speculative demand for money is inversely related to the rate of interest (rather than to security prices). As interest rates decline, security prices increase and vice versa. Thus, if interest rates are low and expected to increase, security prices are high and should decline. Under such conditions, individuals will sell their securities and hold their assets in a highly liquid form; that is, the speculative demand for money is high. Similarly, if interest rates are high, the speculative demand for money should be low. The speculative demand for money is illustrated graphically in fig. 3–2 where M_s is the speculative demand and i is the rate of interest.

Now with the three components of demand for money and a given supply of money, the rate of interest is determined very much the way price is determined in any market—by the interaction of supply and demand. If the supply of money is increased by the monetary authorities while demand remains constant, the rate of interest should decline. And if the demand for money increases relative to supply, interest rates should increase.

Without doubt, much of Keynes' work has been omitted from our discussion. We have covered only the financial side of the economy (and

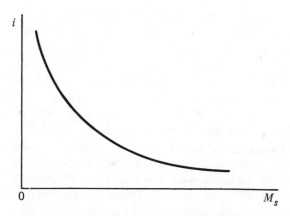

FIGURE 3–2   Speculative Demand for Money

in abbreviated form) in the Keynesian framework. The full Keynesian model also analyzes the factors that influence the level of income, including consumption spending, investment spending, government spending, and net exports. The complete system includes both the financial and producing parts of the economy to demonstrate how the rate of interest and the level of income are interdependent. What is important for our purposes is that Keynes developed a system in which the components of the demand for money could be identified. These components, when combined with the supply of money, offer one explanation of the determination of the rate of interest. For our purposes, one of the problems with the liquidity preference approach is that it excludes the role of financial institutions. In addition, with the exception of money and securities such as bonds, no financial assets are included.

Loanable Funds Framework

Whereas the liquidity preference approach emphasizes the reasons for holding money (preferring liquidity), the loanable funds approach to determining interest rates emphasizes the reasons for lending and borrowing funds. In other words, with lenders as suppliers and borrowers as demanders of funds, the loanable funds framework simply brings together the supply and demand elements in the market for loanable funds to determine the rate of interest. As in the liquidity preference approach, we are abstracting from reality since no single interest rate exists. Our objective is to identify factors that influence all interest rates.

The supply of loanable funds consists of three elements: current saving, increases in the supply of money, and hoarding and dishoarding. The saving component originates with households, businesses, and government. Household saving represents the after-tax disposable income that is not spent for consumer goods. Saving by the business sector is considered identical to retained earnings. In other words, business saving represents the part of after-tax income that is not distributed to shareholders in the form of dividends. Government saving is usually ignored on the supply side and included as a component of the demand for loanable funds because government saving is usually negative (government expenditures typically exceed receipts). The second supply component, changes in the supply of money, is exogenously determined by Federal Reserve policy (it is determined outside the system and thus is not functionally related to variables such as income and interest rates). Hoarding and dishoarding, the third supply component, is the difference between the amount of money people desire to hold and the amount they actually hold. If people are holding smaller cash balances than they desire, hoarding occurs. Dishoarding occurs when the money actually held exceeds the balances people desire to hold.

Before we combine these components to examine the shape of the supply of loanable funds curve, we must first turn to the determinants of the components. As we have discussed, saving is positively related to the level of income. Once the level of saving has been determined by the level of income, the rate of interest becomes important as a determinant of the form of saving. In other words, the individual's decision to hold such funds in the form of money or interest-paying assets is influenced by the interest rate. Hence this component of the supply of loanable funds increases as interest rates rise. The hoarding-dishoarding component is perhaps best explained by recalling our discussion of the speculative demand for money in the liquidity preference framework. Figure 3-2 showed that as interest rates rise, the prices of securities decline. Responding to the decline in security prices, individuals attempt to reduce their speculative balances by purchasing the lower-priced securities. This is the equivalent of dishoarding and represents an increase in the supply of loanable funds. Conversely, with low interest rates, security prices are high and speculative balances increase as individuals switch from securities to cash balances—all of which is equivalent to a decline in the supply of loanable funds.

Thus saving is determined by disposable income, while the form of saving is influenced by the rate of interest. Of the two remaining components, changes in the supply of money are dictated by Federal Reserve policy, and dishoarding (hoarding) is determined by the interest rate. Once the components are combined, the net effect is to assume, as illustrated in fig. 3-3, a positive relationship between the rate of interest and the supply of loanable funds.

The demand for loanable funds emanates primarily from the business and government sectors. Businesses require funds to support expenditures for plant, equipment, and inventories. To derive the demand for loanable funds by the business sector, any funds generated internally

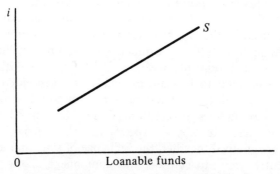

FIGURE 3-3 Supply of Loanable Funds

(after-tax profits not paid in the form of dividends to shareholders) must be subtracted from total business expenditures for plant, equipment, and inventories. Since the factors that influence the level of business investment are covered in detail in chapter 7, we will consider them from a non-technical point of view in this chapter. To illustrate these determinants, let us consider the job of a vice-president in charge of finance. One of the vice-president's tasks is to evaluate the proposed capital expenditures by various departments within the firm and advise top management which proposals should be accepted or rejected. To accomplish this task, the vice-president needs some common basis for comparing the various projects. One approach to this process, called **capital budgeting**, entails the calculation of the rate of return on the proposed projects. As long as the rate of return exceeds the cost of funds, the project is a candidate for acceptance; if the cost of funds exceeds the rate of return, the project is typically rejected outright. Many other factors, such as the risk associated with a project, make this process more complicated than our discussion seems to imply. The process of capital budgeting will be covered in detail in part 2. For the purpose of this chapter, the relationship between the rate of interest (a major part of a firm's cost of funds) and the rate of return is significant. Once the various rates of return on the proposed projects are computed, the level of total investment varies inversely with movements in the rate of interest. If interest rates fall, some projects previously rejected because the rate of interest exceeded the rate of return may become feasible. And as interest rates rise, projects that were previously acceptable, but only by a narrow margin, may be rejected. When this same analysis is extended to include the entire economy, we can see the inverse relationship between the rate of interest and the level of investment.

The government is included as a component of the demand for loanable funds framework because governmental expenditures typically exceed revenues. The natural tendency is to assume that government expenditures are dictated by economic policy and as such are insensitive to interest rates. This assumption is generally valid for expenditures by the federal government. Expenditures by state and local governments, however, are influenced by the rate of interest. Their expenditures are not dictated by goals such as full employment, growth, price stability, and an acceptable balance-of-payments position. Without such goals, state and local governments tend to increase expenditures when interest rates are low and restrict spending as interest rates rise. In addition, these governmental units are sometimes subject to regulations that prohibit them from borrowing at interest rates above a specified level. When all government expenditures are grouped together, the influence of state and local borrowing is sufficiently strong to consider this component of the demand for loanable funds as being inversely related to the rate of interest.

The demand for loanable funds and the interaction between the supply and demand curves to determine the rate of interest are illustrated in simplified form in fig. 3-4. Although it may appear from fig. 3-4 that the rate of interest (utilizing the loanable funds approach) is determined like the price of any other commodity, a few warnings should be mentioned. First we have covered the loanable funds framework in a simplified manner to provide a general understanding of the determination of interest rates using this approach. Unlike the supply and demand curves for a typical product, these curves are not independent. Furthermore, our illustrations of the curves would be different in a more rigorous examination of the same topic. For example, the demand for funds by the federal government, if shown separately, would be a vertical line since it is insensitive to the rate of interest. And if state and local governments faced a restriction on the maximum interest rate that could be paid, that component of the demand curve would not be a straight line. Rather, it would be downward sloping and, at the stated interest rate, would become parallel to the horizontal axis since no demand for funds can exist at higher rates. Moreover, the loanable funds approach provides only a partial equilibrium. While it indicates the current status in the financial market, it ignores the other

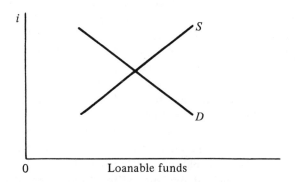

FIGURE 3-4   Supply and Demand for Loanable Funds

parts of the system such as the level of income, the impact of the creation of new financial intermediaries on the supply of loanable funds, and international economic conditions. The list of precautions is far from complete. However, the point should be clear. While the loanable funds approach to the determination of interest rates is fairly simple and easy to understand, one should be aware of its shortcomings and what it is and is not attempting to accomplish.

PRICE EXPECTATIONS AND INTEREST RATES

Any discussion of interest rates is incomplete without considering the impact of inflation. For example, in the financial transaction between the black sheep of the family and his wealthy brothers the stated interest rate is 9%, but if prices increase 12% over the life of the loan, the wealthy brothers will discover they have charged an interest rate that is actually a negative 3% (which means the two wealthy brothers paid the third brother to borrow the money). But how could this occur? From their statement, it seems unlikely that they would give their brother such favorable terms to please their father as he looks down from his eternal home. More likely, the two wealthy brothers did not anticipate the size of the increase in prices. The statement is often made that debtors benefit during periods of inflation because they repay loans with cheaper dollars. This is true only if creditors underestimate the rate of inflation. If the wealthy brothers had anticipated a 12% inflation rate, they may have charged their brother something closer to 20%. From our example, it is easy to see that expectations of changes in prices have an impact on all interest rates.

To be more specific, interest rates tend to be high (low) when people expect rising (falling) prices. For many years economists have believed that changes in interest rates tend to lag behind changes in the level of prices, thus obscuring the relationship between price level changes and interest rates. The lags exist because individuals look at price changes in the past to form their expectations regarding the future. The lags tend to lengthen for long-term bonds because individuals tend to look further back over time. It appears that after 1960 this lag has been dramatically reduced because of institutional factors. Whatever the duration of lags, it is clear that price expectations have a direct influence on interest rates. Changes in interest rates in response to changes in price levels occur primarily in the long run, while changes in short-term interest rates are more appropriately explained by examining the supply of and demand for loanable funds.

FACTORS CAUSING DIFFERENTIALS AMONG INTEREST RATES

So far we have approached interest rates as if one rate existed. We now turn to factors that explain why differentials exist among interest rates. For example, why can we usually get a higher return by purchasing a bond issued by AT&T with a 20-year maturity than if we bought a Treasury bill issued by the United States government with a maturity of 90 days? The factors that explain such differential returns include maturity, risk, callability, taxes, and marketability. All these factors could affect the return on any one type of security. For simplicity, however, when we consider each factor we will assume that all the other factors are the same for all securities.

Maturity: The Term Structure of Interest Rates

To be consistent with our assumption above, in this section we assume that all factors other than maturity are held constant. The relationship between yield and maturity is typically illustrated by a yield curve. Such a curve, shown in fig. 3–5, measures the yield to maturity on the vertical axis and the number of years to maturity on the horizontal axis. In order of frequency, representative curves in fig. 3–5 include the ascending yield curve, which is the most common, followed by the descending and flat yield curves. But more important than knowing that ascending yield curves are more common, one should ask why differentials exist or do not exist among yields of securities that differ only with respect to maturity. In an attempt to answer this question, three basic theories exist including the liquidity premium theory, the expectations theory, and the segmentation theory.

According to the liquidity premium theory, an ascending yield curve is considered normal. The expectation that an ascending yield curve exists is based on the premise that the prices of long-term bonds fluctuate more than the prices of short-term bonds. With the greater variance in long-term bond prices, more risk is associated with the long-term bonds. Reacting to the risk, lenders tend to prefer short-term bonds, thus forcing up the prices of short-term bonds and decreasing their yield. Hence an upward-sloping yield curve is considered normal.

The expectations theory is based on the premise that long-term rates are equal to the average of short-term rates over a long period of time. According to this theory, the term structure is determined by the future interest rates that investors expect. If they expect interest rates to rise, the yield curve should be ascending; if they expect interest rates to decline, the yield curve should be descending; and if they expect no change in interest rates, the yield curve should be horizontal. For example, a potential bond-

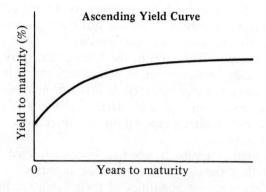

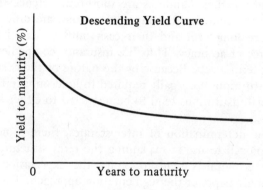

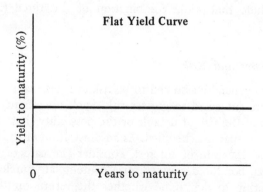

FIGURE 3-5   Representative Yield Curves for Corporate Bonds

holder who wants to invest funds for five years could buy either a single bond with a five-year maturity or a new one-year bond in each of the next five years (reinvesting in a new one-year bond as each bond matures). If investors expect lower interest rates in the future, thus driving the price of bonds up and yields down, they can maximize their return by purchasing the single bond with a five-year maturity. As investors move to longer-term bonds, the prices are bid up and yields decline relative to the short-term bonds. Thus the net result of expectations of lower interest rates is a descending yield curve.

The segmentation approach, which is commonly used by financial analysts, asserts that there is a tendency for investors to match the lives of their assets with the maturities of their liabilities. For example, recall from our discussion in chapter 2 that commercial banks must maintain liquidity because their liabilities are short-term. Hence they tend to invest in short-term securities. Insurance companies are different because their liabilities are long-term and their cash outflows can be forecasted with a high degree of accuracy. Thus life insurance companies hold large amounts of long-term assets. Because of the nature of their liabilities and because some institutions are legally required to hold only certain types of securities, financial institutions tend to be restricted to either long-term or short-term assets.

As with the determination of interest rates, there is no consensus about which approach to use in explaining the term structure of interest rates. Academic economists tend to prefer the expectations approach, while financial analysts prefer the segmentation approach. The logic of all three approaches is appealing. However, no one approach has been proved a clearly superior representation of reality. Until such proof is available, one must conclude that some combination of the three theories best describes reality.

Interest Rates and Risk

Lenders are generally assumed to be risk averters, requiring a greater return as they are subjected to greater risk. Such uncertainty can be expressed in terms of the risk of default or the possibility that the borrower will not be able to repay as scheduled. As an illustration of the relationship between risk and the rate of interest, consider the case of a corporate bond. As potential bondholders (creditors) contemplate purchasing bonds, they are attempting to determine whether the return on the bonds is sufficient to compensate for the risk associated with the bonds. A logical starting point is to determine the return (expressed as a percent) on a bond without any risk of default. Such a riskless rate would be approximated by the return on a security issued by the federal government. Given the riskless rate of return, the objective is then to determine how much additional risk is associated with the corporate bond and how much additional return is sufficient to compensate for the risk. To achieve this objective, one must determine the factors that contribute to the risk of default. These factors include risk characteristics peculiar to the firm issuing the bonds and the environment in which the firm operates. Like a banker determining whether to lend to an individual, the potential bondholder considers the ability and willingness of the company to repay its obligation. In other words, by utilizing certain financial ratios, the investor asks whether the firm has (and will have in the future) the capacity to pay the interest and principal on the bonds. In addition, the investor tries to determine what the record indicates about the company's repayment of its obligations and the impact a recession would have on all these factors.

Our discussion has been grossly oversimplified because these factors will be discussed in greater detail throughout the remainder of the book. At this point all we need to recognize is that potential bondholders subject themselves to greater risk only if they expect greater returns. To increase the expected return, potential bondholders require a higher interest rate, a lower price (which increases the yield), or some combination of the two.

Call Provisions and Interest Rates

If a company defaults, bondholders may not get their money back on time or at all; with call provisions, bondholders may get their money back before they desire. The call provision in bonds provides the issuer of the bonds the option of retiring the bonds (paying them off before maturity) at various times. For the issuer, the call provision is desirable; if interest rates decline the bonds can be retired and replaced with bonds bearing the new (lower) interest rate, thus minimizing the cost of financing. For the bondholders, however, this provision represents a risk because their funds have to be reinvested at a lower rate of return if the bonds are retired during a period of low interest rates. To compensate for this risk, bondholders require a higher interest rate or a lower price (thus increasing the yield) on such bonds.

Taxes

Another reason for expecting differentials among interest rates is the tax structure. Two common examples are taxes on capital gains and the tax-exempt status of municipal securities. To see why such differentials can be attributed to the capital gains tax, let us examine the case of a wealthy individual who is considering two bonds, one with a high **coupon** (interest) **rate** and one with a low rate. A preliminary examination of the two securities reveals that the bond with the high coupon rate has a higher yield before tax than the bond with the low coupon rate. However, wealthy individuals prefer capital gains to interest payments because the latter are taxed at the ordinary income tax rate while capital gains (if the security is held over 12 months) are taxed at a maximum of approximately 25%. If the lower-coupon-rate bond provides bondholders with greater return in the form of capital gains than the bond with the high coupon rate (as it should if other factors are equal), wealthy individuals prefer the former because the after-tax yield is actually greater.

The opposite is true for municipal (state and local) securities. Unlike corporate securities, state and local government securities provide interest that is exempt from federal income taxes. Thus pretax yields on the tax-exempt municipal securities are often considerably lower than the pretax yields on nonexempt securities. Capital gains on municipal securities, however, are not exempt from federal income taxes. When investors examine these tax considerations, they therefore commonly prefer high-coupon over low-coupon municipal bonds.

Marketability

Any time the purchase of an asset is being contemplated, whether it is a security or a business, the potential purchaser should ask several questions. If adverse conditions prevail at some time during the life of the asset, can the asset be sold? How long will it take to sell the asset? And if there is a buyer, can the asset be sold without incurring a loss? In other words, how marketable is the asset? Assuming that other characteristics of the asset are the same, the answers to these questions can explain considerable differentials among interest rates (or yields). Although the same analysis applies to any asset, such rate differentials may be more easily examined by using securities as an example. When securities are initially issued by a corporation, they are sold to investors in the primary market. When these investors are contemplating their purchase, they should direct considerable attention to the secondary market, or the part of the market that enables investors to sell the securities to another investor on short notice at a later time. When a well-developed secondary market exists for the security, little (if any) additional return is required to compensate for the risk associated with marketability. However, if the issuing company is a closely held corporation (owned by a relatively small number of individuals), marketability becomes an issue of paramount importance since there may be virtually no buyers in the secondary market. In such a situation, potential investors would demand relatively high expected returns. As we will see in chapter 4, one of the functions of money and capital markets is to minimize the risk associated with marketability.

SUMMARY

An understanding of interest rates is critical to a number of occupational groups and individuals, including managers of financial intermediaries, financial managers, and investors. To promote this understanding, this chapter examined two approaches, the liquidity preference approach and the loanable funds framework, to explain the determination of interest rates in general. In addition, the impact of inflation on the level of interest rates was explored. Finally, the factors that cause differentials among interest rates, including maturity, risk, call provisions, taxes, and marketability, were examined.

QUESTIONS

1. Discuss the liquidity preference and the loanable funds approaches to determining the rate of interest.
2. Discuss the three elements that constitute the supply of loanable funds, and explain how each component is determined.
3. How does the rate of interest affect capital budgeting decisions?
4. Explain the relationship between price expectations and interest rates.
5. According to the liquidity premium theory, why is an ascending yield curve considered normal?
6. Why is a call provision considered desirable from the issuer's point of view but undesirable from the bondholder's point of view?
7. Why would an individual prefer capital gains over interest payments?
8. Suppose you are a corporate treasurer. The current yield curve is ascending. The corporate officers feel that the market's expectations, as reflected in the yield curve, will in fact be reflected in reality. The vice-president of finance feels that rather than issue long-term (25-year) debt now, the firm should arrange for short-term financing at the current time and issue long-term debt later. She asks your opinion. What would you advise?

SELECTED REFERENCES

HENNING, CHARLES N.; PIGOTT, WILLIAM; and SCOTT, ROBERT HANEY. *Financial Markets and the Economy*. Englewood Cliffs, N.J.: Prentice-Hall, 1975; part 4.

POLAKOFF, MURRAY et al. *Financial Institutions and Markets*. Boston: Houghton Mifflin, 1970; chs. 2, 3, 21, and 22.

ROBINSON, ROLAND I., and WRIGHTSMAN, DWAYNE. *Financial Markets: The Accumulation and Allocation of Wealth*. New York: McGraw-Hill, 1974; ch 6.

4   Money and Capital Markets

Money isn't everything, and
don't let anyone tell you different. There are other
things, such as stocks, bonds, letters of credit,
traveler's checks, checks, drafts.

With the possible exception of our discussion of yield curves, we have not yet explicitly distinguished between the short-term (**money**) and long-term (**capital**) **markets** for funds. To properly set the scene for the remainder of the book, we have to consider this difference now, for two reasons. First, much of the financial manager's time must be allocated to investment and financing decisions. That is, he must decide which assets the firm should acquire (both current and long-term assets) and find the funds to purchase these assets (both short-term and long-term financing). In the search for funds he represents only one of many components of the financial system. Because he is competing with others for available funds, he has to be familiar with the nature of the money and capital markets, the securities included in both markets, and current developments.

Second, as we will see in part 3, the investor is searching for places to put his money to work. And just like the financial manager, his maturity requirements may vary. That is, he may want to buy a security for 90 days, or he may want to purchase a bond with a maturity of 20 years. Whether the investor wants to maintain a strong liquidity position and invest in short-term securities or invest for a long period of time, he wants to know all the options that are available. Thus, like the financial manager, the investor has a vested interest in being knowledgeable about the money and capital markets. This chapter is one more step in establishing the environment for decisions to be made by financial managers and investors. Its purpose is to provide both groups with a knowledge of the nature and role of the money and capital markets as well as the financial instruments that make up these markets.

THE MONEY MARKET

The money market consists of a group of institutions that exist for the purpose of bringing together lenders and borrowers of short-term funds. It provides a network of exchange for assets that are near-money in nature. Specifically, the money market (which is usually characterized by instruments having a maturity of one year or less) facilitates short-term financing and assures the liquidity of short-term financial assets. To see why the money market is so important, recall from chapter 2 that commercial banks' liability structures require them to maintain an optimal balance among safety, return, and liquidity in their portfolios of loans and investments. In essence, this means that they must maintain a high degree of liquidity (that is, they must be able to convert their assets into cash very quickly with a minimum risk of loss). For this reason commercial banks are a significant part of the money market, both as a source and a user of funds.

A discussion of the relationship between money and capital markets is presented later in this chapter. First we will examine the basic types of financial instruments found in the money market. In addition to having short-term maturities, these instruments are typically issued in large denominations by institutions possessing a very high quality of credit.

TREASURY BILLS AND NOTES Treasury bills are obligations of the United States Treasury Department and are backed by the full faith and credit of the United States government. They are issued with maturities of up to one year (including issues with maturities of three, six, and twelve months) and are generally considered the most liquid of investments. Bills can be bought, with various days remaining until maturity, from others who purchased them on or since the date of issue. They are issued in bearer form, which means they do not carry the investor's name (and, as such, must be carefully safeguarded). Treasury bills do not bear interest; instead they are sold at discount, which means the return an investor earns is the difference between the price paid and the face value (which will be received at maturity). Treasury bills can be purchased in denominations of $10,000, $15,000, $50,000, $100,000, $500,000, and $1 million. The income from Treasury bills is exempt from state and local government income taxes but is subject to federal income taxes. Relative to other money-market instruments, Treasury bills do not normally offer a very high yield. Still, they are the most popular of all the instruments.

Their popularity stems from their liquidity rather than their return. They have the highest safety and can be sold more quickly than any other money-market instrument.

In addition to their importance as an investment for holders of short-term excess funds, Treasury bills are also important to the federal government. They are utilized by the United States Treasury Department to obtain funds to finance the programs of the government. They also represent the primary instrument through which the Federal Reserve conducts open-market operations on a day-to-day basis to influence the size of the money supply.

Along with typical Treasury bills carrying maturities of up to one year, the Treasury has (since 1951) issued a special type of bill called the **tax-anticipation bill** (commonly called TABs). These securities provide the Treasury with a source of funds and at the same time satisfy the maturity requirements of corporations. TABs are issued to attract funds that corporations accumulate for the payment of taxes at a future date. Thus the corporation has a security that generates a return and matures at precisely the time the funds are needed to make the tax payments.

Treasury notes, like Treasury bills, are direct obligations of the United States government. One factor that differentiates them is that they are intermediate-term obligations and have maturities that range from one to five years. As such, they might be more appropriately considered instruments of the capital market. We will, however, discuss them briefly at this point because as they approach maturity (within one year of maturity) they are considered part of the money market. Unlike the bills, Treasury notes bear interest, paid semiannually by either coupon or check. They can be purchased in denominations of $1000, $5000, $10,000, $100,000, and $1 million. Notes, like bills, are exempt from state and local income taxes but subject to federal income taxes. With the exception of the maturity and payment of interest, Treasury notes are very similar to bills. They are popular with commercial banks because they are safe and liquid yet provide maturities to satisfy the intermediate-term needs of the banks.

UNITED STATES GOVERNMENT AGENCY SECURITIES Like Treasury notes, securities issued by United States government agencies fall into both the money and capital markets, with most having a maturity of from one to five years. These securities are typically obligations of federal agencies or government-sponsored agencies; the agencies rather than the federal government guarantee the payment of interest and principal. Government agency securities are nearly as safe and liquid as Treasury bills and have become popular instruments in recent years since they offer higher yields than bills. Federal agencies participating in this market include the Export-Import Bank, Federal Housing Administration (FHA), Government National Mortgage Association (GNMA), Postal Service,

Tennessee Valley Authority (TVA), and the United States Railway Association. Federally sponsored agencies include the Federal Home Loan Banks (FHLBs), Federal Home Loan Mortgage Corporation, Federal Intermediate Credit Banks (FICBs), Banks for Cooperatives, and the Student Loan Marketing Association.

A significant development in recent years has been the Federal Financing Bank (FFB). The FFB was established in 1974 to coordinate federal and federally assisted borrowing programs. Coordination was considered necessary because the demand for funds created by these programs was increasing faster than the supply of credit. The FFB is authorized to buy or sell obligations that are issued, sold, or guaranteed by other federal agencies. To carry out its objectives, the FFB incurs debt for the purpose of lending to other agencies. Federally sponsored agencies (along with the FFB) have become a significant factor in the money market in recent years. The magnitude of their activity is indicated in table 4–1.

COMMERCIAL PAPER The oldest money market instrument in the United States, **commercial paper** represents a source of funds available to large, well-known corporations for up to 270 days. The maximum 270-day maturity, along with certain other conditions, exempts the paper from SEC (Securities and Exchange Commission) registration. In essence, commercial paper refers to short-term unsecured promissory notes issued by large corporations such as CIT Financial Corporation and General Motors Acceptance Corporation (GMAC). The typical denominations

TABLE 4–1 Debt Outstanding of Government Agencies (Millions of Dollars; End of Period)

	1973	1974	1975	1976	1977
Federal Home Loan Banks	15,362	21,890	18,900	16,811	18,345
Federal Home Loan Mortgage Corporation	1,784	1,551	1,550	1,690	1,686
Federal National Mortgage Association	23,002	28,167	29,963	30,565	31,890
Federal Land Banks	10,062	12,653	15,000	17,127	19,118
Federal Intermediate Credit Banks	6,932	8,589	9,254	10,494	11,174
Banks for Cooperatives	2,695	3,589	3,655	4,330	4,434
Student Loan Marketing Association	200	220	310	410	515
Total of Federally Sponsored Agencies	60,037	76,659	78,632	81,427	87,162
Federal Financing Bank	—	4,474	17,154	28,711	38,580

Source: *Federal Reserve Bulletin.*

are $25,000, $50,000, $100,000, $250,000, $500,000, and $1 million. Like Treasury bills, commercial paper is usually issued in bearer form and sold at a discount.

Commercial paper provides the issuing firm an alternative to bank loans and other sources of short-term financing. In addition to being a lower-cost form of financing than bank loans, commercial paper is believed to enhance a corporation's image since usually only firms with an excellent credit standing can participate in this market. Rating agencies such as Standard & Poor's rate the quality of bonds and commercial paper to indicate the degree of risk associated with the debt. Events in recent years have caused some concern regarding the reliability of the commercial paper ratings and the corporate image aspect. In the late 1960s firms such as utilities and bank holding companies began issuing commercial paper. During this period several defaults occurred which were extremely unusual for this type of instrument. In addition, when the Penn Central Transportation Company filed for bankruptcy in 1970, it had $82 million in commercial paper outstanding. The result of these events has been an alteration of the image of the commercial paper market. Despite these difficulties, commercial paper remains a significant element in the money market. In early 1977 approximately $55 billion in commercial paper was outstanding.

NEGOTIABLE CERTIFICATES OF DEPOSIT   To most people a certificate of deposit (CD) refers to an agreement in which funds are to be left on deposit for a specific period of time. For example, an individual agrees to keep $1000 on deposit at a commercial bank for four years. In return the bank agrees to pay a return of 7½%, more than could be earned on a passbook savings account at the same institution. In the money market the arrangement is the same. The **negotiable CD** (NCD) is a bank receipt given in exchange for a deposit; the bank agrees to return the amount of the deposit, with interest, to the holder at a specified date in the future. The primary difference is the size of the deposit. The denomination can vary according to the original buyer and the bank, with the range typically running from $25,000 to $10 million. While CDs have existed for a long time, NCDs date only from 1961.

NCDs are also different from CDs in that, being negotiable, they can be traded in the secondary market before maturity. However, because business firms, which are the major holders of NCDs, tend to hold them until maturity, the secondary market for them is smaller than for Treasury bills. The maturity of NCDs ranges from 1 to 18 months. Activity in the NCD market has increased rapidly since their inception in 1961. In 1968 outstanding NCDs in denominations of $100,000 or more totaled $24 billion, and by early 1977 more than $65 billion was outstanding.

BANKERS' ACCEPTANCES   A **bankers' acceptance** is a negotiable time draft drawn on a bank by a drawer ordering the bank to pay to him or another party a specified sum of money at a future date. The bank accepts the draft, thus indicating its willingness to make the payment. Commonly called two-name paper, bankers' acceptances are one type of a class of credit instruments called bills of exchange.

The use of this money-market instrument typically arises from trade with foreign countries. For example, suppose that a Japanese manufacturer of cameras wants to sell its product to an importer in the United States. The importer in the United States asks his bank to send the camera manufacturer a letter of credit authorizing him to draw a time draft on the bank with a specified maturity. The Japanese exporter might sell or discount the draft at his Japanese bank (to obtain his money) before the United States importer has paid for the cameras. The bank in Japan would then send the discounted draft to the bank in the United States for acceptance and discount (the draft is accompanied by supporting documents such as the bill of sale). The United States bank sends the importer the supporting documents so he can take possession of the cameras. If some time still remains before maturity (which is up to six months for most acceptances), the bank in the United States can either hold the acceptance as an earning asset until maturity or sell it in the secondary market. At maturity the United States importer pays the bank and the transaction is complete.

FEDERAL FUNDS   In chapter 1 we discussed the role of the Federal Reserve System in attaining our economic goals. We also covered the reserve requirement for commercial banks. If these banks hold more funds than required, the difference is called **excess reserves**. Rather than let such funds stay idle and not generate a return, an obvious incentive exists for commercial banks to put the money to work. This is the role of **federal funds** in the money market. Federal funds are simply the excess reserves one commercial bank has available to lend to another commercial bank. For example, small rural commercial banks (country banks) often have excess reserves while large commercial banks in metropolitan areas often need funds to meet the reserve requirement. The federal funds rate is the rate that lending banks charge the borrowing banks for the use of the funds. The maturity of this type of transaction is usually one day. Reserve requirements must be met on a daily basis (on average) over the week, which runs from Thursday to Wednesday. No funds are typically lent during the first part of the statement week. Rather, the banks wait until the end of the week approaches. When it becomes obvious that the bank has excess reserves (on average) for the week, it lends the money in the federal funds market to a bank that is short of the reserve requirement (normally on Wednesday).

Compared to other money-market rates, the federal funds rate is very volatile because reserve requirements must be met on a daily basis (at times the rate has been as high as 20%). The funds rate, however, is watched closely as an indicator of the money market, monetary policy, and economic conditions in general. The federal funds market is considered very important since it operates at the center of the money market and the commercial banking system.

REPURCHASE AGREEMENTS   Repurchase agreements (RPs) are much more specialized and are used by fewer market participants than other money market instruments. The typical RP entails the sale of other money market instruments with the stipulation that after a specific period of time the original seller will buy back the securities at a predetermined price. The purpose of RPs is to match the maturity needs of buyers and sellers of the securities. For example, an investor who wants to invest funds for only ten days can survey the money market for a security that matures in ten days. If none satisfies his requirements, he could buy a security with a maturity greater than ten days and sell it when the funds are needed. If he needs the funds in ten days to make a payroll, for example, this arrangement would not be acceptable because the money market is volatile and he may not have sufficient funds to make the payroll. Given the conditions in this hypothetical case, an RP is a feasible option. By using the RP, the investor can purchase a money market instrument (for example, a Treasury bill) with a longer maturity but with the agreement that the seller will purchase it back in ten days at a predetermined price. Thus our investor has successfully invested his funds and is assured of having sufficient funds for his payroll.

RPs can also be used by the Federal Reserve in its open-market operations. To temporarily influence the supply of money, it can use RPs just as the investor does. In other words, the Fed buys government securities with the understanding that the original seller will repurchase them at a predetermined time. Thus the money supply increases for this same period of time. If the Fed wants to decrease the money supply for a short period of time, it can use a reverse RP. Under this arrangement the Fed sells securities, thus decreasing the supply of money, and simultaneously agrees to repurchase them at a specified time in the future. You are probably wondering why the Fed would utilize RPs or reverse RPs. If the Fed wants to increase the supply of money, why not just buy securities via open-market operations? The answer to this question relates to market reaction to monetary policy. For example, if the Fed increases the supply of money through normal open-market operations, the market might infer that the Fed intends to stimulate the economy and react accordingly. If, however, the Fed wants to increase the supply of money for a short period of time for reasons other than stimulating the economy, RPs are a logical tool. The use of RPs minimizes the reactions of participants in the money market because they know when the initial purchase of securities takes place that this action will be reversed within a short period of time.

THE EURODOLLAR MARKET   Eurodollars are deposits denominated in United States dollars but placed in banks outside the United States. To see why such deposits might exist, first consider the following background information. Until recently, the United States dollar has been stable relative to many other currencies. Its stability makes it a natural candidate for use as a **vehicle currency**—a currency utilized by two countries to finance trade when the country issuing the currency is not one of the countries engaging in trade. This is admittedly a very simple treatment of a fairly complicated subject. However, one can see that if trade is to take place and a vehicle currency is going to be utilized, then the parties engaging in trade must maintain an inventory of the currency. For example, to carry on day-to-day transactions and meet seasonal needs, importers must maintain working balances in all currencies from the countries in which they trade. Rather than requiring the maintenance of balances in numerous currencies, trade can take place with a minimum of complexity if one currency acceptable to all parties can be utilized. Playing this role is the function of the Eurodollar in particular and **Eurocurrency** in general. The term Eurocurrency is used because such deposits do not have to be denominated in United States dollars. They could just as easily be Swiss francs or German marks. However, most of these deposits are held in banks located in Europe. Eurodollars are simply a specific type of Eurocurrency that constitute a majority of the Eurocurrency market. Some have suggested, with merit, that the real reason for the popularity of Eurodollars is that they skirt interest rate ceilings on funds in the United States.

THE CAPITAL MARKET

In contrast to the money market, which brings lenders and borrowers of short-term funds together, the capital market exists to facilitate long-term financial arrangements between providers and users of capital. The role of the capital market is to allocate long-term capital to the most productive uses. To some extent this discussion overlaps the discussion of financial intermediaries in chapter 2. For example, new funds flowing into the capital market come from the savings of consumers and business. Positioned between this source of funds and the users are financial intermediaries such as life and casualty insurance companies, pension funds, commercial banks, savings and loans, and mutual savings banks. Thus our discussion of capital markets overlaps, but it is augmented by our discussion of financial intermediaries in chapter 2. Our discussion here is a spin-off of chapter 2 since our objective at this point is to examine the submarkets of the so-called capital market.

THE MARKET FOR GOVERNMENT SECURITIES Presidential candidates invariably project that they will balance the budget. Once in office, they invariably fail to do so. They soon learn in their on-the-job training that

TABLE 4–2   Government Spending, Taxing, and Borrowing (Billions of Dollars; End of Period)

Year	Federal Government Spending	Total Tax Receipts	National Debt
1966	134.7	130.9	329.5
1967	158.3	149.6	341.3
1968	178.8	153.7	369.8
1969	184.5	187.8	367.1
1970	196.6	193.7	382.6
1971	211.4	188.4	409.5
1972	232.0	208.6	437.3
1973	247.1	232.2	468.4
1974	269.6	264.9	486.2
1975	326.1	281.0	544.1
1976	365.6	299.2	631.9
1977	401.9	356.9	709.1

Source: *Economic Indicators.*

their promises must be economically as well as politically feasible. In other words, the only thing that seems really invariable is the continued growth of the federal government. The increase in government spending must be financed through increased taxes, government borrowing, or both. The data in table 4–2 demonstrate the increases in government spending, taxes, and borrowing that have taken place from 1966 to 1977. The activity in the borrowing column has a direct influence on the capital market. While government spending increased almost 200% from 1966 to 1977, tax receipts increased only 173% over the same period. To close this gap, government borrowing (the national debt) increased 115% during the 1966–1977 period. Thus it is easy to see that the government, through government securities, plays a significant part in the capital market.

To examine the market for government securities, we will look at the demand and supply aspects of the market. On the demand side of the market is, of course, the federal government. Statistics such as those in table 4–2 always raise questions about the reasons for such rapid increases in government expenditures. When you read about capital budgeting in chapter 7, you may ask why government expenditures cannot also be evaluated by comparing the benefits and costs involved. Proposals have been made to apply capital budgeting techniques to government expenditures, and the Carter administration proposed a move toward zero-based budgeting (that is, every department or agency starts with essentially no budget and justifies all proposed expenditures). The only problem is that the vast majority of the proposals remain proposals. Government expenditures generally have increased to finance war, to pull the economy out of recessions or depressions, and to fund new social programs. Because of the nature of these reasons, expenditure decisions must often be made without explicit cost-benefit analysis.

Whatever the arguments for adding financial logic to the government budgeting process, if a gap exists between government spending and receipts, the Treasury is charged with generating the funds. To do its job, the Treasury must, like other borrowers, recognize that suppliers of funds have differing maturity requirements and offer securities with maturities to satisfy those requirements. The maturity structure of the debt, which has tended to become shorter, is part of debt management. Debt management by the Treasury is typically segmented into new borrowing and refunding. New borrowing generally has a greater impact on the capital market than refunding since on net it draws money out of the market. Refunding has less impact since the Treasury is simply issuing new debt to pay off debt that is maturing. As such, refunding does not (on a net basis) take funds from the market.

When the Treasury enters the market with an offering, either on a new cash or refunding basis, the Treasury Department itself takes care of the majority of the sales work. This sales effort is augmented by commercial banks and government securities dealers who are the principal underwriters of government securities. Nevertheless, Treasury officials, like other issuers of securities, must price securities attractively to lure buyers into the market. Securities that are priced too high will not sell. The buyers of government securities include commercial banks, foreign monetary authorities, individuals, state and local governments, savings and loans, mutual savings banks, insurance companies, pension funds, and nonfinancial corporations. The primary reason for holding government securities is not their return but their liquidity. Being the most risk-free type of security available, the return on these securities is low relative to other forms of investments, but because of the size of the secondary market for government securities, they can be converted into cash with little risk of loss.

THE MUNICIPAL BOND MARKET   The principal participants on the demand side of the municipal bond market (for funds) are state and local governments (some special authorities are created for the purpose of issuing bonds). While the primary advantages of the government securities market are safety and liquidity, the primary attraction of municipal bonds is their tax-exempt status. Funds generated from the issue of municipal bonds are commonly used for capital expenditures in education, water and sewer systems, and roads. In the 1960s industrial revenue bonds were heavily used to finance projects such as industrial parks in order to attract new industry to cities and states. This practice, however, has been considerably curtailed since Congress limited the size of such issues. Another trend for municipalities in recent years has been an increasing use of pollution control revenue bonds. Municipalities use the proceeds of these bonds to purchase pollution-abatement equipment, which is then leased to private corporations, and the revenue from the lease is used as security for the bonds. Thus the savings associated with the tax-exempt status of the bonds are passed along to private industry.

The exempt status of municipal bond interest from federal taxes determines the type of investor state and local governments must attract. These investors have historically been financially conservative and in high marginal-tax brackets. Included in this group are commercial banks, high-income individuals, nonfinancial corporations, and casualty insurance companies. While the tax-exempt status of municipal bonds continues to attract investors in the high-income range, the degree of conservatism of these investors is open to doubt. New York City's highly publicized financial difficulties, along with the recognition of similar problems in other areas of the country (particularly urban areas), have caused many investors to question the degree of safety historically assigned to municipal bonds.

THE CORPORATE BOND MARKET   Corporate bonds usually offer the investor a larger return than federal government and municipal bonds. This difference stems from the tax-exempt status of municipals and from the different degrees of risk associated with these securities. Even bonds of so-called blue-chip companies, where the risk of default is negligible, offer the investor some additional return over the yield on government securities. Corporate bonds are contractual agreements between the issuing company and the bondholder stipulating that the company will make interest payments over the life of the bond and repay its face value at maturity. While bondholders are often called investors, they are more appropriately classified as creditors since they are actually lending funds to the company. From the company's point of view, bonds are another source of external financing, in contrast to earnings generated within the firm and retained as a source of funds. Once a company decides to issue bonds, it either sells them publicly (in which the firm is assisted by investment bankers) or tries to place them directly with institutions (direct placement).

The purchasers of corporate bonds include life insurance companies, pension funds, state and local governments, and individuals. When we discussed the municipal bond market, we noted a change in investors' attitudes toward the safety of municipal bonds. In many cases the same change can be seen in the corporate bond market. Over the past 15 years corporate debt has roughly tripled. A first impression from this statistic might be that business has discovered the advantages of financial leverage (expanding more rapidly and making additional profits by using other peoples' money). The other side of this line of reasoning is that as a firm increases its use of debt, the capacity for repayment must increase by approximately the same amount if the firm is to remain as well off. But as corporate debt in the United States has increased in the last 15 years, the capacity for repayment has generally declined. Thus it is reasonable to expect that institutions and individuals who purchase corporate bonds will question their quality just as they have questioned the quality of municipal bonds.

THE MORTGAGE MARKET A mortgage is a legal instrument that provides the lender with a lien on the land and structures attached to the land. Mortgages are typically divided into four classifications: one-to-four family units, multifamily, commercial, and farm. At the beginning of 1977 more than 60% of mortgage debt outstanding was for one-to-four family units. In recent years, however, higher construction costs have decreased the ability of families to purchase single-family homes. Accordingly, if inflationary trends continue, more and more families may have no alternative but to shift to multifamily housing. Despite this trend, the basic component of the demand for housing continues to be owner-occupied homes. This demand depends on a number of variables including the number of marriages, the number of children in these families, and the attitude of the public toward home ownership.

The mortgage market is also categorized by the maturity of loans, the market in which the mortgage is sold, and the basic type of mortgage. To a degree the construction process represents a link between the short-term market for money and longer-term mortgage loans. It is common for builders to obtain a short-term construction loan to finance projects until construction is completed and the unit is sold. The purchaser then arranges for long-term mortgage financing and uses the proceeds of this loan to pay the builder, who then repays the construction loan. In view of government involvement in the mortgage market in recent years, the distinction between the primary and secondary market for mortgages has become significant. An example of such government involvement was the establishment of the Federal Home Loan Mortgage Corporation (or Freddie Mac) in the 1970s. The objective of Freddie Mac is to increase the availability of mortgage credit for housing by creating a secondary market for conventional mortgages. These moves by the government to create a more effective secondary market in residential mortgages have been designed to increase the ability of mortgages to compete more effectively for funds in the capital market. The primary suppliers of funds include savings and loans, mutual savings banks, commercial banks, and life insurance companies. Buyers of mortgages analyze the capacity to repay these obligations differently from other creditors in the capital market. While investors in the municipal and corporate bond markets have begun to question the capacity of the issuers to meet their repayment obligations, buyers of mortgages have tended to put more emphasis on the value of the real estate mortgaged as a measure of the quality of the mortgage. In view of the rapid increase in consumer debt in recent years, deeper analysis of repayment ability may be a healthy change.

THE MARKET FOR EQUITIES   Since an entire chapter is devoted to stocks in part 3, this discussion of equities is held to a minimum. Note, however, how the market for equities fits into our basic coverage of the capital markets. Common stocks differ from corporate bonds in several respects. Whereas bonds represent creditor claims, common stock represents ownership in a corporation. If a firm liquidates, the bondholder has a prior claim on assets. Because of this prior claim and the obligation of the corporation to pay interest and principal to the bondholder (the firm is not legally obligated to pay the common shareholder anything), common stock is considered riskier than corporate bonds. To compensate for this greater risk, investors expect to earn a higher return from common stock than they would from corporate bonds of the same firm.

Another difference between common stock and bonds is that common stock has no maturity date. Thus, if liquidity is to be provided in this market, both primary and secondary markets must exist. That is, a primary market for common stock must exist to facilitate the original issue of stock by companies, and a secondary market must exist to enable shareholders to resell their securities if they desire to liquidate their positions. To provide this liquidity, the over-the-counter (OTC) market and organized exchanges (such as the New York and American Stock Exchanges) exist.

THE EUROBOND MARKET   Just as Eurodollars (a type of Eurocurrency) exist to provide short-term liquidity for importers and exporters, Eurobonds exist to provide an international market for funds on a longer-term basis. Eurobonds are debt securities denominated in a currency other than that of the country in which the bonds are originally sold. Most of the bonds (which originated in London and are sold primarily in Europe) are denominated in United States dollars. To see how these bonds work, consider the case of a foreign subsidiary (located in Germany) of a company headquartered in the United States. If the subsidiary decided to raise funds externally by issuing bonds, it would have two options. It could float the issue and have the bonds denominated in German marks. These bonds are called foreign bonds. Or it could float the issue but have the bonds denominated in United States dollars. In this case the bonds could be sold in Germany along with other European countries and are called Eurobonds.

MONEY AND CAPITAL MARKETS:
AN OVERVIEW

Without doubt, our discussion of the money and capital markets has been very superficial. The material discussed in this chapter often forms an entire course on money and capital markets. Our objective, rather than to duplicate a course in money and capital markets, has been to provide an introduction to the role played by the money and capital markets along with the basic instruments that exist in each market. The money and capital markets are arbitrarily separated by the one-year maturity distinction. However, they are very much alike in their attempt to facilitate the transfer of financial assets in their particular domain and provide liquidity to the participants in the markets. In addition, we have seen that both the money and capital markets are international in scope.

A knowledge of the money and capital markets is valuable to the financial manager and the investor. Both individuals are very likely to have short-term and long-term needs for funds and/or a desire to invest funds for short as well as long periods of time. The money and capital markets can satisfy their needs. The money market deals in so-called esoteric financial assets, including instruments such as Treasury bills, government agency securities, commercial paper, CDs, bankers' acceptances, federal funds, RPs, and Eurodollars. This market is typically thought to be physically located in New York City where the large money-market banks are headquartered. However, it is national in scope because of a network of commercial banks and securities dealers. As such, it is a sophisticated system for facilitating open-market transactions in highly marketable short-term debt instruments.

The capital market facilitates the issue and trade of intermediate- and long-term securities. Although we examined this market from an individual-security point of view, it is typically subdivided into three parts —the bond market, the mortgage market, and the stock market—which together form an efficient market in which existing funds are attracted to the highest bidders. In addition, it augments the size of the pool of funds since by operating efficiently, it lowers the rate of return that is required on investments and increases the rate of return on savings.

SUMMARY

Financial managers and investors are likely candidates to use the money and capital markets. It is therefore important for these individuals to understand how each market functions and to be familiar with the instruments of each market. To satisfy this need, this chapter has covered the role of the money and capital markets in transferring financial assets and providing liquidity to the participants. In addition, the characteristics of the instruments in the money and capital markets were presented.

QUESTIONS

1. Define money market and capital market. Discuss the function of each and the differences between the two.
2. List and define the money market instruments.
3. List and discuss the components of the capital market.
4. Explain the usage of tax-anticipation bills and the reasons for their issuance.
5. Why was the Federal Financing Bank established?
6. The corporate image of firms with excellent credit standings has historically been enhanced by the successful issuance of commercial paper. Why has concern developed in recent years regarding the reliability of commercial paper ratings and the corporate image?
7. What is the role of federal funds in the money market and the basis of its importance?
8. Why is it more desirable for the Federal Reserve to use repurchase agreements to increase the supply of money for a short period of time than to buy securities via open-market operations?
9. Differentiate between Eurodollars and Eurocurrency.
10. Define debt management and discuss the impact of debt management by the Treasury on the money and capital markets.
11. Discuss the reasons for the establishment of the Federal Home Loan Mortgage Corporation.
12. Why is common stock considered riskier than corporate bonds, and how is this risk differential compensated for?
13. What are Eurobonds, and how are they used?

SELECTED REFERENCES

DOUGALL, HERBERT E., and GAUMNITZ, JACK E. *Capital Markets and Institutions.* 3rd ed. Englewood Cliffs, N.J.: Prentice-Hall, 1975.
GUP, BENTON E. *Financial Intermediaries: An Introduction.* Boston: Houghton Mifflin, 1976.
HEMPEL, GEORGE H., and YAWITZ, JESS B. *Financial Management of Financial Institutions.* Englewood Cliffs, N.J.: Prentice-Hall, 1977.

HENNING, CHARLES N.; PIGOTT, WILLIAM; and SCOTT, ROBERT HANEY. *Financial Markets and the Economy*. Englewood Cliffs, N.J.: Prentice-Hall, 1975; part 3.

POLAKOFF, MURRAY et al. *Financial Institutions and Markets*. New York: Houghton Mifflin, 1970; chs. 19, 20.

ROBINSON, ROLAND I., and WRIGHTSMAN, DWAYNE. *Financial Markets: The Accumulation and Allocation of Wealth*. New York: McGraw-Hill, 1974; parts 2, 3.

5 Bringing the Financial and Economic Systems Together

*Business is so bad that even the
people who never pay have stopped buying.*

Our primary objective in part 1 has been to establish the environment in which decisions are made by financial managers and investors. To accomplish this objective, we have attempted to justify each of the components of this part of the book. Still you may have the feeling that you have been exposed to the basic topics but that they are just parts of a puzzle. The purpose of this chapter is to "get it all together." As we now proceed to bring the financial and economic systems together, you will see that the rate of interest is the thread that runs through both systems.

THE FINANCIAL SYSTEM

Chapters 2, 3, and 4 were intended to substitute for much of the material that would ordinarily be included in a course on financial markets and institutions. Although texts in this area are generally out of date and rather boring because of the nature of the material, the material they include is very important. Successful financial managers and investors must be familiar with the types of financial instruments and institutions that exist to facilitate the flow of funds from savers to investors. Thus you should consider chapters 2 and 4 as supporting material. They were written to provide an overview of financial instruments and institutions. However, if we continue to talk about markets, the concept of price must eventually surface. Herein lies the importance of chapter 3, which covered the determination of interest rates. Our coverage must eventually focus on the market for money and the price of money—the rate of interest. Hence, while the financial instruments and institutions represent supporting information, the rate of interest represents the heart of our study of financial markets and institutions.

Recall from chapter 3 that two approaches, liquidity preference and loanable funds, are used to explain how interest rates are determined. The liquidity preference approach isolated the demand for and the supply of money. This approach assumes that the supply of money is a given quantity and views the demand for money in terms of three motives for preferring liquidity: the transactions motive, the precautionary motive, and the speculative motive. With the three components of demand and a given supply, the rate of interest is determined very much like price is determined in any market—by the interaction of supply and demand.

While the liquidity preference approach emphasizes the reasons that people hold money (prefer liquidity), the loanable funds framework emphasizes the reasons people lend and borrow funds. Thus lenders are suppliers of funds, and borrowers are demanders of funds. Once the two are brought together by the loanable funds approach, the interaction between supply and demand determines the rate of interest.

Although we mentioned that most financial analysts tend to use the loanable funds approach, we should reemphasize that the approach one uses is a matter of preference because both approaches yield the same result. We will maintain our neutrality and let you decide for yourself. However, as we proceed to link the financial system and the economic system, our approach is a logical extension of the liquidity preference approach. Both the liquidity preference and loanable funds approaches present only the financial side of the picture. An understanding of the entire system must also encompass the factors that influence the level of income. In other words, both the financial and producing parts of the economy must be included. Before turning to this task, we will first review a few of the more significant parts of chapter 1.

THE ECONOMIC SYSTEM

Our objective in chapter 1 was to provide an insight into the economic (and noneconomic) goals that have been established in the United States and how the economic system works to attain those goals. Without doubt, financial managers and investors must understand the goals of full employment, economic growth, price stability, and an acceptable balance-of-payments position. Without such knowledge, they are unlikely to be able to react to a change in monetary or fiscal policies, let alone forecast the change and act before it occurs. In addition to understanding typical relationships, financial managers and investors must be able to interpret and react to the unusual—for example, the stagflation recently experienced by the United States and the trend toward noneconomic goals. Our financial managers and investors must be able to interpret the financial impact of such unusual situations. However, an inability to interpret the usual almost guarantees an inability to interpret the unusual.

Most people would agree that the firm's most important goal is to maximize its value for its owners, the shareholders. Part 2 is intended to provide insight about how to maximize the value of the firm. Using the same logic, one can conclude that the bottom line or objective for the economy is the level of output or gross national product. In chapter 1 we indicated that the expenditure approach is one way of viewing total output or GNP for the economy (the goal of economic growth). With this approach we are basically looking at the components of the demand for final output: consumption expenditures, investment expenditures by the business sector, government spending, and net spending for our exports by foreigners (exports minus imports). To see how we get to the bottom line for the economy, recall from chapter 1 the determinants of our four expenditure categories. Consumption expenditures are positively related to the level of disposable income. Thus, given an increase (decrease) in disposable income, brought about either by an increase (decrease) in wages or a decrease (increase) in taxes, we would expect an increase (decrease) in consumption expenditures. The determination of government spending is not as simple as that for consumption expenditures. Government spending at the federal level (fiscal policy) is often influenced by its use as a tool to attain stability in the economy to achieve our economic goals. As such, we cannot isolate any specific factors that we can consistently rely on to serve as determinants of government spending. The demand for final output is also affected by trade outside the United States (which is determined on the basis of the theory of comparative advantage). To include such trade in our analysis, we must regard exports to other countries as a stimulant to our economy and imports as a stimulant to the economies of other countries. The final component of the demand for final output, investment by the business sector (which is partially a function of the rate of interest), is critical in the link between the financial and economic systems. Even though all the components of the demand for final output are very important to us as financial managers and investors, the investment area is where much of the action takes place.

LINKING THE ECONOMIC AND FINANCIAL SYSTEMS

With this brief review of the economic and financial systems, we proceed now to show how the two are interrelated. As an example, recall eq. 1-2 ($\uparrow m \rightarrow \downarrow i \rightarrow \uparrow I \rightarrow \uparrow GNP$) through which we briefly discussed the process by which a change in the supply of money changes the level of GNP. By bringing together the financial and economic systems, we can explain processes like this and their interim steps much more vividly. In other words, in addition to understanding the relationship between a change in the money supply and a change in GNP, you should also understand the relationships between the money supply and interest rates, interest rates and investment, and investment and GNP.

To link the two systems requires more specific terminology. The financial side of the picture illustrates how the commodity money is traded and how its price (the interest rate) is determined by the forces of supply and demand. The result, interest rate determination, is the same whether we think in terms of the liquidity preference approach or the loanable funds approach. Now we can be more precise about the economic system. Specifically, when we refer to the economic system we are actually referring to the output or production (sometimes called the real sector) part of the system. In other words, we are interested in the output of goods and services produced in the system, the reasons for changes in the level of output, and the sources of demand for the output. To a considerable extent, the real sector operates very much like the financial sector. A supply as well as a demand for goods and services exists. Further, as this market does its job, the interaction of supply and demand establishes prices for goods and services. While both the financial and producing sectors have their separate roles, they cannot operate in isolation. A great degree of interrelation exists. To see how this works, we will use two illustrations. First, we will utilize our previous example in which the initial change occurs on the financial side through a change in the supply of money. Our second illustration comes from the producing side, through a change in government spending.

Stimulus from the Financial Side

To examine the first case in more detail, we will assume that after a careful review of current economic conditions, the monetary authorities at the Federal Reserve have concluded that some economic stimulus is needed. To achieve this stimulus, they have decided to use open-market operations. Thus they buy government securities. These purchases inject more money into the system; the net short-term result of this action is lower interest rates. To observe this process, we will utilize both the liquidity preference and loanable funds approaches.

Using the first approach, we see that the money supply increases but the level of income does not change immediately. With the level of income (output) unchanged, no more money is demanded to carry on day-to-day transactions (the transactions demand for money remains constant). With the same transactions demand and a larger money supply, more money is available to satisfy the speculative demand for money, and the interest rate declines. The decline in the interest rate is illustrated graphically in fig. 5-1 in the move from point 1 to point 2 (this graph was originally discussed in fig. 3-2).

We can obtain essentially the same result by using the loanable funds approach. With this method we are isolating lenders and borrowers of funds. If the supply of loanable funds increases (as a result of an increase in the money supply) relative to the demand for loanable funds, the rate of interest declines. Thus, as a result of the decision by the monetary authorities to stimulate the economy by increasing the supply of money, the financial sector is sending signals to the producing sector through the reduction in the interest rate.

Let us now observe how signals from the financial sector are interpreted and reflected in the real sector. Although the primary participants in this sector in terms of demand for output are consumers, businesses, government, and foreigners, most of the action takes place in business investment. To see how this process works, consider an example. The financial manager of a hypothetical firm takes proposals for capital expenditures from the various departments, ranks them in order of potential return, and

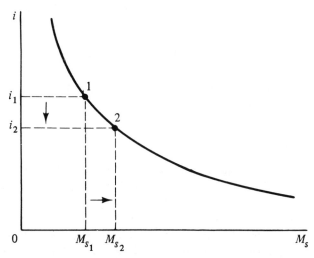

FIGURE 5-1   Speculative Demand for Money (M_s)

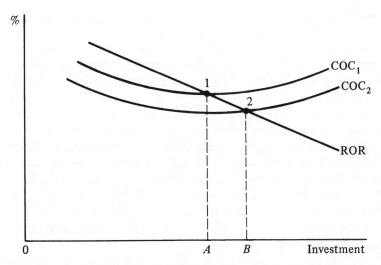

FIGURE 5–2   Investment and the Cost of Capital

recommends that the chief executive officer accept some projects and reject others. One approach to ranking the projects entails the calculation
of the rate of return for each project; part of the process must also include
an assessment of the risk associated with each project. With the projects
ranked by rate of return and other things equal, they are accepted as long
as the rate of return exceeds the cost of funds generated to finance the
expenditures (the cost of capital). In simplified form this process is
demonstrated in fig. 5–2. The rate of return (ROR) is downward sloping
and shows that projects with the highest ROR are undertaken first. On
the cost side, the cost of capital (COC) is used rather than explicitly
utilizing the rate of interest. Although interest rates have a significant and
positive impact on the cost of capital, other factors such as the risk of the
firm also affect this variable. Prior to any activity in the financial sector,
our hypothetical firm is investing OA at the point where the COC_1 and
ROR schedules intersect. When the Federal Reserve increases the supply
of money and interest rates decline, the COC for our firm drops from
COC_1 to COC_2. Other things equal, the firm moves to the new intersection of COC_2 and ROR (point 2) and increases its investment by AB.
Because other firms in the economy face similar situations, total business
investment for the economy increases.

The next step in the process is relatively simple. Recall from eq. 1–1
that $GNP = C + I + G + (X - M)$. If investment ($I$) increases and
no offsetting declines occur in any of the other components on the right
side of the equation, GNP increases. Within this step, however, other
factors must be considered. As the business sector invests in plant and
equipment, other sectors of the economy are stimulated to build the plant

and produce the equipment, stimulating employment and income in these sectors. In addition, the higher level of income stimulates consumption expenditures for all types of goods. Thus, as we move from the increase in investment to the increase in GNP, the system has generated an increase in the demand for the higher output that resulted from the higher level of investment.

To summarize, we have demonstrated the interrelationship between the financial and producing sectors. With the original stimulus occurring in the financial sector, we have demonstrated how an increase in the supply of money eventually affects the level of GNP. Between these two events, we discussed how the financial system, either through the liquidity preference or loanable funds framework, signals the producing sector. In the producing sector, we viewed the reaction to the reduction in interest rates in terms of the level of investment and, with interim steps, in terms of gross national product.

Stimulus from the Producing Side

The stimulus can just as easily originate in the production sector. We will extend our discussion of fiscal policy, introduced in chapter 1, to indicate in more detail how such policy affects the financial sector. Assume, as we did in chapter 1, that a decision is made to stimulate the economy by an increase in government spending for anything from paper (so more forms can be printed) to ball-point pens. Businesses that produce these goods must gear up to fill the orders. If they have been operating at less than capacity, they can now utilize existing equipment, hire additional employees, and use more raw materials. Income increases because of the larger payrolls and payments for raw materials, and these in turn increase demand for all types of goods and services. If the firms have been operating close to capacity prior to the new orders, they may very well increase their capacity by spending for new plant and equipment. If this occurs, then the sectors building the plant and producing the equipment are positively affected. The result is an increase in GNP.

However, our explanation is incomplete since the increase in government spending must be accompanied by a source of funds. If the increase in government spending is supported by an increase in taxes, the impact is felt primarily in the producing sector. Taxing individuals and businesses reduces their demand for final output, thus offsetting to a considerable extent the stimulative effect of the increase in government spending. This method of generating the funds also has an impact on the financial sector: saving is reduced, so the supply of funds to the money and capital markets diminishes.

As an alternative to taxes as a source of funds, the government could turn to the financial sector and sell government securities, thus operating with a budget deficit. If the economy is operating at less than capacity (that is, business investment is low and the supply of funds therefore exceeds the demand for funds in the financial markets), the expanded demand for funds by government should not appreciably increase interest rates. If, however, the demand for funds by businesses is high and the supply of and demand for loanable funds are approximately equal, the result may be considerably different. Unless something happens to relieve the pressure in the financial markets, interest rates will increase considerably and affect the producing sector. Specifically, the process we described in fig. 5–2 begins to work, but in reverse. The increase in interest rates increases the cost of capital to the business sector, and investment in plant and equipment declines. Thus the stimulative impact of the increase in government spending on GNP is eventually offset by the depressing effect of the decline in investment. This concept is, of course, the "crowding out" that we discussed in relation to monetary and fiscal policies in chapter 1. In an attempt to ease the pressure in the financial sector and avoid the possibility that government spending will crowd out business investment, the Federal Reserve could increase the supply of money (thus monetize the debt). Monetizing the debt dampens the upward pressure on interest rates and makes loanable funds available to satisfy the demand from government and business. However, pursuing this course of action runs the risk of setting off a round of inflation.

In the two previous sections of this chapter, we extended our discussion of monetary and fiscal policies from chapter 1. Our intent thus far has been to provide insight into the relationship between the financial and producing sectors. Since monetary policy is housed in the financial sector and fiscal policy is more closely related to the producing sector, you can begin to see that chapters 1–4 are not four separate chapters, but the framework for discussing two subsectors, financial and producing, that together create the environment in which financial managers and investors make decisions. We have used government spending and a change in the money supply as illustrations, but any of the components can initiate a change that can affect both the financial and producing sectors. In other words, an increase in business investment or a decline in the demand for loanable funds by one of the nongovernment components could have just as easily set off a disturbance. Let us turn now to a preview of parts 2 and 3.

SETTING THE STAGE

The objective of financial managers should be to maximize the value of the firm for its owners, the shareholders. The purpose of part 2 is to acquaint you with the basic decisions that financial managers confront in their attempts to attain their objectives. These decisions include investments, financing, and dividend policy. Optimal investment decisions, both short-term and long-term, maximize the profitability generated from the operations of the firm. As financial managers utilize the tools for making investment decisions, they must simultaneously consider the sources of funds to support their contemplated investment expenditures. Thus they must determine whether the needed funds can be generated internally. If not, can they obtain the funds externally? And if the funds are available externally, what is the optimal mixture of debt, equity, and preferred stock that minimizes the cost of capital to the firm? As they make these decisions, financial managers must determine the impact of each potential source of funds on the firm's ability to pay the shareholder a satisfactory dividend. Finally, we cannot stress too strongly that all these decisions must be made with awareness of the concepts covered in part 1. After our coverage of the basic financial decisions that must be made within the firm, we will "get it all together" for the financial manager in chapter 10.

Shareholders, because they are owners of the firm, are obviously just as interested as financial managers in the objective of maximizing the value of the firm. The shareholder's return is going to take the form of appreciation in the price of the common stock, in dividends, or both. Since the success of financial managers in providing both types of return hinges on their ability to maximize return and minimize the cost of capital through optimal investment and financing decisions, shareholders are obviously interested in the financial manager's decisions. Further, since the success of financial managers in making these decisions determines the capacity of the firm to repay its debts, the creditors of the firm also have a common interest.

Part of our objective in part 3 is to discuss the analysis one might use in the valuation of common stocks and fixed-income securities. Since investors may hold securities of many types, we provide a framework for making decisions regarding portfolios of securities. Once again, like financial managers, investors cannot make effective investment decisions without having one eye on the financial and economic systems.

QUESTIONS

1. Discuss the role of chapters 2, 3, and 4 in establishing the financial system.

2. Describe how the financial and economic systems are interrelated.

3. In view of your answer to question 2, describe in detail how an increase in the supply of money will eventually affect GNP.

4. In view of your answer to question 2, describe in detail what impact an increase in government spending could have on the economic and financial systems.

5. Suppose a firm's cost of capital will be different in the future. Would this affect the attractiveness of projects undertaken two years ago?

2 FINANCIAL MANAGEMENT

6   Understanding Financial Statements

*"For heaven's sake, stop your
perpetual worrying," said one businessman to his
distraught friend. "Do as I have done—consolidate all
worries into three: creditors, business deficits,
and simple insolvency."*

To analyze a company's financial position, one must understand its accounting statements. The two statements of primary interest are the balance sheet and the income statement; both are contained in the annual report and in quarterly statements sent to shareholders. While these documents represent an historical record of the company, they are typically utilized to determine where the company is and in what direction it can be expected to move. There has been great controversy over the relative value of the information contained in the statements. Since a company can report most transactions in a number of ways, financial data of companies in different industries (and many times, data of companies in the same industry) are not strictly comparable. Although intercompany and interindustry comparisons are difficult, evaluating the same firm over a period of time is less a problem. However, even this seemingly simple comparative analysis can prove hazardous.

Since different individuals and companies are interested in different aspects of a firm, given pieces of financial information can assume various degrees of importance. For example, short-term creditors may find most of the information in which they are interested in a statement of assets and liabilities, while potential investors may place more importance on the historical record of earnings growth. Both may be interested in all the available information, but some data may have more relevance to a particular problem. In addition, the importance of individual types of financial data changes over time. In the middle and latter 1960s many investors cared little about anything but growth in a company's earnings; a more recent trend has been to scrutinize the balance sheet (assets and liabilities) more carefully.

TYPES OF FINANCIAL STATEMENTS

There are two major types of financial statements, the balance sheet and the income statement. These in turn are used to derive additional statements. For example, a statement of retained earnings is a cumulative summary of the present and prior income statements, while a sources and uses of funds statement is calculated from the current and prior year's balance sheet and the current income statement.

The Balance Sheet

Table 6–1 (pp. 80–81) illustrates a typical balance sheet. This financial statement shows what a firm owns (its assets) and how it obtained the funds to purchase these assets (its liabilities and net worth). Balance sheets are typically constructed so that assets appear on the left side, liabilities and net worth on the right. Assets are sometimes found at the top of the page, followed by liabilities and net worth. Both assets and liabilities are listed in order of liquidity, with those that can be converted into cash most easily appearing first. Assets and liabilities are divided into two categories—short-term and long-term. Short-term assets include cash marketable securities, inventories, accounts receivable, and prepaid expenses. These items are relatively liquid and will generally be converted into cash within one year. Similarly, short-term liabilities such as accounts payable, short-term loans, and wages, taxes, and dividends payable (generally termed accruals) require payments by the company within one year. Long-term assets and liabilities are less liquid. The former include investments in other companies, intangible assets such as goodwill, and fixed assets such as land, plant, and equipment. These assets are normally not converted into cash as are current assets, but are kept by the company to produce its output. Long-term assets such as plant and equipment are gradually worn out in the production process, and this deterioration is accounted for in depreciation. Long-term liabilities consist primarily of debt that matures in over one year. The last category to appear on the liability side of the balance sheet is stockholders' equity or net worth. This segment includes capital stock entered at par value, capital paid in excess of par, and earnings retained by the company rather than paid to stockholders as dividends.

The Income Statement

While a balance sheet shows a firm's financial position at a particular point in time (end of quarter or end of fiscal year), an **income statement** such as that illustrated in table 6–2 (p. 82) matches revenues and expenses over a period of time. Expenses are deducted from revenues to calculate net income or net loss for the accounting period. A corporation's annual report covers revenues and costs for a period of one year; the company may also send shareholders a quarterly financial statement. A corporation's accounting, or fiscal, year does not necessarily correspond to the calendar year and thus does not always end on December 31.

While the basic configuration of most income statements is the same, many variations exist among industries and even among companies within the same industry. For example, some companies provide more detail about various income and expenditure categories than others. More important variations can occur when different accounting methods are employed. One method that has gained increasing attention in recent years is the accounting procedure used in recording inventory costs. Some companies use the most recent inventory purchases in figuring the cost of goods sold; other companies use the cost of the earliest existing inventory. The method of computation can have a large impact on the level of earnings reported to shareholders. Another significant variation occurs in the recording of depreciation. Since wear and tear of fixed assets can be accounted for by widely differing methods, this expense can be made larger or smaller depending on the method used. Consequently income can be made larger or smaller since, with a given level of revenues, income varies inversely with expenses.

The Statement of Retained Earnings

The **statement of retained earnings** or statement of earned surplus, displayed in table 6–3 (p. 83), summarizes changes in retained earnings in the owners' equity portion of the balance sheet from the beginning to the end of a fiscal period. In addition to the net income and common stock cash dividend items illustrated in table 6–3, the statement also includes cash dividends on preferred stock and stock dividends on common stock if any are paid during the period. It may also contain changes that affect previous statements of earnings. Note that retained earnings does not indicate the amount of cash the firm has.

The Statement of Changes in Financial Position

A statement of changes in financial position, sometimes called a sources and uses of funds statement, is useful in determining where a firm is spending funds and how it is providing for these expenditures. Such a

Table 6-1 The Blazer Corporation, Consolidated Balance Sheet, December 31, 1977 and 1978 (Thousands of Dollars)

	1978	1977	
Assets			
Current Assets			
Cash and short-term securities	$ 90	$ 75	Valued at lower of cost or market value
Accounts and notes receivable	256	296	What customers and others owe to Blazer
Inventories	285	329	Holdings of raw materials, work in process, and finished merchandise, valued at lower of cost or market
Prepaid expenses	20	25	Bills paid ahead of time
Total Current Assets	651	725	
Other Assets			
Domestic Movies, Inc.	116	105	Miscellaneous assets and investments in nonconsolidated subsidiary companies
Greater Overseas Corp.	59	52	
Other Investments	45	42	
Total Other Assets	220	199	
Fixed Assets			
Land	17	17	Long-lived assets valued at original cost
Buildings	199	193	
Equipment	614	564	
Total Fixed Assets	830	774	
Accumulated Depreciation	406	375	Wear and tear to fixed assets, recovered from Blazer's customers
	424	399	
Total Assets	$1295	$1323	

TABLE 6-1 *Continued*

	1978	1977	
Liabilities and Shareholders' Equity			
Current Liabilities			
Accounts payable	$ 180	$ 211	Owed by Blazer to suppliers, employees, and others
Accrued liabilities	20	20	
Installments of long-term debt	15	15	Past borrowings soon due to be repaid
Accrued taxes	34	25	Taxes owed but not yet paid
Dividends payable	5	6	Dividends declared but not yet paid
Total Current Liabilities	254	277	
Long-Term Debt	385	400	Money borrowed and not due to be repaid within the next 12 months
Deferred Income Taxes	185	205	Taxes owed but not currently payable because taxes for public reporting and taxes for tax reporting may differ
Shareholders' Equity			
Preferred stock	11	11	Funds originally contributed by Blazer's shareholders
Common stock, 50¢ par value; authorized 30,000 shares; outstanding 20,000 shares	10	10	
Capital surplus	200	200	Additional funds received from shareholders from sale of stock above par value
Retained earnings	250	220	Earnings reinvested in the business
Total Shareholders' Equity	471	441	
Total Liabilities and Shareholders' Equity	$1295	$1323	

TABLE 6-2 The Blazer Corporation, Statement of Consolidated Income, Year Ended December 31, 1978 (In Thousands of Dollars; Per Share Amounts in Dollars)

Net Sales	$1752	Amount receivable or received from customers
Foreign management fees	5	
Interest and other income	14	
	1771	
Cost of Products Sold	1422	Amount owed or already paid for wages and materials
Depreciation	31	Noncash provision for wear and tear on fixed assets
Selling, general, and administrative expenses	175	Funds paid or owed for commissions, advertising, salaries, and general expenses
Interest charges	35	Cost of borrowed money
	1663	
Income Before Income Taxes	108	
Taxes on income	47	Funds paid or owed for federal and state income taxes
Net Income	$ 61	Earnings available for dividends and reinvestment
Per Share of Common Stock	3.05	Net income divided by number of shares of common stock outstanding

TABLE 6–3 The Blazer Corporation, Statement of Retained Earnings, December 31, 1978 (In Thousands of Dollars)

Balance, beginning of year	$220
Net income	61
	$281
Cash dividends on common stock, $1.55 per share	31
Balance, end of year	$250

statement indicates whether a firm is financing expansion internally through normal operations or externally by selling new long-term debt or equity.

Data for the funds statement in table 6–4 (p. 84) are found in Blazer's balance sheet and income statement. Since a flow occurs over a period of time, it is necessary to compute changes in balance sheet items between two statement dates. Sources are provided by changes that reduce assets or increase liabilities and net worth items. Funds are used when asset values increase or when liability and net worth items decline. For example, the sale of 20-year bonds increases long-term debt—a liability—and provides an inflow of funds for the firm. Conversely, an increase in net plant and equipment—an asset—represents a use of funds and requires an offsetting change somewhere else. The financing might be provided by operations, by the sale of debt or stock, or by a decrease in working capital.

Although some statements are used to discover sources and applications of cash, most are employed to determine changes in working capital. Since working capital is composed of current entries on the balance sheet, net changes can occur only because of transactions in items other than current assets and current liabilities. Consequently, if a customer pays a bill due the company, no change occurs in working capital since one current asset is merely replaced by another (accounts receivable by cash). On the other hand, the sale of new common stock, taken by itself, tends to increase working capital. In the statement shown in table 6–4 uses exceed sources by $51,000, reducing working capital by the same amount. The bottom portion of the statement displays changes in each component of current assets and current liabilities. The summary indicates that the primary result of the change was a reduction of accounts receivable and inventories.

TABLE 6–4 The Blazer Corporation, Statement of Changes in Financial Position, Year Ended December 31, 1978 (In Thousands of Dollars)

Financial Resources Provided By		
Net income	$ 61	Funds from profits after taxes
Add (deduct) items not affecting working capital		
Depreciation	31	Expenses that reduce profit on the income statement but require no cash outlay
Deferred income taxes	(20)	
Provided from operations	72	
Proceeds from additional long-term debt	38	Funds generated from increasing long-term liabilities or decreasing long-term assets
Proceeds from sales of property, plant, and equipment less gains included in net income	7	
	117	
Financial Resources Used For		
Expenditures for property, plant, and equipment	63	Funds expended by increasing long-term assets or decreasing long-term liabilities
Increase in investment, advances, and other assets	21	
Reductions of long-term debt	53	
Cash dividends	31	Cash dividends paid to stockholders
	168	
Increase (decrease) in working capital	$(51)	

TABLE 6–4 *Continued*

Summary of Changes in Working Capital

Increase (Decrease) in Assets

Cash and short-term securities	$ 15
Accounts and notes receivable	(40)
Inventories	(44)
Prepaid expenses	(5)
	(74)

(Increase) Decrease in Current Liabilities

Accounts payable	31
Accrued liabilities	—
Installments of long-term debt	—
Accrued taxes	(9)
Dividends payable	1
	23

Increase (Decrease) in Working Capital	$(51)

SPECIAL PROBLEMS WITH FINANCIAL STATEMENTS

Financial statement analysis can hold pitfalls for the unwary. Similar transactions can be recorded in a number of acceptable ways, and some of the more important financial insights are not found in the formal statements but in footnotes to the report.

Valuation of Inventory

For many firms inventory is the largest single item among current assets. Although it is increased and reduced over the production cycle, most companies keep some minimum level on hand. Since inventory may be purchased at widely varying costs during periods of unstable prices, the company must decide for accounting purposes the cost of the inventory that has been consumed. If the inventory has been purchased during a period of rising prices, the firm has on hand some lower-cost units purchased in the past; at the same time it has some units bought at the current higher price. Reported profits will be higher or lower depending on which portion of inventory the company records it is using. There are two major methods of accounting for inventory in cost of goods sold—**first-in, first-out** (FIFO) and **last-in, first-out** (LIFO). Under the former, the first goods acquired are also the first ones sold, leaving the more recently purchased units still in inventory. Under LIFO the last units purchased are the first ones sold, leaving the first units in the remaining inventory. During a period of rising prices, the firm can report a lower cost of goods sold and thus a higher profit by using first-in, first-out inventory accounting. Unfortunately, the higher profit also entails a larger tax liability. Suppose a firm has 300 units of inventory valued at $10 per unit on hand on January 1 and makes the following purchases.

Date	Units	Price/Unit	Cost
Beginning	300	$10	$3000
April 1	400	12	4800
July 12	300	13	3900
September 1	500	16	8000
December 3	400	16	6400

On December 31 the company has 500 units remaining in its inventory. Since it acquired 1600 units during the year to add to a beginning inventory of 300, the company consumed 1400 units in the course of business (300 + 1600 − 500 = 1400 units).

Using FIFO, the cost of goods sold would be

$$300 \times \$10 = \$ \ 3,000$$
$$400 \times \ 12 = \ \ 4,800$$
$$300 \times \ 13 = \ \ 3,900$$
$$400 \times \ 16 = \ \ 6,400$$
$$\overline{1400} \qquad \overline{\$18,100}$$

and the value of the remaining inventory would be $8000 (500 units $\times$ 16 = $8000).

However, if LIFO is used in valuing inventory, the cost of goods sold would be

$$200 \times \$12 = \$ \ 2,400$$
$$300 \times \ 13 = \ \ 3,900$$
$$500 \times \ 16 = \ \ 8,000$$
$$400 \times \ 16 = \ \ 6,400$$
$$\overline{1400} \qquad \overline{\$20,700}$$

and the value of remaining units is $5400 [(300 $\times$ \$10) + (200 $\times$ \$12) = $5400].

If the company had sales of $30,000 and other expenses of $5000 during the year, its tax liability and reported profits would appear as shown in table 6–5. Although the first-in, first-out method of inventory accounting has the effect of showing increased profits during a period of rising prices, it also results in higher taxes. This is the case even though the change in profits is brought about by the method of accounting rather than by actual operations. The inflation experienced during the 1970s induced a number of companies to change from FIFO to LIFO in order

TABLE 6–5 Effect of Inventory Valuation on Earnings

	FIFO		LIFO	
Sales		$30,000		$30,000
Cost of Goods Sold				
Beginning inventory	$ 3,000		$ 3,000	
Purchases	23,100		23,100	
	26,100		26,100	
Ending inventory	8,000	18,100	5,400	20,700
Gross profit		11,900		9,300
Other expenses		5,000		5,000
Income before taxes		6,900		4,300
Taxes on income (50%)		3,450		2,150
Net Income		$ 3,450		$ 2,150

to reduce their tax liability and improve cash flows. The deterrent to last-in, first-out accounting is that the company must report lower profits to stockholders since the Internal Revenue Service requires that firms using LIFO for tax purposes also use it for financial reporting purposes.

A third method of valuing inventories is through average cost. Under this type of costing, the firm determines a weighted average of the cost of an item and uses this basis as the inventory valuation. For example, the total costs for all orders are added together and the result is divided by the number of units purchased.

Measuring Depreciation

Depreciation is a cost allocation (not involving a flow of cash) to account for the wear and tear of assets over a period of time. Since the actual deterioration of these assets—whether physical or economic—is highly subjective, there has been much disagreement about how charges should be estimated. One starting point, and one over which management has little control, is establishing the value of the asset that is subject to depreciation. Generally accepted accounting practice dictates that this value is the amount actually invested in the asset or its historic cost. Even here, however, accuracy is criticized since original cost grossly understates the cost of replacement during a period of inflation. The result is an inability to replace deteriorated plant and equipment through depreciation reserves.

Equally important is the appropriate period over which an asset should be depreciated. Since a shorter estimated life results in larger expenses (even though no cash outlay is required) and lower taxes, corporations generally like to use relatively short life spans. To limit this inclination, the Internal Revenue Service has established a set of estimated lives for specific assets. Another counter to this tendency is the lower income that is reported to stockholders due to the large depreciation expenses.

Three basic methods of depreciation are used today: (1) service-life methods (operating hours or units of production), (2) straight-line method, and (3) accelerated methods (declining balance or sum of-the-years' digits). All these are accepted by the Internal Revenue Service for tax purposes. A company may choose one method for reporting income to the IRS and another for reporting income to shareholders. The general practice is to minimize income and thus taxes for reports to the IRS, while showing stockholders a higher earnings figure. This option of different reporting practices for owners and the IRS is not allowed in inventory valuation.

SERVICE-LIFE METHODS   The **service-life methods** include estimating depreciation based on either the probable operating hours or the units of production expected during an asset's lifetime. In the former method, depreciation is calculated on a per-hour basis and charged off as hours of use are accumulated. For example, if a machine costs $10,000 and has an estimated useful life of 1000 hours, depreciation is recorded at $10 ($10,000/1000 hours) for each hour it is used. With the units-of-production method of recording depreciation, the total number of output units an asset can be expected to produce is estimated. Depreciation is then calculated on a per-unit basis and recorded as output units are accumulated. If the asset in the previous example is estimated to produce 100,000 units over its lifetime, depreciation is charged off at $.10 ($10,000/100,000 units) per unit.

Both of these methods generate depreciation expenses that fluctuate over the life of the asset, with a greater amount of use resulting in a correspondingly higher charge for depreciation. Not only do they generate the greatest charges when income is high, they also give a more accurate representation of physical deterioration.

STRAIGHT-LINE METHODS **Straight-line depreciation** charges off an equal amount of an asset's cost during each year of its life. Unlike the service-life methods, this type of depreciation is not concerned with equipment utilization or productivity. For example, a piece of equipment costing $10,000 with an expected life span of 10 years is charged off at $1000 ($10,000/10 years) per year under the straight-line depreciation method.

ACCELERATED METHODS The two most common methods of using accelerated depreciation are declining balance and sum-of-the-years' digits. Both of these allow larger depreciation charges in the early part of an asset's life and smaller charges in the latter part. As in the case with the service-life and straight-line methods, charges equal to original cost are made over the entire estimated life of the asset.

The declining-balance method is tied to the straight-line rate. For most assets the Internal Revenue Service currently allows a maximum of twice the straight-line rate to be taken against book value. Book value in a given year is equal to an asset's original cost minus the depreciation charges already accumulated. To illustrate, for an asset with a ten-year life, the declining-balance rate is 20%, or twice the straight-line rate of 10%. The 20% rate remains the same throughout the life of the asset although the basis against which it is taken declines each year. This depreciation is calculated as follows.

Year	Depreciation Expense	Accumulated Depreciation	Book Value
0			$10,000
1	.20 × $10,000 = $2,000	$2,000	8,000
2	.20 × 8,000 = 1,600	3,600	6,400
3	.20 × 6,400 = 1,280	4,880	5,120
.	.	.	.
.	.	.	.
.	.	.	.
10	.20 × 1,342 = 268	8,926	1,074

Since this method results in a positive book value at the end of the estimated useful life of the asset, the firm switches to straight-line depreciation in the last year and writes off the entire amount ($1342). An alternative is to switch to the straight-line method in an earlier year in order to charge off the entire original cost. This change may be made without the approval of the IRS.

While the declining-balance method determines depreciation by taking a constant percentage of a declining book value each year, the sum-of-the-years' digits method takes a declining percentage of an asset's original cost each year. The depreciation rate in the latter method is given as a fraction. The denominator in the fraction is found by summing the years of life over which the asset is expected to last ($1 + 2 + 3 + \ldots + 10 = 55$ for a 10-year asset), while the numerator is the number of years remaining in the asset's life ($10, 9, 8, \ldots, 1$). The denominator remains the same throughout the asset's life, and the numerator is reduced by one each year. For an asset with an expected life span of 10 years, the fraction is 10/55 the first year, 9/55 the second year, 8/55 the third year, and so on. Rather than adding the years of the asset's life to find the denominator, a simplifying equation can be used:

$$\text{Sum-of-the-years' digits} = N(N + 1)/2 \qquad \text{6-1}$$

where N is the number of years over which the asset is to be depreciated. For a piece of equipment with an expected life of 10 years, the formula reads:

$$10(10 + 1)/2 = 110/2 = 55$$

The larger write-off in the early years of an asset's life under sum-of-the-years' digits method of accounting is shown in the following illustration of a $10,000 piece of equipment with an expected life of 10 years.

Both the declining-balance and sum-of-the-years' digits methods protect larger amounts of earnings from taxation during the early years of an asset's life. In addition, they probably more accurately appraise the asset

Year	Depreciation Expense	Accumulated Depreciation	Book Value
0			$10,000
1	10/55 × $10,000 = $1,818	$ 1,818	8,182
2	9/55 × 10,000 = 1,636	3,454	6,546
3	8/55 × 10,000 = 1,455	4,909	5,091
.	.	.	.
.	.	.	.
.	.	.	.
10	1/55 × 10,000 = 182	10,000	0

being depreciated since resale values generally decline more rapidly during the early years. Primarily for the first reason, companies generally choose one of these methods in reporting income to the Internal Revenue Service.

SALVAGE VALUE   The previous illustrations were simplified by assuming that the asset being depreciated had no resale, or salvage, value at the end of its estimated life. Since this is not always the case, it is sometimes necessary to include a **salvage value** in the calculation. With the declining-balance method, no adjustment is necessary until the final year's expense is recorded. In this year the difference between the book value and the salvage value is taken as the depreciation charge. For example, in the illustration used, a $1000 salvage results in a depreciation expense of $342 ($1342 − $1000) during the tenth year. With each of the other methods, salvage value is initially deducted from original cost to determine the amount that can be depreciated over the life of the asset. Using the straight-line method in the example, the annual amount that can be depreciated is $900 (.10 × $9000), rather than $1000 (.10 × $10,000) with no salvage value. Using sum-of-the-years' digits, depreciation in the initial year is $1636 (10/55 × $9000) rather than $1818 (10/55 × $10,000). In each case the ending book value equals the salvage value.

Calculating Earnings per Share

In its most elementary form, earnings per share (EPS) is found by simply dividing the earnings available to common stockholders by the average number of common shares outstanding. Unfortunately, because of the complexities in financing modern corporations, this type of calculation may be misleading. Accepted accounting practice now requires that many companies publish statistics on both primary earnings per share and fully diluted earnings per share. The former is found by dividing earnings available to common stockholders by the average number of common shares and the share equivalents outstanding. Common stock equivalents include shares that would be issued through the exercise of outstanding warrants and options and, in some cases, the new shares created by the conversion of convertible securities. Fully diluted EPS is calculated by considering the effect of all potential dilution on earnings per share. In this method all convertible securities are used in calculating potential dilution.

FINANCIAL RATIOS

Since interest in a company's financial status depends on the particular concern of the analyst, ratios can be calculated to provide different information. For example, although stockholders should be concerned with all aspects of a firm's financial picture, a limited number of areas, such as profitability, will probably occupy most of their attention. Conversely, short-term creditors are generally more interested in measures of liquidity.

Ratio analysis involves two types of comparison. The first is the comparison of ratios of a given firm with industry averages or with similar companies. This indicates whether figures on a firm's balance sheet or income statement are "out of line" with the figures on financial statements of similar companies. Industry statistics for use in ratio analysis are available from firms such as Dun & Bradstreet and Robert Morris Associates. A second type of analysis involves comparing the present ratios with past ratios. This type of examination can be useful in discerning whether certain segments of a firm's financial picture are deteriorating or improving and what can be expected in the future. Many times this is accomplished by plotting trend lines of a company's ratios.

Financial ratios are usually categorized according to (1) how rapidly assets can be turned into cash, (2) how efficiently the firm is employing its assets, (3) what portion of assets is being financed by debt, and (4) how profitably assets are being used. We will classify ratios into the following four types, which correspond to these descriptions: (1) liquidity, (2) activity, (3) leverage, and (4) profitability. Some of the most significant ratios in each of these categories are listed in the following section. Financial data for constructing the ratios are from the balance sheet and income statement found earlier in this chapter.

Liquidity Ratios

These ratios indicate the ability of the firm to meet its maturing obligations. Since these obligations require payment of cash within a relatively short period of time, the more easily the firm can turn its assets into cash or the more cash it already has, the better its ability to fulfill its short-term obligations.

1. CURRENT RATIO   This measure of current assets and current liabilities is probably the best-known of all ratios. Supposedly, a higher ratio indicates that a firm is more liquid and better able to meet its short-term obligations. This can be misleading, however, since not all current assets are equally liquid. The current ratio for Blazer Corporation at the end of 1977 is

$$\text{Current ratio} = \frac{\text{Current assets}}{\text{Current liabilities}} = \frac{\$651,000}{\$254,000} = 2.56 \qquad \textbf{6-2}$$

2. QUICK RATIO   Often called the acid-test ratio, the quick ratio is an accurate test of liquidity since inventories (the least liquid component of current assets) are deleted. For Blazer this ratio is

$$\text{Quick ratio} = \frac{\text{Current assets} - \text{Inventories}}{\text{Current liabilities}} = \frac{\$651,000 - \$285,000}{\$254,000} \qquad \textbf{6-3}$$
$$= 1.44$$

Activity Ratios

These ratios attempt to show how effectively the firm is utilizing its assets. This category consists primarily of ratios measuring turnover, which indicates how rapidly assets flow through into sales.

1. INVENTORY TURNOVER   Inventory is an expensive asset because it normally earns no direct return, so this ratio is designed to show how effectively a company converts its inventory into sales. A slow-moving inventory (and resulting low turnover ratio) tends to lower profits. In this ratio cost of goods sold is sometimes used instead of sales since inventory is valued at cost while sales are carried at market prices. In addition, inventory is sometimes averaged over the year instead of being recorded at its year-end value. With sales in the numerator and year-end inventory in the denominator, the inventory turnover for Blazer is

$$\text{Inventory turnover} = \frac{\text{Sales}}{\text{Inventory}} = \frac{\$1,752,000}{\$285,000} = 6.15 \qquad \textbf{6-4}$$

2. RECEIVABLES TURNOVER   This ratio simply measures the number of times accounts receivable are turned into sales each year. Although credit sales are generally used, if these are not specified in the financial statements, total sales can be substituted. A ratio that is low in comparison with the same ratio of similar firms may indicate that a large portion of receivables is past due. Blazer's receivables turnover is

$$\text{Receivables turnover} = \frac{\text{Sales}}{\text{Accounts receivable}} = \frac{\$1,752,000}{\$256,000} = 6.84 \qquad \textbf{6-5}$$

A similar ratio in measuring the effectiveness of a company's credit policy is the average collection period. This ratio indicates the number of days the firm must wait for payment after making a sale; it is computed by dividing sales per day into receivables. For Blazer the average collection period is

$$\text{Average collection period} = \frac{\text{Receivables}}{\text{Sales per day}} = \frac{\$256,000}{\$1,752,000/360 \text{ days}} \qquad \textbf{6-6}$$
$$= 52.6 \text{ days}$$

3. TOTAL ASSET TURNOVER   Total asset turnover indicates how efficiently resources are used in generating output. This ratio has some

drawbacks in the short run (for example, a firm would lower its turnover by purchasing new equipment), but it can be used with other ratios to give a good indication of a company's efficiency. Blazer's total asset turnover is

$$\text{Total asset turnover} = \frac{\text{Sales}}{\text{Total assets}} = \frac{\$1,752,000}{\$1,295,000} = 1.35 \qquad 6\text{--}7$$

Leverage Ratios

Financial leverage occurs when the firm obtains a portion of its assets with the proceeds from fixed-cost financing. The payments must be made regardless of profitability, thus implying that greater leverage subjects the firm to more risk, because unforeseen circumstances may prevent the company from meeting its fixed-payment schedule. Leverage is not necessarily bad, since it can be used to increase income available to stockholders. Therefore one must recognize that leverage can work both for and against the firm.

1. DEBT RATIO   The ratio of total debt to total assets is commonly referred to as the debt ratio. The numerator includes all debt on the balance sheet including current liabilities. This ratio measures the percentage of funds supplied by creditors. Blazer's debt ratio is

$$\text{Debt ratio} = \frac{\text{Total debt}}{\text{Total assets}} = \frac{\$824,000}{\$1,295,000} = .64 \qquad 6\text{--}8$$

2. DEBT-TO-EQUITY RATIO   This ratio is directly related to the debt ratio and is probably the most commonly used measure of leverage. It is found by dividing a firm's total debt by shareholders' equity. As with the debt ratio, a higher debt-to-equity ratio shows a greater proportion of funds contributed by creditors and a resulting higher level of financial risk. Blazer's balance sheet indicates a debt-to-equity ratio of

$$\text{Debt-to-equity ratio} = \frac{\text{Total debt}}{\text{Shareholders' equity}} = \frac{\$824,000}{\$471,000} = 1.75 \qquad 6\text{--}9$$

3. TIMES INTEREST EARNED   This ratio measures the number of times annual interest charges are covered by earnings before interest and taxes. The before-tax figure is used since interest is a deductible item for income tax purposes and the firm's ability to cover interest charges is thus not affected by the tax payments. This ratio indicates the extent to which earnings could fall during adverse economic conditions and still enable the firm to meet its interest obligations. The coverage for Blazer is

$$\text{Times interest earned} = \frac{\text{Earnings before interest and taxes}}{\text{Interest expense}}$$
$$= \frac{\$143,000}{\$35,000} = 4.09$$

6–10

A similar, but more inclusive ratio, is fixed-charge coverage. This measures the ability of the firm to cover all fixed expenses including interest, leases, and rentals. To obtain fixed-charge coverage, the additional expenses are added to both the numerator and the denominator of the times interest earned ratio.

Profitability Ratios

Profitability ratios measure profit in relation to either sales or investment. These ratios are of great significance to the company's owners and to its creditors. Like other ratios, profitability measures must be analyzed over a period of time, and the pitfalls of using reported earnings must be taken into account.

1. GROSS PROFIT MARGIN This ratio is a measure of the return on sales and is computed by dividing sales into gross profit (sales less cost of goods sold). It is an indicator of the company's pricing policy and the efficiency with which output is produced. Blazer's gross profit margin is

$$\text{Gross profit margin} = \frac{\text{Sales} - \text{Cost of goods sold}}{\text{Sales}}$$
$$= \frac{\$330,000}{\$1,752,000} = 19.0\%$$

6–11

2. NET PROFIT MARGIN The net profit margin indicates the relative efficiency of the firm after all expenses including taxes are considered. The ratio is found by dividing sales into net profit after taxes. Blazer's net profit margin is

$$\text{Net profit margin} = \frac{\text{Net profit after taxes}}{\text{Sales}} = \frac{\$61,000}{\$1,752,000} = 3.5\% \quad \text{6–12}$$

3. RETURN ON TOTAL ASSETS The return on total assets is calculated by dividing net profit after taxes by total assets. This ratio is a gauge of the company's return on its aggregate investment. The return on total assets for Blazer is

$$\text{Return on total assets} = \frac{\text{Net profit after taxes}}{\text{Total assets}}$$
$$= \frac{\$61,000}{\$1,295,000} = 4.7\%$$

6–13

4. RETURN ON NET WORTH   The return on net worth measures the firm's after-tax profits in relation to the stockholders' investment. An extraordinarily high return on net worth may result from a large amount of debt in the company's capital structure. When this ratio is considerably higher than return on total assets, a close look at the company's capital structure is warranted. Blazer's return on net worth is

$$\text{Return on net worth} = \frac{\text{Net profit after taxes}}{\text{Net worth}}$$
$$= \frac{\$61,000}{\$471,000} = 13.0\%$$

6–14

A similar but more restrictive ratio measures the return on common stock equity. This ratio considers only the common stockholders' investment. To obtain this, cash dividends on preferred stock are subtracted from net profit after taxes in the numerator, and the par value of preferred stock is subtracted from net worth in the denominator.

SUMMARY

Understanding how to interpret a firm's financial statements is crucial to both the financial manager and the investor. This applies to the primary statements—the balance sheet and the income statement—and to statements derived from these. The most common method of using financial data is ratio analysis. The ratios are utilized to compare one firm with another and to track a single firm's financial status over time.

In examining financial statements one must understand that there are a number of acceptable methods of recording similar transactions. As a result, financial managers and investors have to understand how the data in the financial statements were obtained.

QUESTIONS

1. Describe the contents and purpose of the balance sheet.
2. What is the difference between short-term and long-term assets? List examples of each.
3. Name some different accounting methods employed in preparing the income statement that will cause a variation in income.
4. How is a statement of changes in financial position useful to a firm?
5. Name the two major methods of accounting for inventory, and explain the difference between the two methods in terms of results on profits.
6. In determining depreciation expense, a company may choose one

method for reporting income to the IRS and another method for reporting income to the shareholders. What is the purpose of this, and why do companies generally choose either the declining-balance or sum-of-the-years' digits methods in reporting income to the IRS?

7. Here are the beginning inventory and data on purchases of the Hattaway Company:

Date	Units	Price/Unit	Cost
Beginning	50	$60	$3000
Jan. 14	110	50	5500
Feb. 2	70	55	3850
Feb. 15	80	65	5200

On February 28 the company had 100 units remaining in its inventory. Determine the cost of goods sold using (a) the LIFO method; (b) the FIFO method.

8. Define the following four types of ratios: (a) liquidity, (b) activity, (c) leverage, and (d) profitability. Explain who would primarily be concerned with each type of ratio.

9. The following information was taken from the financial statements of the Ribray Corporation. Calculate the following ratios: (a) current ratio; (b) quick ratio; (c) inventory turnover; (d) receivables turnover; (e) total asset turnover; (f) debt ratio; (g) gross profit margin; (h) net profit margin; (i) return on total assets.

Ribray Corporation
Balance Sheet
December 31, 19—

Assets

Current Assets:		
Cash	$ 40,000	
Receivables	65,000	
Inventory	175,000	
Total Current Assets		$280,000
Fixed Assets:		
Plant equipment	45,000	
Building	75,000	
Total Fixed Assets		120,000
Total Assets		$400,000

Liabilities

Current Liabilities:		
Accounts payable	$ 55,000	
Notes payable	45,000	
Total Current Liabilities		$100,000
Long-term Liabilities:		
Long-term debt		65,000
Total Liabilities		165,000

Capital

Net Worth	235,000
Total Liabilities and Capital	$400,000

Ribray Corporation
Income Statement
For Year Ended December 31, 19—

Sales	$600,000	
Cost of Goods Sold	300,000	
Gross Profit		$300,000
Expenses:		
Operating expenses	125,000	
Depreciation expense	12,000	
Interest expense	3,000	
Total Expenses		140,000
Net Income Before Taxes		160,000
Taxes (50%)		80,000
Net Income After Taxes		$ 80,000

SELECTED REFERENCES

GITMAN, LAWRENCE G. *Principles of Managerial Finance.* New York: Harper and Row, 1976. ch. 3.

HAMPTON, JOHN J. *Financial Decision Making: Concepts, Problems, and Cases.* Reston, Va.: Reston Publishing Co., 1976. ch. 5.

HELFERT, ERICH A. *Techniques of Financial Analysis.* Homewood, Ill.: Richard D. Irwin, 1977. ch. 2.

KRONCKE, CHARLES O.; NEMMERS, EDWIN E.; and GRUNEWALD, ALAN. *Managerial Finance: Essentials.* St. Paul, Minn.: West Publishing Co., 1976. ch. 11.

PHILIPPATOS, GEORGE C. *Essentials of Financial Management.* San Francisco: Holden-Day, 1974. ch. 3.

SCHALL, LAWRENCE D., and HALEY, CHARLES W. *Introduction to Financial Management.* New York: McGraw-Hill, 1977. ch. 11.

SOLDOFSKY, ROBERT M., and OLIVE, GARNET D. *Financial Management.* Cincinnati, Ohio: South-Western Publishing Co., 1974. ch. 12.

VAN HORNE, JAMES C. *Financial Management and Policy.* Englewood Cliffs, N.J.: Prentice-Hall, 1977. ch. 25.

7 Investment Decisions: Short-Term and Long-Term

A man was telling a friend that he was starting a business in partnership with another fellow.
"How much capital are you putting in it?" the friend asked.
"None. The other man is putting up the capital, and I'm putting in the experience."
"So, it's a fifty-fifty agreement."
"Yes, that's the way we're starting out. But I figure in about five years I'll have the capital and he'll have the experience."

Investment decisions are one part of an equation that determines the profitability of a firm. In fact, such decisions are the single most important determinant of a firm's profitability since superior investments can make an enterprise profitable despite poor decision making in other areas. Likewise, regardless of how well other areas are administered, poor investment decisions eventually lead to disaster.

It is generally agreed that the real goal of a firm's management should be to maximize the wealth of its owners. Even if one believes that this is the goal toward which management should strive, some argue that many managers are concerned primarily with their own survival in high-paying jobs. As a result, high-risk, high-return investment opportunities may be rejected in favor of alternatives that offer less risk and lower returns. This could be the case even though shareholders may desire the high-risk, high-return options. That the owners of a firm really have little say in its operation is nothing new. The structure of the large modern corporation, with its widely dispersed ownership, leaves management with a relatively free hand since significant stockholder input in the decision-making process is both time-consuming and expensive. Smaller firms, whose ownership is less diluted, present correspondingly fewer difficulties for stockholders.

The actual process of maximizing shareholder wealth is not nearly as easy as may be assumed, for it is not only a firm's profits that must be considered, but also the risk taken to generate these profits. For example, the financial manager must determine the most appropriate financing alternatives. The company must decide whether dividends should be paid and, if so, how much. In addition, the company can usually choose from among a number of production processes having different proportions of fixed and variable costs. The results of these and other decisions, which often seem isolated from the actual investment process, are important determinants of both profitability and risk. This chapter is devoted only to investment decisions; financing and financial structure decisions are discussed in chapters 8 and 9.

THE INVESTMENT DECISION

Many factors must be considered in deciding where money can best be invested. The financial manager must consider the alternatives in light of existing economic circumstances, but future conditions may be even more important. Long-term assets may require the commitment of a firm's funds for decades. Overlooking important trends and future perspectives can lead to the acquisition of an asset that is initially profitable but less than desirable over its entire life. Hence an understanding of the variables discussed in part 1, such as projections of gross national product and interest rates, is important for any financial manager.

A decision to invest involves the acquisition of an asset that the company hopes will be profitable. Profitability is perhaps a poor choice of words since the firm is really interested in an asset that produces a positive cash flow rather than simply an increase in reported profits. Although cash flows and reported profits may seem compatible, chapter 6 showed that this is not necessarily the case. Cash is available for reinvestment, while reported profits may result only in increased taxes and an actual reduction in cash. Thus cash flow is the crucial variable in analyzing any investment proposal.

Since nearly any type of investment program, whether for the acquisition of short-term or long-term assets, involves costs as well as benefits, the financial manager is working with incremental cash flows. Hence we must consider only the differential in cash flows resulting from an investment option. Increased cash outflows in the form of higher overhead, maintenance, labor, and taxes must be deducted from increased receipts in evaluating a new proposal. In addition, implementing a new project may reduce cash flows in existing operations of the firm. For example, the introduction of a new detergent by a large soap manufacturer will surely draw sales from some of its existing products as well as from the products of its competitors. All these changes must be taken into account in computing incremental cash flows.

The financial manager must consider not only the absolute change in cash flows, but also the timing and certainty of the changes. Cash cannot be reinvested until it is actually received, so cash generated at an early date is more valuable than an equal amount of cash to be received some time in the future. Since this concept of timing is more relevant to long-term than short-term proposals, it is covered in more detail in the section on long-term investments.

The certainty of cash flows is an appropriate variable for both long-term and short-term investments. Investors generally try to avoid uncertain returns; thus two proposals with the same amounts and timing of cash flows but different certainties of receiving the flows should result in a preference for the project with the greatest certainty. For example, suppose a financial manager is considering the three proposals indicated in table 7–1. Each project produces a flow in only one period. Proposal A has a 10% probability of a $1000 cash flow, a 20% probability of a $2000 flow, a 40% probability of a $3000 flow, a 20% probability of a $4000 flow, and a 10% probability of a $5000 flow. The five probabilities sum to 100%, implying that there are no other possibilities for proposal A. The expected cash flow of this proposal is equal to

$$(\$1000)(.10) + (\$2000)(.20) + (\$3000)(.40) + (\$4000)(.20) \\ + (\$5000)(.10) = \$3000$$

TABLE 7–1   Expected Cash Flows from Investment Proposals

Proposal A		Proposal B		Proposal C	
Probability (%)	Cash Flow ($)	Probability (%)	Cash Flow ($)	Probability (%)	Cash Flow ($)
10	1000	5	1000		
20	2000	20	2000		
40	3000	50	3000	100	3000
20	4000	20	4000		
10	5000	5	5000		
100		100		100	

A general notation for expected cash flow is

$$\overline{C} = C_1P_1 + C_2P_2 + C_3P_3 + \ldots +C_nP_n \quad \text{or} \quad \overline{C} = \sum_{x=1}^{n} C_xP_x \qquad 7\text{-}1$$

where

$\overline{C}$ = expected cash flow

x = possible outcome with $x = 1, 2, \ldots, n$

C = each possible cash flow

P = probability of each outcome

The expected cash flow from proposal B is

$$(\$1000)(.05) + (\$2000)(.20) + (\$3000)(.50) + (\$4000)(.20)$$
$$+ (\$5000)(.05) = \$3000$$

and the same calculation for proposal C is

$$(1.00)(\$3000) = \$3000$$

Hence the expected cash flow from all three proposals is the same. Even though all three have equal expected cash flows, they are not necessarily equally desirable. Proposal C is the only one with a certain outcome. The remaining two proposals may result in a flow greater or less than $3000. This uncertainty of the outcome for proposals A and B makes them more risky and less desirable than proposal C. The risk factor might be compensated for if A and B offered greater expected flows than C, but when the expected flows are equal the alternative with the most certain outcome is the most desirable. The possible results of each proposal are displayed in fig. 7-1 in what statisticians term discrete probability distributions.

Since most investment proposals offer a large number of possible outcomes, instead of the few shown in each case in fig. 7-1, it is generally necessary to display a probability distribution as a curve instead of a set of lines. Figure 7-2 illustrates two proposals similar to A and B. The horizontal axis measures all possible outcomes of the investment in terms of dollars of cash flow, and the vertical axis measures the probability of each outcome, so the area under each curve is equal to 100%. In other words, no other result is possible.

A comparison of the two distributions shows that the possible outcomes of proposal D are less tightly bunched than the outcomes of pro-

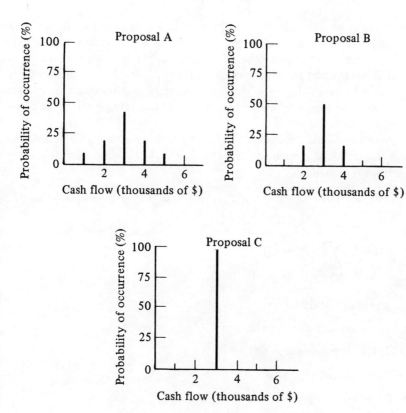

FIGURE 7-1   Discrete Probability Distributions

posal E. The dispersion, or tightness, of a distribution can be used as a measure of the risk associated with a project. Since the dispersion of the distribution for proposal D is greater than that for proposal E, we can say that more risk is associated with the expected outcome of proposal D.

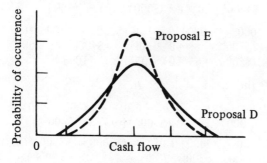

FIGURE 7-2   Continuous Probability Distributions

Proposal C is an example of the ultimate in risk avoidance: it has only one possible outcome and no dispersion. A realistic example of such a risk-free investment is the purchase of a United States Treasury bill or a deposit in an insured bank or savings and loan. In each case the resulting cash flow is known with certainty. Unfortunately, not many such risk-free investments are available, and when they are, the rate of return is correspondingly small.

A conventional measure of the dispersion of a probability distribution is the **standard deviation**. The standard deviation is calculated using the following equation:

$$\sigma = \sqrt{(C_1 - \overline{C})^2 P_1 + (C_2 - \overline{C})^2 P_2 + (C_3 - \overline{C})^2 P_3 + \ldots + (C_n - \overline{C})^2 P_n}$$

or

$$\sigma = \sqrt{\sum_{x=1}^{n} (C_x - \overline{C})^2 P_x} \qquad\qquad 7\text{-}2$$

where

σ = standard deviation

x = possible outcome with $x = 1, 2, \ldots, n$

C = each possible cash flow

$\overline{C}$ = expected cash flow

P = probability of each outcome

This equation appears somewhat different from the one usually used in an introductory statistics course. The only change is that instead of dividing by the number of possible outcomes (N), we are multiplying by the probability of each outcome. This is necessary because each cash flow is not equally probable.

Using these equations, we find that the standard deviation for proposal A in table 7-1 is

$$\overline{C}_a = (\$1000)(.10) + (\$2000)(.20) + (\$3000)(.40)$$
$$+ (\$4000)(.20) + (\$5000)(.10) = \$3000$$

$$\sigma_a = [(\$1000 - \$3000)^2(.10) + (\$2000 - \$3000)^2(.20)$$
$$+ (\$3000 - \$3000)^2(.40) + (\$4000 - \$3000)^2(.20)$$
$$+ (\$5000 - \$3000)^2(.05)]^{1/2} = \$1095$$

For proposal B the standard deviation is

$$\overline{C}_b = (\$1000)(.05) + (\$2000)(.20) + (\$3000)(.50)$$
$$+ (\$4000)(.20) + (\$5000)(.05) = \$3000$$

$$\sigma_b = [(\$1000 - \$3000)^2(.05) + (\$2000 - \$3000)^2(.20)$$
$$+ (\$3000 - \$3000)^2(.50) + (\$4000 - \$3000)^2(.20)$$
$$+ (\$5000 - \$3000)^2(.05)]^{1/2} = \$632$$

Hence the second proposal has a lower standard deviation and a tighter probability distribution.

If two proposals have significantly different expected cash flows, it is quite likely that the alternative with the largest expected outcome also has the largest standard deviation. An exaggerated example is the case of one project with an expected cash flow of $1 million and a second project with an expected cash flow of $1000. The size of the first project dictates a higher standard deviation except in very unusual circumstances. To compensate for differing project sizes we have to construct a measure of relative risk. We can do this by dividing the standard deviation of a proposal's projected cash flows by the expected outcome. The result, the coefficient of variation, provides an indication of the relative risk of an investment. For projects A and B the respective coefficients are

$$ v_a = \frac{\sigma_a}{\overline{C}_a} = \frac{\$1095}{\$3000} = .365, \qquad v_b = \frac{\sigma_b}{\overline{C}_b} = \frac{\$632}{\$3000} = .211 \qquad 7\text{-}3 $$

We can see that proposal B is less risky than proposal A in both a relative and an absolute sense. The alternatives are somewhat unusual since the expected outcomes are equal.

SHORT-TERM INVESTMENT DECISIONS

Although most people think that only long-term assets contribute to a firm's profits, this is not necessarily the case. While the bulk of profits for many companies derives from longer-lived assets, the proper management of short-term items can have a material effect on profit. The financial manager must decide not only what proportion of funds to commit to current assets, but also how to allocate these funds among the individual components.

The proper level of liquid assets depends on the trade-off between risk and profitability. Liquid assets tend to reduce both profitability and risk. Profitability is reduced because liquid assets usually earn a relatively low rate of return. The most liquid asset, cash, earns no return. Even less liquid current assets such as marketable securities, inventories, and accounts receivable, if held in amounts greater than necessary to conduct normal business operations, can reduce profitability.

Although current assets reduce profitability, holding a greater proportion of assets in the form of current assets also reduces risk. Since current assets can be turned into cash more readily and for a more certain amount than fixed assets, they can help cushion adverse fluctuations in cash flow. Although fixed assets (real estate and equipment) could be sold to satisfy a temporary cash need, such a sale would probably be at prices not advantageous to the seller. In addition, the firm could try to meet a cash problem by increasing its liabilities. For example, a firm could counteract slow payment from credit customers by delaying payments to its own creditors. In this case an increase in accounts payable, a liability item, is being used to offset an increase in accounts receivable, a current asset. Decisions concerning the liability side of the balance sheet are discussed in the next chapter, but note here that there is an important relationship between the liquidity structure of a firm's assets and the liquidity structure of its liabilities.

Cash and Marketable Securities

Cash and marketable securities should be managed to promote the ultimate goal of maximizing shareholder wealth. To do so, it is necessary to compare the benefits and costs of holding these assets. These benefits and costs are, in turn, affected by factors such as fluctuations in sales and receipts, firm size, and growth. Although cash and cash equivalents generally earn a low return, they are necessary to the conduct of normal business operations. This reasoning applies to individuals as well as to corporations. While it may be convenient for an individual to hold large checking account balances, it makes little economic sense since the idle balances could be in income-earning assets such as stocks, government and corporate bonds, or a savings account. While the large checking balance reduces the possibility of being unable to readily meet an obligation such as an emergency medical bill, it also reduces income. On the other hand, a person whose income stream is reduced during a temporary job layoff might have to sell other assets at an inopportune time. Thus the trade-offs between risk and return for an individual apply on a larger scale to the firm.

The first step in properly managing cash is to obtain an accurate projection of the firm's cash inflows and cash outflows—in other words, to prepare a cash budget. Projecting cash receipts and disbursements on a short-, intermediate-, and long-term basis provides a base for proper cash policy. Since net cash flows for most firms vary over time, the financial manager can adjust cash balances to the minimum required for necessary operations. A cash budget is similar to any other budget except that it includes only cash items. Variables such as depreciation, accrued expenses, and credit sales are omitted even though they may have a direct effect on cash flows in another period. For example, credit sales eventually turn into collections, but they do not contribute to cash inflows at the time of sale.

In addition to adjusting cash balances to meet the needs shown by the budget, it is necessary to include a margin for error. An economic slowdown or increase in interest rates may significantly slow collections so that cash receipt projections are not met. Additional balances beyond those normally required could provide a cushion necessary to carry the company through the slow period.

A firm can improve the efficiency of its cash management by accelerating its cash receipts and delaying its cash disbursements. It can accelerate cash receipts in a number of ways: (1) establishing a number of collection centers, (2) requiring customers to mail their payments directly to a centralized lock box where they are picked up by one of the firm's banks, and (3) speeding the deposit of large checks through special handling. One major method of delaying disbursements is to postpone required payments until they are actually due. Depending on the implied interest rate, the firm may wish to pay early enough to take advantage of discounts, but even in these cases payments should be delayed until the latest possible dates on which the discounts are available. Firms with large payrolls can sometimes conserve cash by keeping checking balances sufficient only for checks as they are presented to the firm's bank for payment. Since payroll checks may clear the bank over a period of days, it is not necessary to keep balances to cover the entire payroll on the day the checks are issued.

Because cash is a nonearning asset, the financial manager should attempt to keep any unnecessary balances placed in income-earning investments. Cash may be required in a short period of time, so it is desirable for investments to be short-term. Longer-term securities generally carry a higher yield, but their price volatility is much greater and the extra income may be more than offset by a loss from a price decline in the securities. The price of securities may rise, but the risk of selling at a loss is generally too great to compensate for the potential price gain and higher yield. The relationship between yield and length of maturity is displayed by a yield curve. A typical yield curve is illustrated in fig. 7–3. The upward slope of the curve shows the positive correlation between yield and maturity. This relationship is caused by a number of factors; one is that creditors generally like to lend short term while debtors prefer to borrow long term. Although the prices of long-term securities are more volatile, short-term interest rates generally fluctuate more than long-term rates. As a result, the yield curve might be viewed as a wagging tail, with the end of the tail on the short-term side. At times, short-term interest rates exceed long-term rates. This unusual event leads to a downward sloping curve.

The most common short-term securities used by firms for idle funds are issues of the federal government or its agencies. The market for these investments is so large and active that issues can generally be found to suit any purpose. In addition, the risk of default is negligible since the federal government has the power to print money. Other instruments available to meet short-term investment needs include commercial paper, negotiable certificates of deposit, and bankers' acceptances. Although none

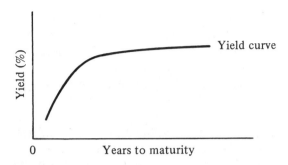

FIGURE 7–3   Relationship Between Maturity and Yield

of these investments is as safe as government obligations, all are relatively secure and can generally be expected to carry higher yields.

If the financial manager is relatively certain of the firm's projected cash flows, the company can purchase securities whose maturity dates coincide with net outflows. However, if the forecasts are subject to uncertainties, it may be preferable to invest on a very short-term or even a day-to-day basis. With a normal yield curve, this added liquidity can be obtained only at a reduced yield. The portfolio of marketable securities is generally designed not to provide the firm with a large source of earnings, but to act as a buffer against net cash outflows and to provide some income on an otherwise nonearning asset.

Accounts Receivable Management

Accounts receivable originate when firms sell their goods and services on credit rather than for cash. Since a large proportion of ultimate sales to consumers and nearly all interbusiness sales are on credit, accounts receivable represent a significant asset on most firms' balance sheets. The cost of carrying this asset may be larger than one might expect. Not only does the firm incur the extra expense of running a credit operation, but it must keep a portion of its funds tied up in receivables. It is this latter cost that is most frequently overlooked. Any time a firm increases the size of an asset (in this case, accounts receivable), it must either provide additional financing or reduce another asset by an equal amount. If the financial executive is managing the other assets efficiently, the second option will prove difficult and it will be necessary to find additional funds. Since it is the carrying of receivables that requires the firm to obtain more funds, the extra cost must be imputed to the receivables. A third cost of selling on credit is the loss from bad debts. Although this expense may be high, it is usually the least important of the three costs.

If the costs of a credit operation are so large, why don't firms sell for cash only? If costs were the only consideration, they probably would. In many instances, however, selling on credit is a desirable or necessary way of conducting business. Competitors may be selling on credit, or the merchandise may be sold to buyers at a time when they find cash payments impossible. In any event, a proper credit policy requires that the financial manager compare the costs and benefits of such an operation. For example, easing credit terms may increase sales enough to more than offset the additional costs of more accounts receivable. On the other hand, collections may be too lax and a tighter credit policy may reduce receivables without greatly reducing sales. Another possibility is to give a discount to customers who pay early. This method might actually increase sales while at the same time reducing accounts receivable. The cost is then a lower average selling price for the firm's product.

Unless the firm has decided to accept all credit applicants regardless of quality, the first step in managing accounts receivable is to establish a credit policy. This involves deciding to whom credit will be offered, in what amounts, and on what terms. While all three are important, careful attention to the first goes a long way toward alleviating problems in the other two. In evaluating a potential credit customer, the firm may want to examine the applicant's past record by checking with banks, credit organizations, and other companies selling to the same customer. An additional step is to examine the applicant's financial statements.

Inventory Management

Inventory is one of the largest assets that many firms carry on their balance sheets. Thus proper management of this asset can have a significant impact on a company's profitability. Excessively large inventories penalize profits through costs that are higher than necessary. On the other hand, keeping inventories too low handicaps sales, thus lowering profits by reducing revenues.

The costs of holding inventories are similar to the expenses of selling on credit and carrying accounts receivable. First, inventories are an asset which require either a reduction in another asset or additional financing. In any case, they require funds which could be invested in some other income-earning asset. Although inventories are constantly being converted into cash through cash sales or the collection of receivables, they are also constantly being replenished by additional purchases. As a result, the firm has a certain amount of cash committed to inventories on a permanent basis. If inventories fall below a certain level the firm cannot function effectively. Inventories also occupy physical storage space which otherwise could be used for a different purpose. In addition, there are costs for security, insurance, and management of the assets. Finally, there is the possibility that the inventory will become obsolete or lose its value while it is being held. On the other hand, unlike accounts receivable, the inventories may increase in value. During an inflationary period this is quite likely.

The problem with keeping inventories too low is that the firm may experience shortages and production inefficiencies. For example, if a company uses several resources in its manufacturing process, running out of just one of them will slow or halt production. Cost savings from a low inventory level may thus be more than offset by lost sales or, at the least, lost production time. Lost sales may also result if a firm schedules output to minimize inventory of finished output. A short burst of larger than expected orders could then send potential customers to the firm's competitors.

As with other assets, a firm should increase its inventories until extra costs from carrying the additional inventories exceed extra revenues that would accrue because of the added holdings. In other words, they should be increased until they drain profits. The correct level of inventories to hold is easier to figure on paper than in actual practice. However, some helpful tools are available.

One method of checking the effectiveness of inventory policy is to use some of the relationships discussed in chapter 6. These indicators of efficient management can be compared with the firm's past ratios or with the ratios of other firms in the same industry. For example, an abnormally low inventory turnover ratio is a good indication that inventory levels are excessively high.

One formal method of calculating proper inventory levels is termed economic order quantity (EOQ). EOQ attempts to determine the average inventory a firm should keep on hand in order to minimize total costs. The model does not take into account the possibility of lost sales or production difficulties encountered with low inventory levels. The formula for EOQ is

$$EOQ = \sqrt{2CS/PK} \tag{7-4}$$

where

C = cost of placing an order

S = units of sales per year

P = price per unit of inventory

K = percentage carrying cost of inventory (cost of storage, losses, and money tied up)

Since carrying costs generally rise at a constant rate as inventory size increases, the relationship between these two variables is linear. On the

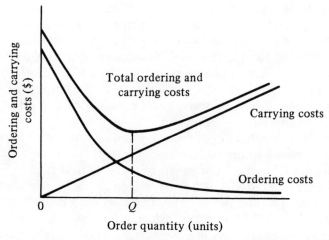

FIGURE 7-4   Relationship Between Order Quantity and Costs

other hand, the cost of placing an order is constant regardless of order size. As a consequence, the higher average inventory levels resulting from large orders cause greater carrying costs and lower average purchasing costs. The relationship between order quantity and costs is illustrated in fig. 7-4. If the firm does not order until its stock is depleted and if inventory is used evenly between order dates, the average inventory level is

Average inventory $= EOQ/2.$ 7–5

LONG-TERM INVESTMENT DECISIONS

Committing a firm's capital to long-term investments is one of the financial manager's most important and difficult jobs. While some of the problems inherent in capital budgeting are similar to those encountered in working capital management, the decisions reached are even more critical since funds are tied up for such long periods of time. Whereas current assets are generally turned into cash in a matter of weeks or months, funds used to acquire plant and equipment may be returned over a decade or more. The resulting lack of flexibility means that once a decision is made and funds are committed, the firm is tied to the consequences for years. The company of course hopes that the consequences are favorable and result in increased cash and profits. Unfortunately, this is not always the case, and the firm may be able to abdicate its investment only at a large loss.

At any given time a company has a number of alternate capital budgeting proposals under consideration. Some will undoubtedly produce more favorable results than others, and it is the job of the financial manager to evaluate each of the prospective investments. Indeed an alternative that has been judged unprofitable in the past might be viewed in a much more favorable light at a later date. If firms could obtain unlimited funds at no cost, the evaluation process would be less critical. However, since only limited funds can be made available over a relatively short time period and since the use of these funds entails a cost, deciding which projects to undertake is very important.

The various methods of evaluating investment proposals depend on the fact that money is more valuable the earlier it is obtained. Cash cannot be used for reinvestment or to pay off debts until it is received. That is why an asset that provides cash flows early in its life is preferable to one that returns an equal flow in later years. In some cases a desire to accelerate these flows may result in an actual reduction in reported, or accounting, profits during the asset's early life, as when a firm uses accelerated instead of straight-line depreciation.

Calculating Cash Flows

Nearly all investments result in both cash inflows and cash outflows. It is only the net change in cash flows that concerns us. In other words, cash outflows originating from an investment must be subtracted from cash inflows that the investment produces. In most cases cash outflows comprise the original outlay to acquire the asset plus annual cash expenditures on such items as labor, maintenance, and materials to keep the asset in operation. Inflows result from additional cash sales or collections plus any salvage value the asset is expected to have at the end of its useful life. For example, suppose a firm is contemplating an investment proposal requiring an initial cash outlay of $100,000. The proposed machine will last four years, and it will require the following additional expenses for materials, labor, taxes, and maintenance:

Year	0	1	2	3	4
Outflows	$100,000	$30,000	$50,000	$50,000	$20,000

The machine produces a product with sales estimated as follows:

Year	0	1	2	3	4
Inflows	0	$60,000	$90,000	$100,000	$30,000

Thus the net change in cash flows that can be expected from acquiring the new machine is

Year	0	1	2	3	4
Cash inflows	$ 0	$60,000	$90,000	$100,000	$30,000
Cash outflows	100,000	30,000	50,000	50,000	20,000
Net change	−$100,000	$30,000	$40,000	$ 50,000	$10,000

Acquisition of the machine thus requires an initial outlay of $100,000 and provides total net inflows of $130,000 during years 1 through 4. In other words, a $100,000 investment returns the original cost plus $30,000 during a four-year period. At first glance this may seem to be a 30% return. However, the time value of money has not been considered. Another proposal with the same initial cost, no net inflows during the first three years, and a net flow of $130,000 in year 4 would provide the same rate of return according to this reasoning.

If potential investments are expected to result in equal net cash inflows throughout their lives, the analysis is somewhat easier. Suppose our hypothetical firm is presented with the three proposals in table 7–2. Lines 1 and 2 show the cost and expected life of each project. Increased sales indicate the cash inflows that will occur. While increased expenses include maintenance and labor (cash outflows), it also lists depreciation, which is not a cash flow. However, since depreciation is an allowable expense in calculating income taxes, it must be included before arriving at taxable income. Income taxes have been computed at 40% of taxable in-

TABLE 7–2 **Annual Cash Flows from Proposed Investment Projects**

	Proposals		
	A	B	C
Initial cost	$100,000	$150,000	$125,000
Expected life	4 years	10 years	10 years
Increased sales/year	$ 50,000	$ 25,000	$ 20,000
Increased expenses/year			
Depreciation	$ 25,000	$ 15,000	$ 12,500
Maintenance, labor, etc.	15,000	5,000	4,500
Total	$ 40,000	$ 20,000	$ 17,000
Increased profit (before taxes)	$ 10,000	$ 5,000	$ 3,000
Taxes (40%)	4,000	2,000	1,200
Increased profit (after taxes)	$ 6,000	$ 3,000	$ 1,800
Depreciation	25,000	15,000	12,500
Increased cash flow	$ 31,000	$ 18,000	$ 14,300

come, leaving after-tax profits equal to 60% of before-tax profits. Since depreciation is a noncash expense, it must be added to after-tax profits in calculating the annual net cash inflow. The only actual cash expenses are operating expenses, such as added maintenance and labor, and additional taxes due to higher profits. If cash inflows derived from increased sales are reduced by these cash outflows, the net cash inflows are the same as those shown on the last line of table 7–2. Since additional sales and expenses are projected to remain the same throughout each project's life, net cash inflows are also unchanged. The next step in evaluating the proposals is to compare the net cash inflows with initial outlays. First, however, we must investigate one of the most important concepts in financial analysis— the time value of money.

The Time Value of Money

Because cash is more valuable the sooner it is received, the time value of money is an important consideration for the financial manager in his decision-making process. The technique employed to equate cash flows in various years is generally referred to as discounted cash flow analysis. Using this analysis we can calculate the present value of a sum of money to be received sometime in the future. If $1 is invested today at a 6% rate of interest, in one year we will have the original investment of $1 plus an additional 6%, or

$$\$1 + (\$1)(.06) = \$1(1 + .06) = \$1.06$$

If the deposit is left for two years the result will be

$$\$1(1 + .06)(1 + .06) = \$1(1.06)^2 = \$1.1236$$

A more general formulation for finding the ending amount of a deposit is

$$FV = P(1 + i)^n \qquad\qquad 7\text{–}6$$

where

FV = amount at end of time period

P = amount invested

i = interest rate per period

n = number of periods the amount invested is left to accumulate

Using this formula we can calculate the future value of any given deposit, at any rate of interest, for any number of periods. As we shall see, this equation can be rearranged to provide other useful financial data. Although the formula provides a framework for finding future value over any number of annual periods, using it for a large number of years would present a problem in mathematical computation. To help with this type of calculation, tables such as table 7–3 are available. This is an abbreviated version of more complete tables that can be found in the back of this book and other financial management texts.

Table 7–3 shows the computed value of $(1 + i)^n$ for various periods

TABLE 7–3   Future Value of $1

Period	1%	2%	3%	4%	5%	10%	15%	20%
1	1.010	1.020	1.030	1.040	1.050	1.100	1.150	1.200
2	1.020	1.040	1.061	1.082	1.102	1.210	1.322	1.440
3	1.030	1.061	1.093	1.125	1.158	1.331	1.521	1.728
4	1.041	1.082	1.126	1.170	1.216	1.464	1.749	2.074
5	1.051	1.104	1.159	1.217	1.276	1.611	2.011	2.488
10	1.105	1.219	1.344	1.480	1.629	2.594	4.046	6.192
15	1.161	1.346	1.558	1.801	2.079	4.177	8.137	15.407
20	1.220	1.486	1.806	2.191	2.653	6.728	16.367	38.338

(n) and interest rates (i). To find the future value of a given deposit, merely multiply the deposit by the appropriate table value. For example, $87 deposited for 15 years at 10% is

$$\$87(1 + .10)^{15} \quad \text{or} \quad (\$87)(4.177) = \$363.40$$

Suppose we need the factor for a period not contained in the table, say 17 years at 4%. To calculate that factor recall from algebra that $x^{n+m} = (x^n)(x^m)$. Then for this example $x^{17} = (x^{15})(x^2)$. Therefore $(1 + .04)^{17} = (1.04)^{15}(1.04)^2 = (1.801)(1.082) = 1.949$.

If deposits are to be made over a number of periods, the table is still useful since each deposit can be multiplied by the appropriate table value for a given interest rate and number of years. Suppose we deposit $150 this year, $200 in 5 years, and $300 in 10 years, all at 5%, and want to calculate the value 20 years from today. The $150 will be on deposit 20 years, the $200 for 15 years, and the last deposit for 10 years. So the future value is

$$\$150(1 + .05)^{20} + \$200(1 + .05)^{15} + \$300(1 + .05)^{10}$$
$$= \$150(2.653) + \$200(2.079) + \$300(1.629)$$
$$= \$1302.45$$

A special case of multiple deposits occurs when equal payments are deposited in consecutive years. For example, if we deposit $150 annually for five years at a 10% rate of interest, at the end of five years the future value will be

$$\$150(1 + .10)^5 + \$150(1 + .10)^4 + \$150(1 + .10)^3$$
$$+ \$150(1 + .10)^2 + \$150(1 + .10)^1$$
$$= \$150(1.611) + \$150(1.464) + \$150(1.331) + \$150(1.210)$$
$$+ \$150(1.100) = \$1007.40$$

This solution assumes that each of the deposits is made at the beginning of each year. If deposits are made at year end, each deposit has one fewer interest earning period, and the future value would be

$$\$150(1 + .10)^4 + \$150(1 + .10)^3 + \$150(1 + .10)^2$$
$$+ \$150(1 + .10)^1 + \$150(1 + .10)^0$$
$$= \$150(1.464) + \$150(1.331) + \$150(1.210)$$
$$+ \$150(1.100) + 150(1.000)$$
$$= \$150(1.464 + 1.331 + 1.210 + 1.100 + 1.000)$$
$$= \$150(6.105) = \$915.75$$

Since each of the deposits is the same, it is possible to factor out this constant dollar amount in solving the problem. When we are confronted with a stream of equal payments in finding future value, we have an annuity. Using table 7–3 we can construct table 7–4, which can be used to solve annuity problems. This table assumes that payments are made at the end, rather than the beginning, of each year. For example, if we make 10 yearly payments of $200 each into an investment earning 4% annually, we merely multiply the table value of 12.006 times the $200 annual payment to calculate a terminal value of $2401.20 at the end of year 10. The future value is computed on the same day the last $200 payment is made, so the last deposit draws no interest. Illustrating the same problem in its full form we have

TABLE 7–4   Future Value of a $1 Annuity

Periods	1%	2%	3%	4%	5%	10%	15%	20%
1	1.000	1.000	1.000	1.000	1.000	1.000	1.000	1.000
2	2.010	2.020	2.030	2.040	2.050	2.100	2.150	2.200
3	3.030	3.060	3.091	3.122	3.153	3.310	3.472	3.640
4	4.060	4.122	4.184	4.246	4.310	4.641	4.993	5.368
5	5.101	5.204	5.309	5.416	5.526	6.105	6.742	7.442
10	10.462	10.950	11.464	12.006	12.578	15.937	20.304	25.959
15	16.097	17.293	18.599	20.024	21.579	31.772	47.080	72.035
20	22.019	24.297	26.870	29.778	33.066	57.275	102.444	186.688

$$FV = \$200(1 + .04)^9 + \$200(1 + .04)^8 + \ldots + \$200(1 + .04)^0$$

If payments are to be made at the beginning of each year, we have

$$FV = \$200(1 + .04)^{10} + \$200(1 + .04)^9 + \ldots + \$200(1 + .04)^1$$

Hence, in the latter example each $200 deposit has one extra interest-earning period, so the future value is greater. To use the annuity table for this example, we must find the future value of an 11-year annuity and subtract one payment. (There is no $(1 + i)^0$ with beginning-of-the-year deposits.) Alternatively we could subtract 1.000 from the table value and multiply the result by the annual deposit. Since table 7–4 does not list an 11-year annuity, we cannot work the previous problem, but we can calculate the future value of an annuity with fewer years. If, at the end of each year, a person deposits $300 for four years in an account earning 5% interest, the future value will be $1293 or $300 × 4.310. If the deposits are made at the beginning of each year, the future value is $1357 or $300 × (5.526 − 1.000). The procedure we used for calculating a factor not listed in table 7–3 does not work for the annuity table.

The previous examples have addressed the problem of the future value of money. With most investment proposals, however, cash is to be received in the future. Consequently, we will now turn our attention to the concept of present value.

The future value of a present sum of money is found through use of the equation $FV = P(1 + i)^n$. By rearranging the equation to solve for P, we can calculate the present value of a future sum.

$$P = FV\left(\frac{1}{(1 + i)^n}\right) = \frac{FV}{(1 + i)^n}. \qquad 7\text{--}7$$

For example, if we are to receive $400 in one year and the discount rate is 4%, the present value is

$$\$400/(1 + .04)^1 = \$400/(1.04) = \$384.62$$

In other words, a deposit of $384.62 earning 4% has a future value of $400 in one year. If the $400 is not to be received for 10 years with a 4% discount, the present value is $400/(1 + .04)^{10} = \$400/1.480 = \$270.27$. Since it becomes laborious to calculate the denominator when a large number of years are involved, tables such as table 7–5 have been developed.

Table 7–5 provides the calculated value of $1/(1 + i)^n$ for various discount rates and various periods. A comparison with table 7–3 shows that the values of that table are simply the inverse of the respective values of table 7–5. If we are to receive a $200 payment in year 2, a $300 payment

TABLE 7–5   Present Value of $1

Periods	1%	2%	3%	4%	5%	10%	15%	20%
1	.990	.980	.971	.962	.952	.909	.870	.833
2	.980	.961	.943	.925	.907	.826	.756	.694
3	.971	.942	.915	.889	.864	.751	.658	.579
4	.961	.924	.888	.855	.823	.683	.572	.482
5	.952	.906	.863	.822	.784	.621	.497	.402
10	.905	.820	.744	.676	.614	.386	.247	.162
15	.861	.743	.642	.555	.481	.239	.123	.065
20	.820	.673	.554	.456	.377	.149	.061	.026

in year 5, and a $700 payment in year 10, the present value of this cash flow when discounted at 5% is

$$PV = \frac{\$200}{(1 + .05)^2} + \frac{\$300}{(1 + .05)^5} + \frac{\$700}{(1 + .05)^{10}}$$

$$= \$200 \frac{1}{(1.05)^2} + \$300 \frac{1}{(1.05)^5} + \$700 \frac{1}{(1.05)^{10}}$$

$$= \$200(.907) + \$300(.784) + \$700(.614) = \$846.40$$

Now let's look at the same problem from a different perspective. If we deposit $846.40 today in an account earning 5% annually, we could withdraw $200 at the end of year 2, $300 at the end of year 5, and $700 at the end of year 10. The total withdrawals of $1200 include interest of $353.60 and would deplete the account.

If an investment returns a constant number of dollars annually for a given number of years, the stream is termed an annuity. We can calculate the present value of an annuity by using table 7–5. For example, if an investment returns an annual cash flow of $500 for five years and the flow is discounted at 10%, the present value is

$$PV = \frac{\$500}{(1 + .10)^1} + \frac{\$500}{(1 + .10)^2} + \frac{\$500}{(1 + .10)^3} + \frac{\$500}{(1 + .10)^4}$$

$$+ \frac{\$500}{(1 + .10)^5}$$

$$= \$500(.909) + \$500(.826) + \$500(.751) + \$500(.683)$$

$$+ \$500(.621) = \$1895$$

Regardless of the size of the annual flow, however, the table values used are always the same as long as the discount rate and number of years are the same. In other words, a five-year flow of $700 annually discounted at 10% would use the same discount factors as those in this example. The $500 flow could be factored out, leaving

$$\$500(.909 + .826 + .751 + .683 + .621) = \$500(3.790) = \$1895$$

TABLE 7–6   Present Value of a $1 Annuity

Periods	1%	2%	3%	4%	5%	10%	15%	20%
1	.990	.980	.971	.962	.952	.909	.870	.833
2	1.970	1.942	1.913	1.886	1.859	1.736	1.626	1.528
3	2.941	2.884	2.829	2.775	2.723	2.487	2.283	2.106
4	3.902	3.808	3.717	3.630	3.546	3.172	2.855	2.589
5	4.853	4.713	4.580	4.450	4.329	3.790	3.352	2.991
10	9.471	8.983	8.530	8.111	7.722	6.144	5.019	4.192
15	13.865	12.849	11.938	11.118	10.380	7.606	5.847	4.675
20	18.046	16.351	14.877	13.590	12.462	8.514	6.259	4.870

To help in this calculation, tables with the individual interest factors already summed are available. Table 7–6 indicates that to find the present value of any five-year annuity discounted at 10% we should use a factor of 3.790. Similarly, a ten-year annuity discounted at 4% is found by using an 8.111 factor. The equation used in finding the present value of a stream of equal payments is

$$PV = (\text{table value})(\text{annual payment}) \qquad \textbf{7-8}$$

The same methodology and tables are useful in solving other problems. For example, if we have $40,000 on deposit earning 5% and want to know how much we can withdraw annually for ten years leaving a zero balance, we simply rearrange eq. 7–8:

$$\text{Annual payment} = \frac{PV}{\text{Table value}} = \frac{\$40,000}{7.722} = \$5180$$

If we have $50,000 and want to withdraw $6000 annually for ten years, what interest must our investment earn? In this case, we rearrange the equation to solve for the table value that, in turn, can be used to find the interest rate.

$$\text{Table value} = \frac{PV}{\text{Annual payment}} = \frac{\$50,000}{\$6,000} = 8.333$$

From table 7–6 we can see that for a ten-year annuity 8.333 lies somewhere between 3% and 4%. Hence, we must earn approximately 3.5% on our investment in order to make the ten $6000 withdrawals.

Capital Budgeting Decisions

Since a firm generally has limited funds available for investment, it must choose among alternative proposals. To determine how these decisions are made, we will cover four major methods of allocating long-term funds: payback, average rate of return, net present value, and internal rate of return. Each of these has advantages and disadvantages, and it may be preferable to use a combination of methods in evaluating proposals.

PAYBACK   The **payback** method refers to the number of periods required for a project to return its investment outlay. Note that the payback is calculated using cash flows rather than reported profits. The proposals listed in table 7–2 have the following payback periods:

Proposal	A	B	C
Outlay	$100,000	$150,000	$125,000
Cash flow/Year	31,000	18,000	14,300
$\text{Payback} = \dfrac{\text{Outlay}}{\text{Cash flow/Year}}$	3.23 years	8.33 years	8.74 years

Since the payback indicates the length of time required to recover an initial outlay of cash, the shorter the payback, the more desirable the investment. Of these three proposals, A is preferable to B or C since its payback period is much shorter. The obvious problem with this method of evaluation is that it does not take into account any cash flows beyond the payback period. In addition, it does not distinguish dollars received early in the payback period from those received later, a disadvantage since dollars are more valuable the earlier they are received.

AVERAGE RATE OF RETURN   Average rate of return is the only evaluation that utilizes accounting profits. It relates the average annual profit to the average annual investment in the proposal. With straight-line depreciation and no salvage value, the average annual investment is equal to half the initial outlay. With a positive salvage value, the average annual investment is

$$\text{Average annual investment} = \tfrac{1}{2}(\text{Initial outlay} - \text{Salvage value}) + \text{Salvage value} \qquad 7\text{–}9$$

In each case the firm recovers its cash outlay through depreciation allowances that accrue gradually over the life of the investment. When an investment has no salvage value, the firm recovers its entire outlay through depreciation.

The average rates of return for the three proposals of table 7–2 are as follows:

Proposal	A	B	C
Outlay	$100,000	$150,000	$125,000
Salvage value	0	0	0
Average annual profit	6,000	3,000	1,800
Average rate of return $= \dfrac{\text{Average annual profit}}{\text{Average annual investment}}$	12%	4%	2.9%

In terms of average rate of return, proposal A is preferable to B and C. However, the first project has an expected life of only four years, while the latter two projects have expected lives of ten years. In addition, this method of evaluating proposals centers on accounting profit, which can misrepresent an investment's economic value. For this and other reasons, average rate of return is not considered one of the better tools for selecting investments.

NET PRESENT VALUE   **Net present value** (NPV) considers the time value of money in comparing cash outflows and cash inflows and allows us to adjust for uncertainty in expected cash flows. Using this method, the financial manager discounts net cash flows at the firm's cost of capital. (Calculation of the cost of capital appears in chapter 9.) The general equation for the net present value is

$$NPV = \frac{C_0}{(1+k)^0} + \frac{C_1}{(1+k)^1} + \frac{C_2}{(1+k)^2} + \cdots + \frac{C_n}{(1+k)^n}$$

or

$$NPV = \sum_{t=0}^{n} \frac{C_t}{(1+k)^t} \qquad \text{7-10}$$

where

   NPV = net present value in dollars

   t = time periods

   C = net cash flow in each time period

   k = cost of capital or discount rate

C_0 is usually the original outlay and a negative flow, while net cash flows C_1 through C_n are generally positive. However, this is not always the case and does not have to be true for the equation to be used. Recall that any variable with an exponent of zero is equal to one. Therefore $(1+k)^0$, the denominator in period zero, is equal to one and the discounted cash flow is C_0. If the investment is expected to have a salvage value, the dollar amount is included in the net cash flow of the final period.

If the firm considering the projects of table 7–2 has a 5% cost of capital, the net present value of proposal A is

$$NPV = \frac{-\$100,000}{(1+.05)^0} + \frac{\$31,000}{(1+.05)^1} + \frac{\$31,000}{(1+.05)^2} + \frac{\$31,000}{(1+.05)^3}$$
$$+ \frac{\$31,000}{(1+.05)^4}$$
$$= (-\$100,000)(1) + (\$31,000)(.952) + (\$31,000)(.907)$$
$$+ (\$31,000)(.864) + (\$31,000)(.823) = \$9926$$

Since the annual cash inflows are equal, the discounted cash flow can be more easily solved as an annuity:

$$NPV = -\$100,000 + \$31,000(3.546) = 9926$$

The net present values of proposals B and C are $-\$11,004$ and $-\$14,575$, respectively.

The basic rule in using this method of project evaluation is that a positive net present value (using the appropriate discount rate) is a signal to implement the proposal because the return on the investment is greater than the cost of funds used to finance it. As a practical matter, the firm might have a limit on the funds it can obtain and be unable to finance every proposal with a positive NPV estimate. Under these circumstances it must choose between projects. One method is to base the relative merit of each project on a ratio of the discounted value of cash inflows to the discounted value of the initial outlay.

INTERNAL RATE OF RETURN   The **internal rate of return** (IRR) is the rate of return on the proposed investment, or the discount rate, that equates the present value of the stream of net cash inflows with the present value of the net cash outflows. Another way of saying the same thing is that the IRR is the rate of discount that leaves the net present value equal to zero. With the net present value evaluation technique, we are given the discount rate as the firm's cost of capital and are required to solve for NPV. With the IRR evaluation method, we are given a NPV of zero and are required to find the appropriate discount rate. In equation form this is

$$0 = \frac{C_0}{(1+r)^0} + \frac{C_1}{(1+r)^1} + \frac{C_2}{(1+r)^2} + \cdots + \frac{C_n}{(1+r)^n}$$

or

$$\sum_{t=0}^{n} \frac{C_t}{(1+r)^t} = 0 \qquad\qquad 7\text{-}11$$

where

$t =$ time period

$C =$ net cash flows in each time period

$r =$ internal rate of return

If the net cash flows are unequal, solving for r becomes a game of hit and miss. Using the appropriate values of table 7–5, we approximate a rate of return and multiply each cash flow by its respective table factor. If NPV is negative, the estimated rate of return is too high and a lower one must be tried. Conversely, a positive NPV indicates too low a rate has been used.

If all the net cash flows except C_0 are equal, the solution is much easier because the cash stream is an annuity. C_0 is usually the initial outlay of the investment and a negative cash flow. Using table 7–6 and the formula $PV =$ (table value) (annual payment), we can transpose C_0 to the left side of the equation making it equal to the present value. Then we merely solve for the table value and find that value in table 7–6 for the appropriate number of years of the annuity.

For example, the table value of proposal A in table 7–2 is

$$\text{Table value} = \frac{\text{Present value of the annuity}}{\text{Annual cash flow}} = \frac{\$100,000}{\$31,000} = 3.226$$

Finding this value for a four-year annuity indicates a rate of return of something between 5% and 10%. Calculating the table value for proposal B yields 8.333 and an IRR of between 3% and 4%. The internal rate of return of project C is between 2% and 3%. The basic decision rule in using IRR as an evaluation technique is to choose projects offering the highest expected internal rates of return.

Choosing a Method Except perhaps for accounting rate of return, each of the capital budgeting methods examined has both good and bad points. The payback method is easy to calculate, but it does not consider cash flows that occur after the payback period or the time value of money during the payback period. The average rate of return is more consistent with current accounting concepts but does not evaluate cash flows or consider the time value of money. The latter two techniques, NPV and IRR, rely heavily on the time value of money, but IRR does not take into account the size of the projects under consideration. As all-inclusive techniques, the last two methods are probably superior, with net present value proving best when the firm's funds are limited.

SUMMARY

Investment decisions are made on the basis of both expected return and risk. An investment's expected return is measured in terms of incremental cash flows and the expected timing of the flows. A project's relative risk is the variability of the incremental flows.

The four methods that are commonly utilized in evaluating long-term investments are (1) payback period, (2) average rate of return, (3) net present value, and (4) internal rate of return. The latter two techniques rely heavily on the timing of cash flows and are generally considered superior methods.

QUESTIONS

1. Why is cash received early more valuable than an equal amount of cash to be received some time in the future?

2. Why do liquid assets tend to reduce both profitability and risk?

3. List the ways a firm can improve the efficiency of its cash management by accelerating its cash receipts and delaying its cash disbursements.

4. Why do most firms sell their goods and services on credit rather than for cash, and what are the firm's costs of running a credit operation?

5. What are the risks associated with carrying inventories that are excessively large? excessively low?

6. Why are long-term investment decisions one of the most important and difficult jobs of the financial manager?

7. Explain the concept of the time value of money.

8. What will $1000 be worth in one year if we invest it at an 8% rate of interest?

9. Suppose we deposit $400 annually for four years at a 5% rate of interest. What will the terminal value be at the end of four years?

10. If we are to receive a $500 payment in four years and the rate of discount is 5%, what is its present value?

11. On April 1 Frank DeZoort bought a swimming pool for $6000 and paid $2000 down. He is to pay the balance in four equal annual payments and 4% interest is computed annually on the unpaid balance. What are his payments each year?

12. Define the four major approaches to capital budgeting, and discuss the advantages and disadvantages of each method.

13. Calculate the internal rate of return for a project that costs $1000 and will net cash flows of $200 in year 1, $300 in year 2, $500 in year 3, and $400 in year 4.

14. If a project costs $125,000 and the rate of discount is 10%, calculate the net present value for the project. The cash flows for the project are year 1: $50,000; years 2–9: $30,000; year 10: $20,000.

15. Walt Woelfel has decided to buy furniture for his new home. After selecting $3000 worth of merchandise he finds the dealer will allow him to pay $500 down and make payments of $600 per year for five years. Alternatively, with no down payment he can pay $700 per year for three years and $1200 at the end of the fourth year. Which option results in the lowest rate of interest?

SELECTED REFERENCES

BRADLEY, JOSEPH F. *Administrative Financial Management.* Hinsdale, Ill.: Dryden Press, 1974. Parts 2, 3.

CHRISTY, GEORGE A., and RODEN, PEYTON F. *Finance: Environment and Decisions.* New York: Canfield Press, 1976. Chs. 26, 27, 28.

DONALDSON, ELVIN F.; PFAHL, JOHN K.; and MULLINS, PETER L. *Corporate Finance.* New York: Ronald Press, 1975. Chs. 6–10.

JOY, O. MAURICE. *Introduction to Financial Management.* Homewood, Ill.: Richard D. Irwin, 1977. Sects. 3, 6.

SCOTT, DAVID L. *Pollution in the Electric Power Industry: Its Control and Costs.* Lexington, Mass.: D. C. Heath & Co., 1973. Ch. 5.

8 Financing Decisions: Short-Term and Long-Term

A borrower is one who exchanges hot air for cold cash.

When we discussed the coordination of asset and liability maturities in chapter 7, we mentioned that heavy emphasis on **current assets** reduces the risk of running short of cash because these assets are generally liquid and can be turned into cash on short notice. We also mentioned that the same strategy tends to penalize profits because more liquid assets are generally less profitable than **fixed assets**. Similar reasoning applies to the liability side of a firm's balance sheet. Short-term obligations are generally less costly, since short-term interest rates are usually lower than long-term rates. But they also subject the firm to greater risk because short-term obligations must be repaid more often.

Financial managers cannot consider the risk-return trade-off of liability management in isolation; they must also compare the structure of liabilities with the firm's asset structure. For example, it may be unwise to engage primarily in long-term borrowing if the firm's assets consist largely of cash, marketable securities, accounts receivable, and inventories. Although long-term borrowing might reduce risk, the higher interest expense characteristic of long-term financing may prove superfluous because short-term assets could readily be sold to meet cash needs. In addition, the firm will probably be paying interest on unnecessary borrowings during part of the year since receivables and inventories are generally seasonal assets. Conversely, utilizing short-term liabilities to finance an asset structure composed mostly of permanent assets may be riskier than the added profitability warrants. If money becomes tight and the firm finds it im-

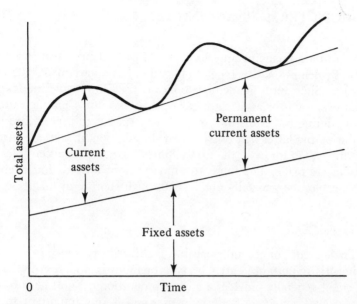

FIGURE 8–1 Financing Requirements for Current and Fixed Assets

possible to roll over (refinance) short-term debt, long-term assets may have to be sold at large price concessions.

The total financing requirements of a firm can be illustrated by a graph such as that in fig. 8–1. A typical firm acquires fixed assets such as plant and equipment and current assets such as cash, receivables, and inventories. Although current assets may fluctuate over time, the firm's operations generally require that some minimum amount of these assets be kept on hand at all times. These assets, which we shall call permanent current assets, gradually expand as the firm grows larger. Since permanent current assets are carried thoughout the year, it may be desirable to finance these assets with permanent funds such as equity or long-term debt. This approach is less risky than using short-term borrowing to cover the permanent component of current assets. Although it also entails the acquisition of higher-cost funds, the funds will be on hand when they are needed. An even less risky posture for the firm is to finance all or a portion of nonpermanent current assets with permanent funds. However, the cost of such a liability structure is the higher cost of permanent funds and the carrying of a portion of these funds when they are not needed to support assets.

What this means is that the financial manager must determine an acceptable safety margin for the firm, keeping in mind that a smaller margin should increase profitability. At the expense of smaller profits (due to the increase in costs), the safety margin can be improved by increasing either short-term assets or long-term liabilities.

SHORT-TERM FINANCING

Short-term financing appears on the firm's balance sheet as a current liability. By definition, this type of obligation has a repayment date of one year or less. Short-term financing is typically used to provide funds for the seasonal expansion of assets. For example, if the firm's products are sold primarily during the Christmas season, the firm has to accumulate inventories during the latter half of each year. In addition, if sales are made on credit rather than for cash, the firm requires financing for receivables until collections are made. The funds to support seasonal needs for inventories and receivables are generally obtained through short-term financing.

Trade Credit

Trade credit, or accounts payable, is the primary source of short-term financing. Its importance varies by type of industry and size of the firm. Trade credit generally provides a greater proportion of short-term funds in the service and wholesale trade industries and is very important to small companies who are usually less able to take advantage of cash discounts.

Accounts payable become a source of financing when the firm does not have to pay for goods on delivery. As a result, the goods that have been purchased are financed by a liability to the seller. The terms of sale dictate the length of time this type of financing can be used for a particular shipment of goods and the cost that it entails. In addition to not requiring a settlement until a given number of days after the delivery of goods, the seller often offers a cash discount for prompt payment. For example, the terms of sale might require full payment by the end of 30 days but provide a 3% discount for payment within 10 days. This arrangement is stated as 3/10, n/30. Terms of 2/15, n/45 indicate that the buyer can obtain a 2% discount if payment is made within 15 days, and the full bill must be paid within 45 days. Since the buyer would like to operate with the seller's money for as long as possible if it entails no additional cost, there are only two relevant payment dates. The first date is the last day to take advantage of the discount; the other is the last day that payment is due in full. For example, with terms of 2/15, n/45 the buyer would not want to make payment on day 20 because it is too late for the discount but 25 days before the bill is due in full. Likewise, the buyer would not be wise to pay on the fifth day since he could obtain the same discount while keeping the funds for an additional 10 days.

If the final day to take the discount and the final day the bill is due in full are the only two relevant payment dates, we can calculate the implied cost of funds if the firm pays on the day the bill is due rather than on the last day for the discount. In other words, we can find the cost of not taking a discount when it is offered. Suppose we purchase goods costing $1000 and the seller has offered us terms of 2/15, n/45. Not paying by day 15 enables our firm to use $980 ($1000 less 2%) of the seller's money for an additional 30 days. The annual interest rate on this short-term financing is

$$\frac{\$20}{\$980} \times \frac{365 \text{ days}}{30 \text{ days}} = 24.8\%$$

Accrued Expenses

Since companies are not required to meet all expenses on the exact date they are incurred, there are liability items on their balance sheets that require periodic payments. These items are called **accrued expenses.** For example, most firms pay their employees weekly or monthly rather than daily. As a result, the firms must account for wages that have been earned but not yet paid. This liability, termed accrued wages, is a short-term source of funds. A similar type of accrued expense is income tax payments, which are made on a periodic rather than a day-to-day basis.

These funds are essentially costless to the firm since no added expense is incurred when payments are made on a periodic basis. As a result, firms generally have no hesitation about using this method of financing. Although this liability is short-term, its absence requires obtaining other funds to finance the assets of the firm. It is sometimes possible to increase the amount of accrued expenses by altering the firm's payment policies. For example, salaries might be paid monthly instead of every two weeks.

Commercial Paper

Commercial paper is a short-term unsecured note. Since these notes are unsecured and negotiable, they are generally issued only by large and well-established companies. Both financial and nonfinancial corporations use this method of raising short-term funds. This mode of financing is not designed to support permanent assets such as plant and equipment. Such a policy could be disastrous if a period of tight money foreclosed the possibility of "rolling over" the paper.

Commercial paper is normally sold to dealers who expect to resell the paper. In some cases, especially with issues by large sales finance companies, the dealers are bypassed in favor of direct sales to investors. Unlike corporate bonds, the paper does not bear an interest rate on its face; rather, it is sold at a discount from its face value, similar to savings bonds. The difference between the price paid and the value at maturity constitutes the interest payment over the life of the paper. The interest rate implied by this discount in price varies considerably over a typical business cycle. Although high-grade commercial paper generally carries a lower interest rate than short-term bank loans of the same maturity, the spread is usually greater during periods of easy money and smaller when funds are more difficult and expensive to obtain.

The maturity of commercial paper is generally 90, 120, 180, or 270 days, and the amount of a single issue ranges from $25,000 upward. This paper is a source of funds for some corporations and an investment vehicle for others. Hence commercial paper in many cases simply represents the borrowing of short-term funds by one firm from another. The large amount of money involved generally prohibits individual investors from entering the commercial paper market.

Short-Term Loans

Short-term loans are generally obtained from commercial banks or finance companies. The funds from this type of loan are usually invested in assets that generate sufficient cash flows or are self-liquidating so that the loan can be repaid within a year. For example, a short-term loan might be used to purchase inventory, which is converted into finished goods and sales. As sales are turned into cash, the loan is repaid.

Short-term loans are classified into two major categories—**secured** and **unsecured**. The former are backed by some form of security such as receivables or inventories, while the latter are merely promises to repay without the backing of any specific assets.

SECURED LOANS   If a potential borrower is not in a strong financial position, the lender may require that acceptable assets be pledged as collateral. The market value of the pledged assets is nearly always greater than the amount of the loan; the difference between the two is the lender's safety margin. If the borrower is unable to fulfill the obligations stipulated in the loan agreement, the creditor can either assume ownership of the asset or have it sold. Since in most cases the lender does not actually want to take possession, he may have to sell the asset at a discount. Primarily for this reason the lender requires that the market value of the pledged asset exceed the amount of the loan.

Virtually any asset acceptable to the lender can be pledged as collateral for a loan. Since creditors generally do not like to take physical possession of an asset in the event of default, they prefer collateral that can be quickly turned into cash. Such collateral might take the form of stocks and bonds issued by subsidiaries or other firms, government securities, accounts receivable, or inventories. Of these, accounts receivable and inventories are particularly important.

Many firms make nearly all their sales on credit; thus accounts receivable can absorb a large amount of short-term funds. As a result, it may be necessary to borrow to support this asset by using the receivables as collateral. Because commercial banks generally do not like to accept accounts receivable as backing for a loan, most potential borrowers turn to commercial finance companies. Accounts receivable are relatively liquid and thus make suitable loan collateral. Still, lenders generally require that only the best-quality receivables be used and that they be worth more than the amount of the loan.

The finance company generally advances money to the borrower on a day-to-day basis as sales invoices are presented. The loans are usually equal to about 80% of the invoice amounts, although the percentage may be higher or lower depending on the financial condition of the borrower and the quality of the invoices. As payments on the receivables are obtained by the borrower, they are turned over to the finance company. Since the finance company has loaned only about 80% of the receivables value, the excess of payments over receivables is returned to the borrower. Note that although the receivables have been pledged as collateral, the borrower is still responsible for uncollectible accounts. As a result, the borrower must continue to shoulder the financial burden of running a credit operation.

Inventories, while generally less liquid than accounts receivable, are also used as collateral for loans. Much of this financing originates with commercial banks. As with receivables, the amount borrowed with this type of loan is less than the value of the collateral. However, inventories can prove more difficult to value and inspect, so inventory that can be easily identified and has a stable value is best suited for collateral purposes.

When pledged as collateral, inventories are handled by a number of different methods. In some cases the collateral is stored in public warehouses and warehouse receipts are turned over to the lender. Because the receipts are required by the warehouse for release of the goods, the lender knows the collateral is secure. Public warehouses are not always handy, and lenders sometimes accept collateral placed on the borrower's property. Under this method (termed field warehousing), a third party leases space in the borrower's warehouse and acts as custodian to the inventory. A third method of inventory financing takes place through trust receipt loans (floor planning). With this arrangement, durable and readily identifiable goods such as appliances and automobiles are used as collateral. The bank agrees to pay the manufacturer or wholesaler for the merchandise as it is ordered by the borrower. The lender is the owner of the goods and receives the invoices even though the merchandise is shipped directly to the borrower. As the goods are sold, the proceeds are used to repay the bank loan.

UNSECURED LOANS   An unsecured loan does not require the pledge of a specific asset or group of assets as collateral. This does not mean that there are no assets backing the loan. Rather, the firm pledges its credit and all its assets that are not being used as collateral for secured loans. In the event of nonpayment, the creditor can begin judicial proceedings and seek a judgment against the firm's assets. However, secured creditors have a prior claim on the specific assets pledged as collateral for their loans.

The most common type of unsecured loan is the line of credit. Under this arrangement the lender agrees to make available to the potential borrower a maximum amount of funds. The line of credit is generally sought by firms that have recurring credit requirements. For example, a company that needs to finance annual inventory buildups might desire such a credit arrangement. If the firm receives a bank commitment of $100,000, it knows in advance that any requests up to that amount will be fulfilled. The length of the agreement may be for any time period, although most lines run for one year and are subject to renewal. Frequently the interest rate is set in the initial arrangement as a function of some other rate, such as the bank's prime rate or the Federal Reserve discount rate. For example, the agreement may specify that the interest rate charged on the line's unpaid balance is to be 1½% more than the bank's prime rate. If the agreement is a binding contract rather than a moral commitment on the part of the lending institution, the borrower usually has to pay a fee— perhaps .4% to .7% annual payment on the entire amount of the line, whether it is drawn down or not.

A second type of unsecured short-term borrowing is the promissory note. In this obligation the borrower agrees to repay both principal and interest on a specific date. In some cases the agreement may require that the borrower make repayment on demand by the lender.

INTERMEDIATE-TERM FINANCING

While short-term sources carry maturities of less than one year, **intermediate-term financing** runs from 1 to 10 years. Many firms use this type of financing to fill the void between short-term funds that are designed to provide working capital and long-term sources that may require a commitment from the firm for 20 years, 30 years, or even longer. In many instances a company is using short-term funds to the maximum extent possible and the capital market is simply inaccessible. In such cases a firm has little choice but to seek intermediate-term financing.

Term Loans

Term loans are made by a number of financial institutions including commercial banks, insurance companies, commercial finance companies, and agencies of the federal government. These loans are generally unsecured and repaid gradually over the life of the loan. Since they are unsecured, the lender must make a commitment based on the potential borrower's projected cash flows and earning power. In addition, since proceeds from the loan may be incorporated into working capital, the lender usually mandates that minimum financial standards be maintained. These requirements might include a minimum level of working capital and a stated current ratio. The agreement may also prohibit the borrower from disposing of specific assets or pledging assets for other loans. To satisfy the creditor that these standards are being met, the borrower must periodically submit audited financial statements.

Term loans are used for a variety of purposes. The proceeds may be used to acquire current assets such as inventories or to carry accounts receivable. They may also be utilized to provide funds between periods of major long-term financing. For example, a firm may need funds until a major expansion project is completed, when it plans to issue long-term debt or common stock. A borrower may also solicit a term loan to acquire equipment. Hence term loans are utilized for nearly every business purpose.

Leasing

Leasing allows a firm (lessee) to acquire the long-term use of an asset without actually owning it. For this right the lessee makes periodic payments to the asset's owner (lessor). Intermediate- and long-term leasing is accomplished through a financial lease. This contract requires that the lessee make payments to the lessor over the life of the lease; in most cases the required payments return to the lessor the original purchase price of the asset plus a return on the investment. At the end of the term of the lease, the asset is generally returned to the owner, although the contract may specify that the lessee has the right to purchase the asset or renew the lease. The agreement specifies that either the lessee or the lessor is responsible for maintenance. If the lessor pays for maintenance, the expense is passed on to the lessee through higher lease payments. An alternate leasing arrangement is the operating lease in which the lessee can cancel the lease before the lessor recovers the full investment (as with a telephone).

In some instances, such as with property in an urban area, it may actually be impossible to acquire ownership of certain assets. In such cases a firm desiring to use the asset has no alternative but to accept a lease from the owner. Such a situation is unusual, however; a more normal situation allows the potential user to choose between purchasing and leasing. For this reason it is necessary to investigate the comparative advantages and disadvantages of each form of financing.

Financial leases may be advantageous from a tax standpoint. The entire amount of a lease payment is deductible from income for tax purposes. For an asset that is owned, only interest charges (on a loan to purchase the asset) and depreciation are deductible. For unimproved real estate, where no depreciation is allowed, the tax advantage of leasing could prove significant. For depreciable assets, however, accelerated depreciation plus interest charges might well result in a greater tax deduction under ownership, especially during the early life of an asset.

A second possible advantage of leasing is that the firm can use its available funds for other more profitable investments. For example, a retailing company might prefer to commit its money to higher-margined inventory items such as automotive products, toothpaste, phonograph records, or clothing rather than to tie it up in real estate and equipment. In fact, many of the larger retail chains lease rather than own the buildings in which they operate. If a firm had an unlimited supply of available capital, leasing for this reason would not be particularly relevant. For most firms, however, unlimited capital is only a dream.

One of the disadvantages of most leases is that ownership of the leased asset remains with the lessor on termination of the agreement. In many instances the asset has only a nominal value at the end of the period, so this disadvantage is relatively unimportant. In other cases, however, this variable must play an important part in the leasing decision, especially for real estate which historically has appreciated rather than depreciated in value.

One type of leasing that has become increasingly popular in recent years is sale and leaseback financing. Under this type of arrangement, a company constructs a building to its own needs and specifications and then sells the asset to another firm or group of investors. The company then leases the asset back from its new owners. This type of contract generally specifies that the lessee can repurchase the property at a predetermined price on termination of the lease. In addition, it allows a company to obtain the tax benefits of leasing while having the exact asset it needs and the right to retain ownership at the end of the lease. Since sale and leaseback is so similar to outright ownership, the contract must be carefully drawn up or the Internal Revenue Service may disallow the tax deductions normally associated with a lease.

A lease obligation is similar to obligations resulting from debt financing. Although a lease is treated somewhat differently from debt in the event of bankruptcy, a lease legally obligates the firm to make specified payments over the life of the agreement. These payments cannot be skipped simply because the firm fails to earn a profit. In fact, since the lessor retains title to the asset, it can generally be claimed rather quickly if payments are missed. Even though financial lease obligations are similar to those of debt financing, they were not generally shown on a firm's balance sheet prior to January 1977. Whereas debt appeared as a liability and the property the debt was used to acquire appeared as an asset, the lease usually resulted in no balance sheet entries other than footnotes. The result was that leasing instead of borrowing and buying tended to make a firm's balance sheet appear "cleaner" and stronger. Financial ratios such as debt to equity and debt to total assets appeared lower when a firm leased. For this reason leasing has been called off-balance-sheet financing. Contracts entered into beginning in January 1977 must appear on the balance sheet.

LONG-TERM FINANCING

Long-term financing includes the sale of common stock, preferred stock, and long-term debt, as well as the use of retained earnings. The sale of stocks and bonds is called **external financing**, since the firm must raise the funds outside the corporation, while the use of funds generated within the firm is termed **internal financing**. Corporations typically go outside for **long-term financing** when internal sources prove insufficient for expansion and replacement purposes. Large numbers of firms have increasingly relied on external sources of funds. In the latter 1960s and early 1970s many companies found themselves overextended with debt.

In raising long-term funds externally, a firm must ordinarily rely on an outsider to help organize and sell the securities. This outsider, the investment banker, is an intermediary between the company needing funds and the investing public. The investment banker either takes the securities on consignment or purchases them outright from the issuing company and resells them to investors. These intermediaries are employed because of their expertise in this area of finance. When using an investment banker, the company issuing the securities must pay a fee based on the size and risk of the issue.

Common Stock

Common stockholders are the owners of a corporation. As such, they bear most of the risks resulting from an unsuccessful operation and receive most of the rewards from a successful operation. The risks are great because the holders of common stock are the last group to receive cash that flows through the company. Before they get anything, other groups such as employees, preferred stockholders, the government, and creditors must be paid. The amount of money these other groups take is at least partially fixed; thus the common stockholders potentially stand to have their return increased considerably during prosperous periods. No cash return is guaranteed or promised to common stockholders. Even during years when the firm is very profitable, its officers are not required to pay cash dividends. In fact, many new and growing firms do not pay dividends as a matter of policy because the funds are needed in the business. Nor does the firm make a commitment to return the contributions of its owners. A stockholder who wishes to terminate ownership must sell the shares to a willing buyer at whatever price can be agreed on.

CONTROL AND VOTING   In theory common stockholders hold control over the management of a corporation since they are generally the only parties allowed to vote for the company's directors. We say "generally" because some issues of preferred stock convey the right to vote, while certain classes of common stockholders (companies sometimes issue more than one class of common) do not have the right to vote. The stockholders' representatives, the members of the board of directors, are then permitted to either control corporate policy or pick officers to direct this policy.

To elect directors of the corporation, a corporate charter specifies the place and date of the firm's annual meeting. In addition to this meeting, other special meetings may be called during the year. It is the annual meeting, however, at which most stockholder business is transacted. While voting for the directors may be the most important ritual of the meeting, other items such as reports of the officers, answers to stockholders' questions, and voting on additional matters are also generally taken care of.

A common stockholder is entitled to one vote for each share of stock owned. The votes may be cast in person or by proxy (given to someone else who is authorized to act for the stockholder). Voting by proxy is allowed since most owners find it inconvenient or impossible to attend every meeting. Proxies are usually solicited by a firm's management at the corporation's (and thus the stockholders') expense. The returned proxies are then used to elect directors nominated by management and to support management policies. Herein lies one of the major stumbling blocks in stockholder control of a business. Since stockholders are geographically separated and have widely varying interests, it is extremely difficult for them to successfully oppose any policy suggested by management. Although a dissident group of owners may solicit proxies from other stockholders, it must do so at its own expense. This places it at a great disadvantage against management, which has all the resources of the corporation at its disposal. Concerned stockholders may also have other issues placed on the proxy statement. These may include management pension benefits, minority representation on the board of directors, and officers' salaries. If management on the proxy statement recommends voting against these issues (as is usually the case), the chance of passage is nearly nonexistent. Hence, although common stockholders are theoretically in charge of a company's affairs, they actually have very little input into the decision-making process.

Corporate charters allow for two methods of voting for directors. Under majority voting, a shareholder is allowed to cast one vote for each share owned for each director's seat up for election. For example, a person owning 50 shares could cast 50 votes for each position on the board. Under this system, a group controlling one share more than 50% of the total shares could elect its entire slate of candidates. In reality a significantly smaller percentage is required since many shareholders do not bother to vote.

The second method of electing directors is called cumulative voting. This system is similar to majority voting in that a shareholder receives one vote for each share owned times the number of positions up for election. However, under cumulative voting the shareholder may accumulate votes and cast the total for fewer positions than are in contention. In other words, the shareholder's votes do not have to be evenly split among the directors up for election. For example, the stockholder owning 50 shares could cast total votes equal to 50 times the number of directors being elected. If 7 positions were up for election, the shareholder could cast 350 votes (50 × 7) for any number of directors. One extreme would be to cast all 350 votes for one position, while the other extreme would be to cast 50 votes for each position—the same result that would occur under majority voting.

The purpose of cumulative voting is to allow the views of minority interests to be represented on the board of directors. Since a minority group may be able to accumulate enough votes to elect at least one director, its views are more likely to be considered.

THE PREEMPTIVE RIGHT   The **preemptive right** is the privilege of current stockholders to purchase additional shares of common stock before they can be sold to outsiders. The purpose of the preemptive right is to permit common stockholders to keep their proportionate ownership in a firm by allowing them to buy new stock in proportion to their existing holdings. For example, suppose you own 300 shares of common stock in a company that has 1 million shares outstanding. Your proportionate ownership is 300/1,000,000 or .03%. If the firm decides to sell an additional 100,000 shares, you are permitted to purchase 30 more shares to bring your total holdings to 330 shares or .03% of the company's new outstanding stock. You are not required to buy the new stock, but you are given the right to make the purchase if you so desire.

When stockholders have the preemptive right, newly issued shares are sold through a rights offering. Stockholders receive one right for each share owned. Depending on the proportionate increase in the number of shares desired by the company, a given number of rights plus cash is required for the purchase of each new share. Suppose a firm wishes to sell a new stock issue that will increase the number of shares outstanding by 10%. If you own 200 shares, you will receive 200 rights. Since a 10% increase in your holdings would require the purchase of 20 shares, you will need 10 rights (200 rights/20 shares = 10 rights per share) plus cash to buy each new share. The company's decision on the number of shares to issue is actually dictated by the amount of funds it wishes to raise through the stock offering and the price at which its stock is selling. For instance, if the firm requires $300,000 in new equity capital and it can sell a new stock issue at $30 per share, it needs an offering of 10,000 shares ($300,000/$30).

To entice existing shareholders into purchasing the new issue, the company offers them stock at less than the current market price. For example, it might set the price of new shares at $22 if the current market price is $25. The difference between the subscription price ($22) and the market price ($25) gives the stockholders' rights a value since they are a necessary part of purchasing new shares at the below-market price. The value of one right depends on three variables: (1) the subscription price, (2) the market price, and (3) the number of rights required to purchase one share of stock. The formula to calculate the value of a right is

$$R = (M_r - S)/(N + 1) \qquad\qquad\qquad 8\text{--}1$$

where

$R =$ the value of one right

$M_r =$ the market price of the stock with the right included

$S =$ the subscription price of the new shares

$N =$ the number of rights needed to buy one new share

If five rights are required to purchase new shares in our example, the value of one right is

$$R = (\$25 - 22)/(5 + 1) = \$3/6 = \$.50$$

A current stockholder who does not wish to purchase the new shares may sell the rights to someone else. The firm's underwriter generally establishes a resale market for the rights, so selling them is not much of a problem. Since the rights have a value, it is in the interest of the shareholder to either exercise them by purchasing stock or to sell them to someone else who wishes to use them. It is not in the stockholder's interest to set the rights aside and ignore the stock offering. This fact practically assures the company of a successful sale.

On a specific date set by the company's officers (the ex-rights date), new purchasers of stock will not receive rights to the offering. On that date the market price of the company's stock should theoretically decline by the value of one right, or by $.50 in this example. The stock then sells ex-rights at $24.50 ($25.00 − $.50). If we let M_x equal the market price on the date the stock goes ex-rights, the value of a right can be found using the following equation:

$$R = \frac{M_s - S}{N} \qquad\qquad 8\text{-}2$$

In this example

$$R = \frac{\$24.50 - \$22.00}{5} = \frac{\$2.50}{5} = \$.50$$

This analysis assumes that the market price of the firm's stock stays the same prior to the ex-rights date. This, of course, is not generally the case. The result is that the price of the rights fluctuates. In addition, the actual price at which the rights sell does not always equal the theoretical value we have calculated in these formulas.

Preferred Stock

While **preferred stock**, like common stock, represents ownership in a company, it has some of the characteristics of debt. Preferred stock is thus a cross between common stock and debt. Although preferred stock-holders possess no legal right to receive dividends, they do have priority over the owners of common stock. In other words, if the company's directors declare a dividend, they must pay preferred stock ahead of common stock. In addition, if the firm must liquidate, preferred stockholders receive compensation to the extent of their security's par value before any funds can be paid to common stockholders. Compared to preferred and common stockholders, the company's creditors have a prior claim on both income and assets.

Dividends paid to the holders of preferred stock are generally fixed in amount and stated as a percentage of the security's par value. Most preferred stock has a par value of $100 per share. For example, a company's 6%, $100 par value preferred stock would pay a dividend of $6 per year or $1.50 per quarter. (Both preferred and common stock generally pay dividends on a quarterly basis.) If a preferred stock has no designated par value, the dividend is stated as a dollar amount rather than as a percentage. Except in unusual cases, this dividend is the maximum amount the preferred stockholder can expect to receive. This is in contrast to common stock dividends which may increase if profits climb. Because preferred stock is similar to debt (in terms of cash payments to holders), its market price very much depends on the current rate of return on other fixed-income investments. For example, if the current yield on high-grade bonds is 8%, then a 6%, $100 par preferred stock will be selling at well below

$100 per share, even if the company's profits are dramatically increasing.

Nearly all issues of preferred stock have a cumulative feature which requires that skipped dividends must be made up in a future payment period before any dividends can be paid to common stockholders. Thus, if a company's directors do not vote to pay a dividend to the owners of 5% cumulative preferred stock, the arrears of $5 per share must eventually be made up or no dividends ean be paid to holders of the company's common stock. Hence, even though dividends on preferred stock are not a contractual liability, the incentive to meet the obligation is nearly overwhelming. Note that it is the current owner who receives dividends in arrears. Thus if dividends are not voted on cumulative preferred stock and you sell the securities before the arrears are made up, the new owner is entitled to receive the dividends in arrears.

A less common inclusion in preferred stock issues is a participating feature. Participating preferred allows the holders to participate in the firm's net income according to a specified formula. The amount received from the participating feature is in addition to the dividend normally paid. The most prevalent type of participation permits preferred to share equally with common stock when the dividends on common exceed the rate specified for preferred. As an illustration, if you hold 100 shares of 5%, $100 par participating preferred ($5 per share annually), the company's board of directors would be required to pay you an additional $1 per share dividend if it wished to pay common shareholders $6 per share. This type of preferred is very unusual. The maximum dividend that most preferred stockholders can hope to receive is the fixed rate specified on their certificate.

Preferred shareholders are not generally given the privilege of voting for the company's directors unless preferred dividends have been passed a given number of times. Once this occurs, however, the preferred holders are entitled to elect a given number of directors regardless of the number of preferred shares relative to common shares outstanding. Unfortunately, by the time these owners receive a voice in the firm's management, it may be too late to make the feature very meaningful. Preferred stockholders generally do have some control over matters that affect their position with respect to dividends and assets. For example, a proposal to eliminate a preference to certain assets requires the acceptance of a given percentage of the preferred holders.

A great disadvantage of financing with preferred stock is that dividends are not a deductible expense in computing income taxes. If a firm is in the 40% tax bracket, the payment of $1 in preferred dividends requires the generation of $1/(1 − .4) before taxes. To pay $1 in interest requires only $1 before taxes. This single fact has proved to be such a deterrent that few companies rely on preferred stock to any major extent. One of the few exceptions to this is the public utility industry, which can pass the higher capital costs to customers. Many companies have actually retired much of the outstanding preferred. Since preferred stock has no maturity date, the retirements must take place by calling it from stockholders at a predetermined price or by purchasing it in the open market.

Long-Term Bonds

Bonds represent debt of a company, so claims of the holders must be paid before stockholders receive anything. These claims include both interest payments and the return of principal at maturity. A bond obligates the issuing firm to specific interest charges for a given number of years and repayment of the original amount borrowed at the bond's maturity. Bondholders also have priority over stockholders in claims on assets in the event of liquidation. The priorities of the individual claims of bondholders depend on the type of bond held.

Bonds have become a very popular instrument of long-term financing because interest payments are deductible for income tax purposes, in contrast to dividend payments on common and preferred stock which must be paid with after-tax income. As a result, a new 8% bond issue costs the corporation only half as much as a new 8% preferred stock issue (assuming the corporate tax rate is 50%).

PROVISIONS OF BONDS Bonds are issued to the public in a manner very similar to a public stock sale. Investment bankers are generally used to help the firm sell the securities. This intermediary in many cases absorbs the entire risk of selling the issue. The contract between the bondholders and the borrowing company is called an **indenture**. This document specifies what is expected of the firm with respect to interest payments, repayment of principal, pledged property, and restrictions on dividends or more indebtedness. A trustee, such as a bank, is appointed to see that all the stipulations of the indenture agreement are met.

A bond issue may be retired in total at maturity or it may be gradually retired during the years before maturity. In the latter case a sinking fund is used to repurchase a portion of the issue each year. With a sinking fund the firm may either purchase its bonds in the open market or, if the option is available, it may call the bonds from their owners at a predetermined price. The company uses the method that retires the stipulated amount of bonds at the lowest cost. The **call feature** is an important provision to both the firm and its bondholders. Since it allows a company to repurchase its bonds before maturity at a stated price, the holder has to sell at the stipulated price if the bonds are called. In many cases an issue has three to ten years of call protection (a period during which no call can be made). The call price is usually higher than the issue price in order to give the holder some premium in the event of a call. The call price is typically equal to the issue price plus one year's interest during the early call period. The premium gradually declines to zero at maturity. The reason a firm includes a call price in the indenture agreement is not difficult to discern. Should interest rates decline after a bond issue is sold, the call feature lets a company refinance the issue at a lower interest rate.

TYPES OF BONDS   Like other corporate debt, bonds can be either secured or unsecured. The quality of the security (or the lack of it) is an important factor in determining the rate of interest required to sell a bond issue. A company might have to attach "sweeteners," such as options to purchase the firm's common stock, in order to attract buyers, but usually either the firm's promise to pay or the pledge of specific collateral is enough for a successful sale. In the event of liquidation, secured bondholders have a prior claim on assets pledged as collateral. Unsecured bondholders and other general creditors share what is left. Secured creditors who are not paid in full become general creditors.

Secured bonds can have a variety of assets pledged as collateral; the most common type of security is a mortgage on real property. Real property may include machinery, equipment, buildings, or land. A firm may pledge all or only a portion of its real assets in a single bond issue. A company may actually pledge the same property in two different issues. Debt with the first pledge is a first mortgage bond, while debt with the second pledge is a second mortgage bond. The difference is important, since in case of default the pledged asset must be sold to pay claims of first mortgage holders in full before second mortgage holders can be reimbursed. Hence, second mortgage bonds are riskier and carry a higher rate of interest. The value of the pledged property nearly always exceeds the amount of the borrowing.

Other types of secured bonds include collateral trust bonds and equipment trust certificates. The former are secured by stocks and/or bonds (nearly always of other corporations). If the borrower defaults, the collateral is sold to meet creditors' claims. Equipment trust certificates are secured by mobile assets such as railroad cars and airplanes. The equipment is generally easy to sell and is thus a good form of collateral. Since the Penn Central collapse, there has been some concern that the federal government may force a bankrupt utility to keep operating. In such cases the trustee may be unable to sell the equipment to pay creditors' claims.

Bonds backed by the borrower's promise of repayment, but not by any specific asset, are **debentures**. In the event of default, holders of debentures are classified as general creditors with respect to recovery. This positions them ahead of common and preferred stockholders but behind senior creditors. An even lower grade of bond is the subordinated debenture. The claim of this security is inferior to all other secured and unsecured creditors, including straight debenture holders. Since there is a good chance that unsecured bondholders will be unable to recover their full claim in the event of default, the borrower's earning power is an extremely important factor in evaluating the quality of unsecured debt.

Dividends and Internal Financing

The retention of earnings is an important aspect of long-term financing. For many firms it is the largest single source of long-term funds. Even companies with access to external financing may decide not to carry long-term debt because of the added risk and the desire to avoid diluting the position of owners by selling additional common stock. To provide funds for growth and asset replacement, these firms may pay only a nominal dividend. Thus, even when outside capital markets are utilized, retained earnings are almost always an important source of financing.

A corporation (and its stockholders) might prefer to retain a major portion of earnings rather than pay them out to stockholders in the form of cash dividends for a number of reasons. One of the most important is related to the tax consequences for shareholders. With the exception of a $100 exemption for each taxpayer, cash dividends are fully taxable as ordinary income at the stockholder's marginal tax rate. High-income shareholders may pay over half of all dividends in taxes. On the other hand, earnings retained by a corporation presumably enhance the value of its shares of common stock. An owner does not pay taxes on appreciation in the value of stock until it is sold. Even then stock is treated as a capital asset, and gains are taxed at a favorable rate if the shares have been held for over one year. Hence for tax reasons alone many shareholders prefer that a corporation retain earnings instead of paying them out as dividends.

Another reason for retaining earnings is to avoid the dilution of control that may take place with new common stock issues. In addition, the firm may want to avoid the added risk inherent with larger amounts of debt outstanding. One of the best methods of limiting the necessity for outside financing is to retain all or a major portion of earnings.

The firm may be able to earn a greater return on reinvested funds than the stockholder could earn on reinvested dividends. For example, if a company can earn 20% on equity capital, while the stockholder's best alternative is 12% on some other investment of similar risk, it is in the owner's best interest to have the firm retain earnings rather than pay dividends. This does not even consider that the stockholder must pay income taxes on the dividends and can thus reinvest only the remainder.

Most corporations tend to pay relatively stable dividends. In other words, rather than setting dividends at some stated percentage of reported earnings each year, most firms prefer to pay a dividend that increases gradually as earnings expand. Even though earnings may fluctuate from quarter to quarter and from year to year, dividends remain relatively steady under this policy. Some financial managers believe that investors will pay a premium for the stock of a company with a stable dividend policy.

One method of paying a dividend while at the same time conserving cash is to issue the dividend in the form of a stock certificate. Stock dividends do not cost a firm any cash other than accounting, printing, and postage expenses, and stockholders can sell the additional shares if they need money. The tax consequences of such a distribution are more favorable than with cash dividends since a stock dividend is not taxable until the shares are sold (even then the gain is taxed as a return of principal). In theory stockholders are no better or worse off with a stock dividend because their relative ownership position in the company remains unchanged. For example, if an investor owns 100 shares in a firm and the shares are selling at $20 each, the total value of the holdings is $2000. If the firm pays a 5% stock dividend, the investor receives an additional 5 shares. However, the total value of the stockholder's investment remains $2000, because everything else remains unchanged. The same company simply has an additional 5% of common stock outstanding. The stockholder's shares should decline to approximately $19 per share ($2000/105).

SUMMARY

A firm's financing decisions are partially dictated by its asset structure. As a general rule there should be some attempt to match the maturities of assets and liabilities. Short-term funds are obtained through trade credit, accruals, commercial paper sales, and short-term loans from financial institutions. Each of these sources has advantages and disadvantages. Intermediate- and long-term sources of financing include term loans, leasing, common and preferred stock sales, long-term debt sales, and internally generated funds.

QUESTIONS

1. Why must the financial manager compare the structure of liabilities with the firm's asset structure?

2. What is the primary source of short-term financing?

3. Why is it that only large and well-established companies usually issue commercial paper?

4. What are the two major categories of short-term loans and what are their differences?

5. Does a lease appear on the balance sheet? Discuss the implications of your answer.

6. What are the main types of long-term financing?

7. Distinguish between external financing and internal financing.

8. If the common stockholders are theoretically in charge of a company's affairs, why do they actually have little input into the decision-making process?

9. What does the value of a stock right depend on?

10. What are some of the disadvantages of financing with preferred stock?

SELECTED REFERENCES

BRIGHAM, EUGENE F. *Financial Management: Theory and Practice.* Hinsdale, Ill.: Dryden Press, 1977. Part 3.

CLARK, JOHN J.; CLARK, MARGARET T.; and ELGERS, PIETER T. *Financial Management: A Capital Market Approach.* Boston: Holbrook Press, 1976. Chs. 11, 12, 13, and 16.

DONALDSON, ELVIN F.; PFAHL, JOHN K.; and MULLINS, PETER L. *Corporate Finance.* New York: Ronald Press, 1975. Part 3.

LERNER, EUGENE M. *Managerial Finance: A Systems Approach.* New York: Harcourt Brace Jovanovich, 1971. Sect. 3.

PRITCHARD, ROBERT E. *Operational Financial Management.* Englewood Cliffs, N.J.: Prentice-Hall, 1977. Chs. 8–13.

RAY, MARVIN E. *The Environmental Crisis and Corporate Debt Policy.* Lexington, Mass.: D. C. Heath and Co., 1974. Ch. 3.

SCOTT, DAVID L. *Financing the Growth of Electric Utilities.* New York: Praeger Publishers, 1976. Chs. 4, 5.

VAN HORNE, JAMES C. *Fundamentals of Financial Management.* Englewood Cliffs, N.J.: Prentice-Hall, 1977. Sects. 3, 4.

9   Capital Structure, Leverage, and the Cost of Capital

The quickest way to lose your shirt is to put too much on the cuff.

A company's financial structure includes all types of financing, both short-term and long-term. A firm's capital structure, on the other hand, includes only permanent financing. The capital structure generally consists of **common stock**, preferred stock, long-term debt, and retained earnings.

THE FIRM'S CAPITAL STRUCTURE

When a company is initially formed, management must decide how to obtain funds. At least a portion of the financial structure consists of common stock—the contribution of the new owners. Although no retained earnings are possible initially, both short-term and long-term debt can generally be acquired. As the firm expands, new outside sources of financing become necessary. In addition, if the company is profitable, retained earnings should in time provide a portion of financing requirements. In the early years of a company's life, management will probably decide to pay only limited dividends so that most profits can be reinvested. This reinvestment, in turn, enhances the firm's ability to borrow additional funds.

The proportions of financing to be utilized can prove crucial. Using excessive debt increases the possibility of being unable to meet cash obligations. On the other hand, avoiding all debt in the capital structure might penalize the return to stockholders. Hence management should strive to keep a proper balance between debt and equity in the firm's capital structure.

What is proper for one firm may well prove wrong for another. For example, public utilities typically employ large amounts of debt that would be disastrous for companies in other industries. Because of their monopoly positions and generally stable revenues and earnings flows, public utilities can meet the heavy fixed costs of having large proportions of debt. It is quite common for electric utilities to have over 50% of their capitalization in the form of long-term debt. Companies in more cyclical industries, such as construction and mining, would intermittently face bankruptcy (as sometimes happens) with such heavy fixed obligations.

Traditional financial theory suggests that there is some optimal combination of debt and equity in any firm's capital structure. This combination varies from industry to industry, from company to company, and in fact changes over time for the same firm. The optimal combination minimizes the firm's average cost of raising funds. This approach is based on the idea that so long as a firm can earn more on invested funds than it pays to borrow those funds, it can increase the return to common stockholders. Although the inclusion of fixed-income securities in the firm's capital structure introduces the possibility that the firm will be unable to meet the fixed payments, minimizing the proportion of the securities minimizes this risk. As the proportion increases, however, the risk becomes correspondingly greater. The possibility that the firm will be unable to meet the fixed obligations is important to both the firm's owners and creditors. Not only do the owners run the risk of losing all or part of their investment; creditors run the risk that their claims will not be repaid on time or in full. The result is that greater amounts of debt lead both owners and creditors to demand that the firm pay a higher rate of return on their funds. The relationship between the cost of capital and a firm's capital structure is illustrated in fig. 9–1.

Figure 9–1 shows that a firm's average cost of capital declines as small amounts of relatively low-cost debt are incorporated into the capital structure. However, beyond some point the added risk due to increasing the proportion of debt actually causes the cost of capital to rise. The lowest point on the firm's cost of capital curve represents the optimal combination of debt and equity. Note that as the proportion of debt increases, both the cost of debt and the cost of equity increase (since the risk of both creditors and owners increases). Hence debt has an explicit cost (the interest charges incurred) and an implicit cost (the resulting higher cost of equity capital). A common error in evaluating debt as a source of funds is to consider only its explicit cost.

In 1958 Franco Modigliani and Merton Miller developed a theoreti-

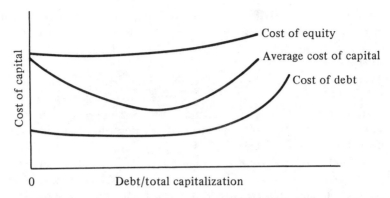

FIGURE 9–1 **Traditional View of the Relationship Between the Cost of Capital and Capital Structure**

cal analysis which showed that a firm's cost of capital is not affected by its capital structure. According to their analysis, the cost of capital remains constant regardless of the proportions of debt and equity and there is no ideal capital structure. Modigliani and Miller argue that it is the asset structure, not the capital structure, that determines the firm's market valuation. Substituting less expensive debt for more expensive equity simply leads investors to discount net income at a higher rate. The relationship between the cost of capital and the firm's capital structure with the Modigliani-Miller analysis is illustrated in fig. 9–2.

The Modigliani-Miller analysis has been criticized on a number of grounds. One of the major criticisms is that the analysis assumes perfect capital markets with no transactions costs and no income taxes. These assumptions are particularly important since they imply that investors

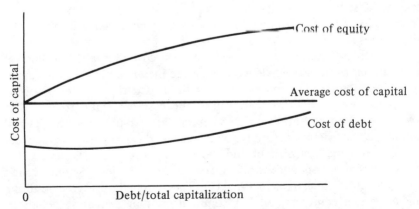

FIGURE 9–2 **Modigliani-Miller View of the Relationship Between the Cost of Capital and Capital Structure**

must be free to sell overvalued securities and buy undervalued securities in order to keep the market values of firms of the same size and risk class equal. In addition, individual investors are assumed to be able to substitute personal debt for corporate debt (borrow against their own portfolios rather than purchasing the common stock of companies with debt in their capital structures).

LEVERAGE AND PROFITS

A firm's cost of funds and financial structure have a direct bearing on profits. The use of assets and financing that require fixed expenditures magnifies profits when sales change. The result can be either favorable or unfavorable depending on whether sales are increasing or decreasing. The relationship between changes in sales and changes in profits is called leverage. Two categories of leverage are discussed in this section—operating and financial.

Operating Leverage

Operating leverage refers to the proportion of fixed costs that the firm employs in its operations. Fixed costs include expenses, such as salaries and depreciation, that do not vary with changes in output. The higher the degree of operating leverage, the greater the change in earnings before interest and taxes (EBIT) for a given change in sales. Hence a firm can increase operating leverage by substituting machinery (fixed costs) for labor (variable costs).

Assets with fixed costs are acquired because the firm believes that sales volume can be increased and that the added revenues will more than cover the additional fixed costs. If the expectation is wrong, the results could be disastrous since declining sales volume will magnify earnings before interest and taxes. The relationship between sales and earnings is more clearly illustrated with break-even analysis.

Break-even analysis permits the financial manager to investigate the relationships among sales, fixed costs, variable costs, and profits. This analysis is necessary before any decision to add new plant and equipment or substitute fixed for variable costs. For example, suppose we are considering the purchase of a new plant that produces widgets. The plant has annual fixed costs of $40,000. Variable costs for labor, materials, and distribution are $15 per widget, while the product sells for $20 per unit. We know that profits (π) equal total revenue (TR) less total costs (TC), or

$$\pi = TR - TC \qquad\qquad 9\text{--}1$$

Since total revenue is equal to the widget's final selling price times output, while total cost is equal to variable costs plus fixed costs, eq. 9–1 becomes

$$\pi = (P \times Q) - [(V \times Q) + F] \qquad\qquad 9\text{–}2$$

where

π = profits

P = selling price per unit

Q = units of output

V = variable costs per unit

F = total fixed costs

In this example, if we projected sales of 13,000 widgets during the first year, our expected profits would be

$$\pi = (\$20)(13,000) - [(\$15)(13,000) + \$40,000]$$
$$= \$260,000 - \$235,000 = \$25,000$$

If we wish to know the level of output for which profits are zero, we simply set the left-hand side of the equation (profits) equal to zero and solve for output (Q).

$$0 = (\$20 \times Q) - [(\$15 \times Q) + \$40,000]$$
$$= (\$20 \times Q) - (\$15 \times Q) - \$40,000$$
$$= \$5Q - \$40,000$$
$$Q = \$40,000/\$5 = 8000 \text{ units}$$

Therefore break-even output is 8000 widgets. Sales of less than 8000 units produce a loss, while sales of more than the break-even level result in a profit. A derivation of eq. 9–2 can also be employed in calculating the break-even volume.

$$Q = F/(P - V) \qquad\qquad 9\text{–}3$$

With the same data eq. 9–3 yields

$$Q = \$40,000/(\$20 - \$15) = \$40,000/\$5 = 8000 \text{ units}$$

Break-even analysis can also be illustrated graphically. Figure 9–3 shows the relationship among revenues, variable costs, fixed costs, and profits for our example. The break-even point occurs where total costs and total revenues are equal. Losses occur at all points below a sales volume of

8000 units, and the amount of the losses is shown on the graph as the vertical distance between the total revenue and total cost schedules. Under the assumptions of the example, the maximum possible loss occurs if the firm shuts down (sales volume is zero). On the other hand, there is no limit to the profits that can be earned so long as volume is expanded. The relationship between profits and sales volume is illustrated in fig. 9-4.

A change in any of the variables affecting total revenues and total

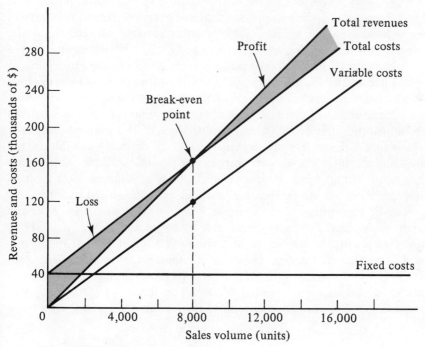

FIGURE 9-3   Break-Even Analysis

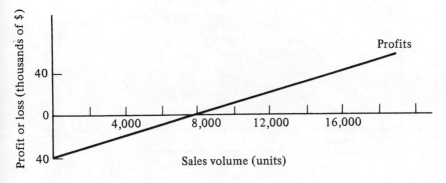

FIGURE 9-4   Profits and Sales Volume

costs alters the break-even output. For example, an increase in fixed costs increases total costs (moves the total cost curve upward) and moves the break-even point to the right. Conversely, a decline in fixed costs lowers the break-even point. An increase in variable costs per unit of output rotates the variable-cost curve counterclockwise to produce a steeper slope (the slope of the variable cost curve is equal to variable costs per unit) and a higher break-even point. A decline in variable costs per unit decreases the break-even level of output. Since the slope of the total revenue curve is equal to the price of the firm's product, an increase in price lowers break-even and a decline in price increases the level of output necessary to reach break-even. Of course, more than one variable can change at the same time. For example, an increase in costs might be accompanied by a price rise so that the break-even point is unchanged. On the other hand, if costs increase at the same time price is reduced, the increase in break-even is even larger than when only one of the variables changes.

Since many of the results inherent with linear break-even analysis are unrealistic, it is necessary to examine some of the assumptions under which figs. 9–3 and 9–4 are drawn. Because all costs are variable in the long run, the inclusion of fixed costs in our example indicates that we are examining a short-run situation. As such, there is some physical limit to how much output can be increased without expanding fixed resources. An unrealistic assumption of the example is that all the variables are linearly related to output. For example, variable costs per unit are given as $15 at any level of output. A more realistic assumption might be that these costs start increasing as the firm begins to approach maximum capacity (see fig. 9–5). The variable and total cost curves would then become more steeply sloped at high levels of output. The linear total revenue curve assumes that the firm can continue to increase its output and sales with-

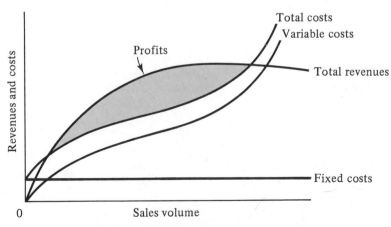

FIGURE 9–5   Nonlinear Break-Even Analysis

out at some point reducing price. If the firm is required to cut price to increase sales, the total revenue curve would be concave downward as shown in fig. 9–5. Because break-even always occurs at the level of output where total cost is equal to total revenue, there are two such points with nonlinear analysis. At output levels between these two points the firm is making a profit. The greatest profit occurs at the level of output where the vertical distance between total revenue and total cost is at a maximum.

Now that we have investigated the variables affecting profits, it is easier to understand the calculation of operating leverage. The degree of operating leverage is the percentage change in profits divided by the percentage change in output, or

$$\text{Degree of operating leverage} = \frac{\%\Delta EBIT}{\%\Delta Q} \qquad \text{9–4}$$

where

$\%\Delta EBIT$ = percentage change in earnings before interest and taxes

$\%\Delta Q$ = percentage change in volume

Operating leverage is calculated at a given level of output. A firm with unchanging revenue and cost curves has differing degrees of operating leverage at various output levels. Another formula for computing the degree of operating leverage is

$$\text{Degree of operating leverage} = \frac{Q(P - V)}{Q(P - V) - F} \qquad \text{9–5}$$

For example, if we calculate the degree of operating leverage at 9000 units of output for the firm in our previous example, we get

$$\frac{9000(\$20 - \$15)}{9000(\$20 - \$15) - \$40,000} = \frac{\$45,000}{\$45,000 - \$40,000} = 9$$

Hence a 1% increase in volume produces a 9% increase in earnings before interest and taxes. The degree of operating leverage at 12,000 units of output is

$$\frac{12,000(\$20 - \$15)}{12,000(\$20 - \$15) - \$40,000} = \frac{\$60,000}{\$60,000 - \$40,000} = 3$$

Financial Leverage

Financial leverage involves the use of funds obtained at fixed rates. Since the cost of these funds does not change when the firm's operating income varies, financial leverage can be used to improve the return to common stockholders. Leverage is favorable when the firm earns more on the assets purchased with fixed-rate funds than those funds cost. Conversely, leverage is unfavorable when the firm earns less on the assets purchased with the funds than the funds cost. For example, if our firm issues bonds with an interest rate of 8% in order to purchase an asset returning 12%, the financial leverage is positive. As a result, the firm earns a larger rate of return on stockholders' investment than if it had financed the new asset through the sale of additional common stock. The firm also earns a higher return than if the investment had not been undertaken. Since financial leverage involves the use of fixed-cost financing in an attempt to increase the return on the stockholders' equity, it is sometimes called "trading on the equity."

A high degree of financial leverage is accompanied by a large amount of risk. A heavy proportion of fixed-income securities, such as debt and preferred stock, in a company's capital structure commits the firm to fixed charges regardless of business conditions. Consequently, there is a greater risk that the company will be unable to meet the required payments. Since creditors and preferred stockholders have a priority claim on both cash payments and assets, financial risk increases the probability that the firm's owners will be unable to recover their investment in the event of adverse business conditions. On the other hand, a capital structure made up entirely of common stock and retained earnings does not commit the firm to any fixed financial charges. Without these fixed charges a company may be able to survive a number of poor years.

To observe the impact of financial leverage, we will examine the results of three possible capital structures for the Rushville Exterminating Company, shown in table 9-1. In each case the firm requires the same amount of funds. However, case A includes mostly common equity, case B incorporates more debt, and case C includes a combination of common equity, debt, and preferred equity. In each example we assume common stock can be sold for $10 per share. The preferred stock in case C must be sold to yield 8% to investors. Debt, which is included in all three capital structures, can be sold to yield 9% in cases A and C. However, because case B includes a heavy proportion of debt (and therefore greater risk) Rushville must pay 10% on its bonds.

In calculating the effect of Rushville's capital structure on its earnings per share of common stock (EPS), assume an EBIT level of $500,000 for each case. If common stock is sold at $10 per share, the outstanding shares are 200,000, 100,000, and 100,000, respectively. Income taxes are computed at 50% of taxable income. The calculations for earnings per share are illustrated in table 9-2.

Although the earnings available for common stockholders are over 25% lower in case B than in case A, earnings per share are significantly higher. The reason is that the financing in case B requires only half as

TABLE 9–1   Rushville Exterminating Company, Balance Sheets for Three Capital Structures

Case A

Current Assets	$ 500,000	Debt (9%)	$1,000,000
Fixed Assets	2,500,000	Common Equity	2,000,000
Total Assets	$3,000,000	Liabilities and Net Worth	$3,000,000

Case B

Current Assets	$ 500,000	Debt (10%)	$2,000,000
Fixed Assets	2,500,000	Common Equity	1,000,000
Total Assets	$3,000,000	Liabilities and Net Worth	$3,000,000

Case C

Current Assets	$ 500,000	Debt (9%)	$1,000,000
Fixed Assets	2,500,000	Preferred Equity (8%)	1,000,000
		Common Equity	1,000,000
Total Assets	$3,000,000	Liabilities and Net Worth	$3,000,000

many shares outstanding. Although case C also has 1 million shares of common stock outstanding, the nondeductibility of preferred stock dividends results in a lower earnings per share than in case B.

Although earnings per share are highest for case B, this capital structure may not be the best of the three. The risk of having two-thirds of Rushville's obligations in fixed-payment debt securities may more than offset the higher earnings per share at the given EBIT level. For example,

TABLE 9–2   The Impact of the Capital Structure on Earnings per Share

	Case A	*Case B*	*Case C*
EBIT	$500,000	$500,000	$500,000
Interest	90,000	200,000	90,000
Earnings before taxes	$410,000	$300,000	$410,000
Income taxes	205,000	150,000	205,000
Earnings after taxes	$205,000	$150,000	$205,000
Preferred stock dividend	0	0	80,000
Earnings available for common stockholders	$205,000	$150,000	$125,000
Common shares outstanding	200,000	100,000	100,000
Earnings per share	$1.02	$1.50	$1.25

if earnings before interest and taxes fall to $300,000, the earnings per share for each of the three cases decline to $.52, $.50, and $.25, respectively. On the other hand, increases in EBIT translate into even more favorable EPS levels for case B. For example, if earnings before interest and taxes climb to $800,000, EPS for cases A, B, and C are $1.78, $3.00, and $2.75, respectively.

To compare the three methods of financing at various levels of EBIT, we can construct an indifference chart. In fig. 9–6 each financing alternative is represented by a straight line showing EPS for possible levels of EBIT. Each line intersects the horizontal axis at the EBIT level at which its respective earnings per share are zero. For example, in case B earnings before interest and taxes of $200,000 result in no earnings for common stockholders. Case A, with lower fixed charges, requires an EBIT of only $90,000 for no earnings per share. Case C is somewhat more difficult to calculate since preferred dividends are paid with after-tax income. Here we must double the preferred dividends (to take account of the 50% tax rate) and add the result to the interest charge. To draw each schedule we need only two points. One can be the intercept of the horizontal axis; the second can be any other EBIT–EPS point, such as one of those calculated in table 9–2.

The intersection of two schedules represents the indifference point,

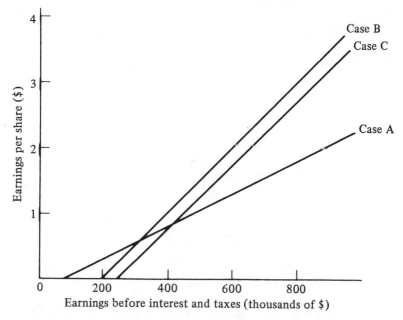

Figure 9–6   Indifference Schedules for the Three Financing Alternatives

or the EBIT level at which earnings per share are the same for each of two methods of financing. To the right of each indifference point, the alternative with the steepest schedule produces the greatest earnings per share. Again, however, the alternative with the highest per-share earnings is not necessarily preferable. A great deal of emphasis must be placed on projected EBIT levels for future years and the expected accuracy of the projections. For example, if we expect annual earnings before interest and taxes of $400,000 over the next several years but are highly uncertain about the accuracy of our projections, we might prefer the capital structure of case A to case B, even though the latter shows a higher EPS.

The level of EBIT at which two schedules intersect is important since it represents equality between earnings per share for two possible capital structures. This point of indifference can be found by using the following equation:

$$\frac{(EBIT - I_1)(1 - t) - D_1}{S_1} = \frac{(EBIT - I_2)(1 - t) - D_2}{S_2} \qquad 9\text{--}6$$

where

$EBIT$ = level of EBIT at which EPS is equal under each method of financing

I_1, I_2 = interest expense (in dollars) of each method of financing

t = corporate income tax rate

D_1, D_2 = preferred stock dividend (in dollars) for each type of financial structure

S_1, S_2 = number of shares of common stock outstanding under each method of financing

Using eq. 9–6 to solve for the indifference point between cases A and C, we have

$$\frac{(EBIT - \$90,000)(1 - .50) - 0}{200,000} = \frac{(EBIT - \$90,000)(1 - .50) - \$80,000}{100,000}$$

$$\frac{.5\ EBIT - \$45,000}{200,000} = \frac{.5\ EBIT - \$125,000}{100,000}$$

$$EBIT = \$410,000$$

Solving for earnings per share at the indifference point, we find that EPS equals $.80. Using the same method of solving for the indifference point of cases A and B we get EBIT and EPS of $310,000 and $.55, respectively. If a capital structure includes no debt or preferred stock, it is only necessary to set I or D equal to zero.

Now that we have discussed financial leverage and the similarities and differences between this variable and operating leverage, it is helpful to examine the calculation of the degree of financial leverage (DFL). The degree of financial leverage at a given EBIT level is simply the percentage change in earnings per share divided by the percentage change in earnings before interest and taxes, or

$$\text{Degree of financial leverage} = \frac{\% \Delta EPS}{\% \Delta EBIT} \qquad 9\text{--}7$$

For example, if earnings before interest and taxes in case A increase from $310,000 to $410,000, earnings per share rise from $.55 to $.80. The percentage increases in EBIT and EPS are 32 and 45, respectively, resulting in a degree of financial leverage of 1.41 (45%/32%). Using the capital structure of case B, we find that an increase in EBIT level from $310,000 to $410,000 results in a rise in EPS from $.55 to $1.05. The degree of financial leverage at the $310,000 EBIT level is 2.84 (91%/32%). The higher DFL in case B is to be expected since debt has been substituted for common equity in the capital structure. A variation of eq. 9–7 that can be employed in computing the degree of financial leverage is

$$\text{Degree of financial leverage} = \frac{EBIT}{EBIT - I - D/(1 - t)} \qquad 9\text{--}8$$

where

$I =$ interest expense (in dollars) on debt

$D =$ dividend expense (in dollars) on preferred stock

$t =$ corporate income tax rate

To illustrate both variations of the DFL formula, we will use case C (the most complicated financial structure of table 9–2). Assume that the corporate tax rate is 75% instead of the 50% used in the table. If earnings before interest and taxes increase from $500,000 to $600,000, EPS rise from $.225 to $.475. The percentage change in each of the variables is 20 and 111, respectively, and the degree of financial leverage using eq. 9–7 is 5.55 (111%/20%). Using eq. 9–8 we see that the DFL is

$$\frac{\$500,000}{\$500,000 - \$90,000 - \$80,000/(1 - .75)} = \frac{\$500,000}{\$90,000} = 5.55$$

Hence, as expected, we arrive at the same answer using either variation of the formula. Note that in eq. 9–8 the preferred dividend is divided by

$(1 - t)$ to account for the fact that these payments must be made with after-tax dollars and are thus more costly than interest. This calculation merely converts the preferred dividend to a before-tax basis.

Total Leverage

Now that we have covered both operating leverage and financial leverage, we can combine the two to consider the impact of total leverage. In other words, we can now determine the effect of a change in sales volume on earnings per share. The degree of total leverage is equal to the degree of operating leverage times the degree of financial leverage, or

$$\text{Degree of total leverage} = \frac{\%\Delta EBIT}{\%\Delta Q} \times \frac{\%\Delta EPS}{\%\Delta EBIT} = \frac{\%\Delta EPS}{\%\Delta Q} \qquad 9\text{--}9$$

As with the examples of operating leverage and financial leverage, the degree of total leverage is calculated at a given level of output.

As an illustration of how total leverage works, we will use table 9–3 to trace both operating leverage and financial leverage. The financial structure is the same as that used by Rushville Exterminating in case B, while the operating structure is constructed for this example. The degree of operating leverage is the percentage change in EBIT divided by the percentage change in sales volume, or 1.50 (.200/.133). The degree of financial leverage is equal to the percentage change in EPS divided by the percentage change in EBIT, or 1.67 (.333/.200). The firm's total leverage of 2.50 can be calculated by dividing the percentage change in EPS by the percentage change in sales volume (.333/.133), or by multiplying the degree of operating leverage by the degree of financial leverage (1.50

TABLE 9–3   The Impact of a Change in Volume on Earnings per Share

Sales volume (units)	150,000	170,000
Sales revenue ($20/unit)	$3,000,000	$3,400,000
Variables costs ($15/unit)	2,250,000	2,550,000
Fixed costs	250,000	250,000
EBIT	$ 500,000	$ 600,000
Interest	200,000	200,000
Before-tax income	$ 300,000	$ 400,000
Taxes (50%)	150,000	200,000
Available to common	$ 150,000	$ 200,000
Common shares	100,000	100,000
EPS	$1.50	$2.00

$\times$ 1.67). The degree of combined leverage may also be calculated by using the following equation:

$$\text{Total leverage} = \frac{Q(P - V)}{Q(P - V) - F - I - D/(1 - t)} \qquad 9\text{--}10$$

where

Q = units of output

P = selling price per unit

V = variable costs per unit

F = total fixed operating costs

I = interest expense (in dollars) on debt

D = dividend expense (in dollars) on preferred stock

t = corporate income tax rate

Using eq. 9–10 to solve for total leverage in this example, we find the degree of combined leverage:

$$\frac{150,000(\$20 - \$15)}{150,000(\$20 - \$15) - \$250,000 - \$200,000 - \$0/(1 - .50)}$$
$$= \frac{\$750,000}{\$300,000} = 2.5$$

Equation 9–9 and table 9–3 illustrate that a firm may increase its total leverage by increasing either its fixed operating costs (plant and equipment) or its fixed financial costs (interest on debt or dividends on preferred stock). A firm operating in an industry that requires large amounts of fixed-expense assets might prefer to reduce total leverage by financing primarily with common stock. Conversely, a company operating in an industry characterized by large expenditures on labor (a variable cost) might feel relatively safe with high financial leverage.

COST OF CAPITAL

In chapter 7 we discussed how investment decisions are based on a project's cash flows discounted by the firm's cost of capital. With the net present value method we concluded that the investment proposal is acceptable if discounted cash inflows are greater than discounted cash outflows. Using the other discounted cash flow analysis (internal rate of return), we determined that a project is acceptable if the internal rate of return is greater than the firm's cost of capital. In either case, one must first calculate the cost of capital.

Very simply stated, a company's **cost of capital** is the rate of return that must be earned on investment projects so that the market price of the firm's common stock remains unchanged. Hence undertaking a proposal that returns less than the cost of capital theoretically lowers the price of the company's common stock. Conversely, investing funds in a project that provides a rate of return higher than the company's cost of capital should increase the market price of its common stock. In the following discussion of how to calculate the cost of each component of a firm's capital structure, we will see how the individual costs are integrated into a single weighted-average cost that can be used in evaluating investments.

Cost of Debt

Because interest payments are deductible for income tax purposes, debt financing has grown in popularity. The tax feature of debt makes it a low-cost source of funds. Although nearly all bond issues are sold at par (maturity value), the issuing company generally realizes slightly less than par value because of underwriting costs to the investment banker. There may also be some additional expenses involved in registering the securities with the Securities and Exchange Commission. If a firm is able to realize the par value of a debt issue, the after-tax cost of this component is

$$C_d = c(1 - t) \qquad\qquad 9\text{--}11$$

where

C_d = after-tax cost of debt

c = before-tax cost of debt (the interest rate)

t = firm's income tax rate

For example, if a company can sell an issue of 20-year bonds at an interest rate of 9% and the firm pays taxes at a rate of 40% of taxable income, the after-tax cost of debt is $.09(1 - .40) = .054$, or 5.4%.

In some cases the cost of debt is greater or less than the coupon rate depending on whether the firm receives less or more than the bond's maturity value. If the company receives an amount other than par value from a bond issue, the approximate after-tax cost is calculated as

$$C_d = \frac{I + (M - P)/N}{(P + M)/2} (1 - t) \qquad\qquad 9\text{--}12$$

where

I = annual dollar interest cost per bond

M = maturity value of the bond

P = net proceeds from each bond

N = number of years to maturity

t = firm's income tax rate

For example, if a 20-year 6%, $1000 par bond is sold to net $800, the after-tax cost is

$$\frac{\$60 + (\$1000 - \$800)/20}{(\$800 + \$1,000)/2} (1 - .40) = \frac{\$70}{\$900} (1 - .40)$$
$$= .047 = 4.7\%$$

In most cases, however, a bond's issue price is not significantly different from its par value and the more complicated calculation is not necessary.

Interest is not the only cost involved in issuing debt. In addition to this explicit cost, we must also account for the effects of debt on the cost of other components of the firm's capital structure. In this section we have discussed only the explicit cost of debt. We will consider the implicit costs when we combine the components into a weighted-average cost of capital.

Cost of Preferred Stock

The cost of preferred stock is relatively easy to calculate. Since preferred stock does not have a maturity date, there is no need to account for any price appreciation or depreciation between the date of issue and the date that holders must be repaid. And since preferred stock dividends are paid with after-tax dollars, there is no need to adjust the calculation by a factor for taxes. The cost of preferred stock is computed by dividing the yearly dividend (in dollars) by the net proceeds that would be received from the sale of each new share. If there is no underwriting cost, the proceeds equal the sale price to investors. Otherwise the underwriting fee (flotation costs) must be subtracted from the sale price in calculating the denominator. The cost of preferred stock is

$$C_p = D/(P - U) \qquad\qquad\qquad 9\text{-}13$$

where

C_p = after-tax cost of preferred stock

D = annual cash dividends per share

P = market price of preferred stock

U = underwriting fee of a per-share basis

To illustrate, if a firm must provide investors with an 8% yield on new $100 par preferred stock and if the underwriting fee averages $2 per share, the cost of preferred is

$$C_p = \frac{\$8}{\$100 - \$2} = \frac{\$8}{\$98} = .082 = 8.2\%$$

The after-tax cost of preferred is considerably higher than the after-tax cost of debt even though in our example the latter was sold to yield a higher rate of return to investors. The reason is that interest payments on debt are a tax deductible expense, while dividends on preferred stock are not. This feature gives debt a significant cost advantage and is the primary reason that new preferred stock is seldom used in financing.

Cost of Common Stock

The holder of a share of common stock receives an entitlement to a proportional share of present and future earnings; thus calculating the cost of this form of financing is considerably more difficult than it is for debt or preferred stock. The latter methods of financing involve fixed annual payments to the holders for as long as the securities are outstanding. With common stock, however, firms may pay varying dividends or even none at all. In many instances companies pay stable dividends that are periodically increased and decreased only under unusual circumstances. Regardless of a firm's dividend policy, estimates of future returns are necessarily imprecise. The question then is how to calculate the cost of common stock.

The price at which a company can sell its stock depends on a number of variables including estimates of earnings per share and dividends, the issuing firm's risk class, and the return available to investors on alternative investments. Other things equal, investors will pay a higher price for a dollar of earnings today if they expect earnings to increase in the future. For example, a firm earning $2 per share in the current year may be able to sell common stock at $30 per share if buyers anticipate that earnings will increase in subsequent years. On the other hand, another company earning $2 per share may be able to sell its shares for only $16 each if investors expect little or no growth in earnings per share.

A stockholder's return is obtained both from cash dividends and earnings reinvested in the company. Presumably, reinvested earnings should increase the selling price of a firm's stock because it enhances future earning power and dividend-paying ability. In other words, the reinvestment of earnings makes it more likely that investors will be able to sell their shares at a higher price than that at which they were purchased.

The most common method of estimating the cost of common stock is the dividend approach. With this method the cost of common is equal to the discount rate that equates the expected future stream of dividends with the price at which the firm can sell a share of stock. This is the same concept as the internal rate of return discussed in chapter 7 (see eq. 7–11), because the firm's cost of common is the same as the investors' return from holding the common.

If a company's dividend is expected to remain at its present level, the cost of common stock is calculated in the same way as the cost of preferred stock (eq. 9–13). However, if dividends are expected to grow indefinitely at a given rate, the cost of common stock is found by using the formula

$$C_e = D_1/(P - U) + g \qquad\qquad 9\text{–}14$$

where

C_e = cost of common stock

D_1 = expected dividends per share in the forthcoming period

P = price at which new shares can currently be sold

U = underwriting fee per share

g = expected growth rate in dividends

As an illustration, suppose a firm is currently paying a dividend of $3 per share on its common stock and that the dividend is expected to grow at an annual rate of 6%. If the company can sell new common stock to the public at $32 per share and $2 per share is consumed in flotation costs, the firm's cost of common stock is

$$C_e = \frac{\$3(1.06)}{\$32 - \$2} + .060 = .106 + .060 = .166 = 16.6\%$$

Note that the price at which a company sells common stock to the public is not necessarily the same as the price at which the company's stock trades in the market. A firm may price the new stock at less than the market price to ensure that the entire issue is sold.

Cost of Retained Earnings

A common misconception among many people outside financial circles is that **retained earnings** is a costless source of funds. This, of course, is not true since these funds could be used to pay cash dividends to stockholders. Stockholders, in turn, could either reinvest the dividends in the firm's common stock or use the money to acquire a different investment of similar risk characteristics. Presumably, stockholders choose the alternative that offers the highest expected return for a given amount of risk. Hence, without a consideration of taxes and frictional costs such as brokerage fees, the minimum cost of retained earnings is the cost of common stock.

If taxes and frictional expenses are incorporated into the cost of retained earnings, the calculation becomes somewhat more complicated. Because dividends are taxable income to individual stockholders (with the exception of a $100 exclusion per individual), income taxes must be paid at the shareholder's marginal tax rate on dividends received, and only the remainder is available for reinvestment. This tax liability tends to lower the cost of retained earnings relative to the cost of common stock. Likewise, a shareholder who reinvests the money received in dividends may have the extra expense of brokerage fees. The reinvestment fee also tends to reduce the cost of retained earnings relative to common stock. Given that shareholders may be able to reinvest fewer dollars than they receive in dividends, the cost of retained earnings is calculated as

$$C_r = C_e(1 - T)(1 - b) \qquad\qquad 9\text{-}15$$

where

C_r = cost of retained earnings

C_e = cost of common stock

T = weighted average of shareholders' marginal income tax rates

b = percentage fee for reinvesting funds

Suppose we use the 16% cost of common stock calculated from eq. 9-14 for computing the cost of retained earnings. If the shareholders' marginal tax rates average 40% and reinvestment fees are approximately 3%, the firm's cost of retained earnings is

$$C_r = .16(1 - .40)(1 - .03) = .093 = 9.3\%$$

Admittedly, calculating the marginal tax rate (on average) for a firm's stockholders is an impossible task. During the process of attempting such a feat, the turnover of shareholders (from trading of the firm's stock) would make obsolete a portion of the data already collected. However, the effects of taxes and reinvestment fees must at least be considered in computing the cost of retained earnings.

Weighted-Average Cost of Capital

Firms generally do not rely on a single source of financing. Even when they do, it is common stock that must be utilized. As we saw, this is the highest-cost component available to the firm. We must now combine each of the individual components into a **weighted-average cost of capital**. It is this weighted average that the financial manager should use in evaluating new investment proposals.

Calculating the weighted-average cost of capital requires two pieces of information for each component of a company's capital structure—the after-tax cost and the proportion of the total capital structure it represents. We have already discussed the component costs, and the weights are easily calculated. A component's weight is the percentage of total capital it represents. For example, if a firm has $200,000 of preferred stock outstanding and a capital structure totaling $2 million, preferred represents 10% of total capital. This 10% figure becomes the weighting factor used for preferred stock. Although in some instances the market value of the components should be used in calculating the weights, it is more common to use book values to simplify the presentation. If book values are used, the weight of each type of financing can be computed from data found in a firm's balance sheet. For example, assume a company has the following capital structure:

Component	Book Value
Debt	$ 400,000
Preferred Stock	200,000
Common Stock	150,000
Retained Earnings	250,000
	$1,000,000

The weighted cost of each component is obtained by multiplying its weight times its respective after-tax cost. If the firm has the component costs calculated earlier in this section, its weighted-average cost of capital would be computed as follows:

Component	Amount	Weight	After-Tax Cost	Weighted Cost
Debt	$ 400,000	.40	.054	.022
Preferred Stock	200,000	.20	.082	.016
Common Stock	150,000	.15	.166	.025
Retained Earnings	250,000	.25	.093	.023
	$1,000,000	1.00		.086

Hence the firm's after-tax cost of capital is 8.6%. This figure represents the minimum return the company should accept from an investment. If the firm undertakes proposals returning less than the cost of capital, the market price of its common stock will decline (assuming unchanged risk). Note that we are working with marginal costs in the cost of capital calculation. The interest rate on bonds issued 15 years ago is not relevant in deciding whether to undertake an investment today. We must compare today's marginal cost of funds with the expected return on investment projects. Similarly, one should use the weights consistent with the way the firm intends, on average, to raise its funds in the future.

An assumption of this analysis is that the firm has already achieved the optimal capital structure. As such, it should continue raising long-term funds in the same proportions as shown on its balance sheet. Although it may not be possible to finance each investment proposal with the given ratios of debt, preferred stock, common stock, and retained earnings, it is possible to keep the proportions constant over a longer period of time. In other words, a firm might raise funds through a debt offering one year and a common stock issue the next year.

SUMMARY

According to traditional financial theory one of the most important decisions of the financial manager is to determine the firm's optimal capital structure. Using the proper proportions of debt, common stock, preferred stock, and retained earnings enables the firm to obtain funds at the least possible cost. Some theoretical studies have challenged this traditional view. Three important concepts were discussed in this chapter: operating leverage, financial leverage, and cost of capital. Operating leverage refers to the proportion of fixed costs that the firm employs in its operations, while financial leverage involves the use of funds obtained at fixed rates. These two are combined to calculate the degree of total leverage. The cost of capital is calculated by finding the cost of each component and weighting it by its respective weight in the capital structure.

QUESTIONS

1. Why should a company strive to keep a proper balance between debt and equity in the firm's capital structure?

2. As the proportion of debt increases, why do both the cost of debt and the cost of equity increase?

3. Explain the concept of operating leverage and how operating leverage affects earnings.

4. Why is break-even analysis necessary before any decision to add a new plant or substitute fixed for variable costs?

5. Suppose we are considering the purchase of a piece of equipment that produces mixers. Fixed costs are $200,000 and variable costs are $35 per unit, while the mixers sell for $50 per unit. If we project sales of 20,000 units, determine the projected profit.

6. What is the break-even point in problem 5?

7. Give an example of favorable financial leverage.

8. Why is debt a low-cost source of funds at a company's disposal?

9. Why is it so difficult to estimate the cost of common stock?

10. Explain how the weighted-average cost of capital is obtained.

11. On December 31, 19x1, the total assets of Wanda's TV Games, Inc. were $1 million. By the end of the next year, total assets are expected to be $1.5 million. The firm's capital structure is considered optimal. Assume that there is no short-term debt.

Debt (7% coupon bonds)	$ 400,000
Preferred Stock (8%)	200,000
Common Stock	150,000
Retained Earnings	250,000
	$1,000,000

New bonds will have a 9% coupon rate and will be sold at par. Preferred will have a 9½% rate and will also be sold at par. Common stock, currently selling at $30 a share, can be sold to net the company $25 per share. The stockholder's required rate of return is estimated to be 12%, consisting of a dividend yield of 5% and an expected growth rate of 7%. The addition to retained earnings for year 19x2 is projected at $50,000, and these funds will be available during the next budget year. The corporate tax rate is 40%.

a. Assuming all asset expansion (gross expenditures for fixed assets plus related working capital) is included in the capital budget, what is the dollar amount of the capital budget? (Ignore depreciation.)

b. To maintain the present capital structure, how much of the capital budget must be financed by equity?

c. How much of the new equity funds needed must be generated internally? externally?

d. Calculate the cost of each of the equity components.

e. Compute the weighted-average cost of equity.

f. Compute an average cost of capital for Wanda's TV Games, Inc. for funds raised during 19x2.

g. According to the information given, would the average cost of capital have been higher or lower if the firm's rate of expansion had been lower? Why?

h. Suppose that the asset expansion was only $300,000, rather than $500,000 and that the flotation cost of common stock made it prohibitively expensive to issue less than about $150,000 of new stock. What does this tell you about sources of funds, cost of capital, and the capital structure for Wanda's TV Games, Inc.? (Do not calculate the cost of capital or the optimal capital structure. Answer in words.)

SELECTED REFERENCES

BRADLEY, JOSEPH F. *Administrative Financial Management.* Hinsdale, Ill.: Dryden Press, 1974. Part 2.

CHRISTY, GEORGE A., and RODEN, PEYTON. *Finance: Environment and Decisions.* New York: Canfield Press, 1976. Chs. 17, 20.

GITMAN, LAWRENCE J. *Principles of Managerial Finance.* New York: Harper & Row, 1976. Chs. 4, 15, 16.

HAMPTON, JOHN J. *Financial Decision Making: Concepts, Problems, and Cases.* Reston, Va.: Reston Publishing Co., 1976. Parts 4, 5.

HELFERT, ERICH A. *Techniques of Financial Analysis.* Homewood, Ill.: Richard D. Irwin, 1977. Ch. 5.

SCHALL, LAWRENCE D., and HALEY, CHARLES W. *Introduction to Financial Management.* New York: McGraw-Hill, 1977. Chs. 6, 12.

SOLDOFSKY, ROBERT M., and OLIVE, GARNET D. *Financial Management.* Cincinnati, Ohio: South-Western Publishing Co., 1974. Part 2.

WERT, JAMES E., and PRATHER, CHARLES L. *Financing Business Firms.* Homewood, Ill.: Richard D. Irwin, 1975. Chs. 4, 10, 11.

WESTON, J. FRED, and BRIGHAM, EUGENE. *Essentials of Managerial Finance.* Hinsdale, Ill.: Dryden Press, 1977. Part 5.

10 Financial Management: Making Decisions Within the Financial and Economic Systems

*Two graduates of the Harvard
School of Business decided to start their own
business and put into practice what they had
learned in their studies. But they soon went into
bankruptcy, and an unlettered old fellow took over the
business. The two educated men felt sorry for him and
taught him what they knew about economic theory.
Some time later the two former
proprietors called on their successor when they heard
he was doing a booming business. "What is the secret
of your success?" they asked him. " 'Taint really no
secret," said the old man. "As you know, schooling and
theory is not in my line. I just buy an article for
$1.00 and sell it for $2.00. One percent profit
is enough for me."*

THE FINANCIAL MANAGER:
MAN IN THE MIDDLE

As we continue through this book, we can begin to see that the financial manager is truly a "man in the middle." On the one hand, he must operate within the environment established by the economy and the financial markets. On the other hand, he must constantly be aware of the factors that outsiders (creditors and investors) are utilizing to evaluate the firm. The purpose of this chapter is to bring together the basic decisions that must be made by the financial manager, as we discussed in part 2. This will be accomplished by demonstrating how the decisions are interrelated as well as how optimal decisions lead to the attainment of the assumed objective of the firm. By relating this discussion to the material from part 1, you can begin to see how such decisions should be made in view of the conditions of the economy and financial markets.

To understand completely the role of the financial manager, a knowledge of financial tools and methodology is not sufficient. One must also understand how basic financial decisions lead to the attainment of the firm's objective. We will assume that the firm is incorporated and that its objective is to maximize the wealth of the owners (shareholders). We emphasize wealth maximization as an "assumed" objective because the objective of management often conflicts with the goal of shareholders. While maximization of owners' wealth is a safe assumption for shareholders, management may at times be more appropriately classified as "satisficers." In other words, rather than considering the maximization of shareholder wealth as the single objective of the firm, management may elect to avoid risks and attempt to earn a return just sufficient to ensure its survival. Although such an attitude is possible, we will assume that the objective of both the owners and management is the same—to maximize the wealth of shareholders. Such wealth can be increased in two ways: through the payment of dividends and increases in the market price of common stock.

In attempting to maximize wealth, the financial officer makes crucial decisions in three major areas: investments, financing, and dividends. The investment decision, as we noted in chapter 7, entails the acquisition of assets expected to be profitable. The financial manager's job is to take capital expenditure proposals from various parts of the firm and rank them in order of priority according to potential return and risk. Utilizing capital budgeting techniques such as the internal rate of return or net present value ensures that only proposals that will contribute the most to the value of the firm are chosen. Although proper decisions regarding capital expenditures are critical to the firm's survival, the financial manager must also make short-term investment decisions. These decisions, which involve cash, marketable securities, accounts receivable, and inventories, rely on many of the same basic concepts utilized in the selection of capital expenditure programs. Just as capital expenditures in a most basic sense entail a comparison of costs and benefits, short-term investments should not be undertaken unless benefits exceed costs.

The investment decision cannot be made without a consideration of financing, the second area of decision making. For example, an increase in sales typically requires an increase in assets to support the higher level of sales. These assets may be financed internally or externally. If the funds must be raised externally, they may be borrowed from a bank, generated by issuing new common or preferred stock, or raised by selling bonds. In deciding how to finance the new assets, the financial manager must consider the costs and risks associated with each source of funds and determine the best combination of financing. If the financial manager succeeds in determining the optimal capital structure, the average cost of capital is minimized.

The third primary decision, the dividend policy of the firm, is considered by many an extension of the financing decision. The financial manager must decide whether to finance the acquisition of new assets internally by retaining earnings (not paying dividends) or externally by selling stocks or bonds. To the extent that new capital can be acquired through the retention of earnings, the firm does not have to rely on the capital markets to raise funds. However, if retained earnings are not sufficient, the firm is forced to finance externally. For example, consider the decision to finance a new plant by selling long-term bonds. Although this transaction requires only that the firm pay the interest and principal on the bonds, such a decision also affects dividend policy. Common stockholders, whose claim on earnings and assets is inferior to that of the new bondholders, may react negatively to the new bond issue thereby causing the stock price to fall and the cost of common stock to increase. If the firm decides to finance the new plant through an issue of common stock, the financial manager must still consider the implications for dividend policy. It may take years for the new plant to become operational, even if demand for the new level of output exists. During this time dividend payments must be made to the new shareholders. Thus, whatever the source of financing, the financing decision must be made with a simultaneous consideration of the company's ability to continue paying dividends.

To summarize, the objective of management should be to maximize the value of the firm (the wealth of the shareholders). To attain this objective, the financial manager must make optimal investment, financing, and dividend decisions. These decisions are interrelated. Investment decisions cannot be made without considering financing decisions, and financing decisions influence, and are influenced by, dividend decisions. Shareholders will interpret information about all these decisions in terms of risk and return. For example if the decision contributes more to the firm's potential return than to its risk, shareholders will react favorably, stock prices will increase, and we will be closer to achieving the objective of the firm. Thus we can see that the financial manager is not making decisions in isolation. In addition to considering the status of the economy and financial markets, he must recognize that his decisions are being monitored by outsiders such as investors and creditors. It is therefore important for the financial manager to be knowledgeable about the factors that outsiders consider in evaluating the firm.

THE FINANCIAL MANAGER AND THE ECONOMY

Optimal financial decisions at the level of the firm are consistent with the economic goals of· the economy. For example, if the financial manager makes optimal investment, financing, and dividend decisions, the firm should grow and profits should increase. To support the higher rate of growth, the firm must hire new employees, thus contributing positively to the national economic goal of full employment. Further, a more rapid rate of growth for the firm is consistent with the goal of economic growth. Optimal investment decisions should increase productivity at the level of the firm, and these increases should enable the firm to sell its output at reasonable prices. In turn, selling its output at reasonable prices contributes positively to the goal of price stability and should put the firm in a favorable competitive position relative to foreign producers of the same product, thus contributing to a favorable balance-of-payments position for the United States.

The fact that optimal financial decisions are consistent with the economic goals is important. However, the financial manager must react to (or, better, anticipate) changes in the state of the economy. Thus the financial manager must understand the goals, how conflicts might arise among the goals, and how monetary and fiscal authorities attempt to attain the goals. To gain an insight into the relationship between the financial manager and the economy, we will examine the way financial decisions should typically be made under various states of the economy.

Assume first that the financial manager foresees a downturn in the economy in the near future, which means that full employment and economic growth will not be attained. Because an increase in unemployment and a decline in GNP typically imply sagging sales for his firm, he must adjust investment and financing decisions. In relation to capital budgeting, the proposed investment must be adjusted downward with the result that the net present value or internal rate of return will be lower. These adjustments will make capital expenditure proposals less desirable and may even render the projects totally unacceptable. When the recession becomes a reality, existing equipment might be more than sufficient to satisfy demand for the product, and some machinery may have to be temporarily shut down. The adjustments in capital budgeting will also be reflected in the financing decision as the need for external financing declines. The dividend decision may also be affected by a projected downturn in economic activity. Dividends on common stock are generally not increased unless earnings are at a sufficient level and likely to remain there. Thus the forecast of an economic downturn may result in a decision to abort or postpone a planned increase in dividends.

Now let us assume that the recession is a reality. Unemployment is relatively high, an acceptable rate of economic growth is not being attained, and our hypothetical firm is operating at 75% of physical capacity. Assume also that the Federal Reserve has been increasing the supply of money in an attempt to decrease interest rates. If the financial manager forecasts a recovery in the economy due to the monetary stimulus, now may be the time to reconsider the investment proposals that were shelved prior to the recession. A critical factor in decisions made by the financial manager is timing. For example, under ideal conditions new machinery should become operational just when existing equipment is not capable of producing enough of the product to satisfy demand. Although ideal conditions rarely if ever exist, the financial manager should attempt to have machinery operational at approximately the same time it is needed. Hence our assumed conditions indicate that a reexamination of capital budgeting proposals is in order at this point. Since it will take time to purchase machinery and have it installed, such decisions must be made before the equipment is needed. Because of the recession this equipment might be available at a lower price than originally estimated, thus increasing the net present value or internal rate of return. In addition, with interest rates lower because of the stimulative monetary policy, the cost of capital should be lower than it was when the projects were postponed. Even though the firm is operating at less than capacity, the time may be right for making investment decisions and obtaining the funds to support the expenditures.

Unfortunately, no cookbook approach exists for making such decisions. Each decision must be made on the basis of prevailing and forecasted economic conditions and the situation of each firm. And although no single approach exists, any attempt to make optimal financial decisions will fail without an understanding of the economic goals, how the goals can conflict, and how the economic system (through monetary and fiscal policies) works to attain the goals.

The financial manager must also consider the financial implications of the noneconomic goals of the government. For example, expenditures for pollution abatement are unique in the typical capital budgeting framework developed in chapter 7. Such expenditures represent a commitment of funds for an asset that is to the firm and its owners unproductive. In other words, this asset generates at most negligible cash inflows while necessitating significant cash outflows. If these costs cannot be passed on to the consumer through higher prices, the net present value for environmental projects is negative and the profitability of the firm is depressed. Another influence on both investment and financing decisions is that new environmental standards may later be established. In other words, equipment installed today to comply with existing standards may become obsolete in five years because of new standards, thus requiring additional expenditures for nonproductive assets. This possibility raises the question of the method of financing the equipment (to comply with existing standards). In chapter 8 we determined that as a general rule the life of assets should roughly correspond to the maturity of the financing. Thus current assets should generally (unless they are permanent current assets) be financed with short-term financing, while fixed assets should be financed on a long-term basis. With respect to environmental expenditures, the financial manager must estimate the life of the asset and, on the basis of the risk and return implications, determine whether long-term financing is consistent with sound financial policy. (Despite the uncertain life expectancy of such equipment, most firms have financed this type of equipment with bonds or long-term leases.) Finally, while such expenditures may reduce the firm's capacity to pay the interest and principal on debt, the future level and stability of dividends may be less certain.

THE FINANCIAL MANAGER AND THE FINANCIAL SYSTEM

Most of our discussion regarding the financial manager and the economy has been related to the timing of investment decisions. Timing is a critical element if the financial manager is to be successful in making financing decisions. Financing requires the issuance of a claim against the firm (stocks, bonds) in exchange for the investor's or creditor's funds. The process is somewhat analogous to selling a product. For example, manufacturers of womens' clothing must constantly be aware of current trends and fashions. Do women plan to wear skirts next spring? If so, do they want miniskirts or maxiskirts? Maybe they will not want skirts at all and prefer pantsuits instead. What price range will be successful? A firm that produces miniskirts to sell at $9.95 when women want pantsuits in the $40 price range will be the industry leader in inventory at the end of the season. Similarly, the financial manager must be constantly aware of the status of the financial system. If his financing decision is the equivalent of producing miniskirts at $9.95, the firm, at best, will not minimize the cost of capital and, at worst, may be subjected to external capital rationing (the firm may simply not be able to generate the funds needed to support the acquisition of assets). If, on the other hand, the financial manager is aware of the trends in the money and capital markets, he will more than likely have better access to funds and achieve the objective of minimizing the cost of capital. The purpose of this section is to aid the financial manager in avoiding the financial equivalent of producing the $9.95 miniskirt. To achieve this objective, much of our discussion about the financial manager and the financial system revolves around timing and the financing decision.

The financing decision is typically thought of in terms of determining the appropriate financial structure (or the optimal combination of the various sources of financing) to achieve the objective of minimizing the average cost of capital. For example, assume that the financial manager, after examining the operating characteristics of the firm, decides to increase the proportion of debt in the financial structure by issuing $100 million of 20-year bonds to finance the construction of a new plant; current conditions in the capital market indicate that bonds of this maturity and quality must yield 6¾%. Thus, over the 20-year period, interest payments of $6.75 million must be made each year.

A more comprehensive approach, if we assume the firm has enough flexibility that construction of the new plant can be postponed, is to examine the current status of the capital market and determine what future interest rates are likely to be. If interest rates (and therefore the cost of capital) are likely to increase, the manager should decide to proceed with the construction of the plant and the bond issue. On the other hand, if interest rates are likely to decline during the next six months, the manager must decide whether to postpone the project in an attempt to reduce the average cost of capital. Rather than pay the annual interest of $6.75 million, the firm might be able to float the bonds in six months at a cost of 6% or $6 million in interest expense per year. Although 75 basis points (3/4 of 1%) may not seem that important, it appears more significant when expressed in dollars. In our example, the decision to wait six months will save the firm $750,000 annually, or $15 million over the 20-year period. Our example is not intended to imply that a firm would always decide to wait six months. Many other factors must also be considered. First, this decision must be made in present value terms. In addition, it might not be possible to postpone the project. Even if it is possible, inflation might increase the cost of construction, thus offsetting the interest saving. Further, there is no guarantee that long-term interest rates will fall from 6¾% to 6%. Thus this decision must be made by comparing the expected costs, benefits, and risks. Our example is intended to show that to achieve his objectives, the financial manager must understand the financial system and its role in establishing the environment in which he operates.

A first step in understanding how the financial manager must function in the financial system is to be aware of the relationship between savers and investors and the role that financial intermediaries play in bringing the two together. For example, recall from fig. 2–1 and the accompanying descriptions that saving, as a source of funds, flows to investors in the form of either direct finance or indirect finance (with financial intermediaries positioned between savers and investors). The financial manager should be aware of trends, either to direct or indirect finance, so that he can be successful in tapping the money and capital markets when funds are needed. At the same time, he must recognize that the relationship between saving and investing could change. For example, if saving declines because income declines, or if the system of financial intermediaries is operating inefficiently, funds that would otherwise have gone to support projects with lower rates of return will disappear. In other words, funds will flow only to the most profitable investment projects (thus the premium on making optimal investment decisions) and, irrespective of cost, funds will not be available to marginal firms.

The financial manager must also be familiar with the various types of intermediaries and their investment objectives. As they channel funds from savers to investors, financial intermediaries determine the types of securities they purchase primarily by the nature of their liabilities. Thus the financial manager should follow trends in the growth of various types of intermediaries to help him decide what type of security to issue. The financial manager who is unaware of such trends may be neglecting this potential demand for the firm's securities. For example, assume the financial manager needs external funds and is indifferent between intermediate- and long-term financing at a time when commercial banks (which must lend funds on a short- or intermediate-term basis) have considerable excess reserves. If he does not consider this trend and decides to finance via long-term bonds, he has failed to consider a potential source of low-cost financing.

Finally, but certainly not least important, the financial manager must be knowledgeable about the factors that determine interest rates. Without such knowledge, he will be in a poor position to forecast movements in interest rates and, therefore, the cost of capital. If the financial manager is aware of current trends in interest rates, he can react rationally to the trends. But more important, an understanding of the factors determining interest rates permits him to project trends so that he can act before rates change instead of reacting after they have changed.

To a degree, the financial manager is like a collector of paintings. Just as the collector purchases paintings, the firm (with the financial manager as its representative) buys money. And just as the collector wants to keep abreast of factors influencing the price of paintings in general, as well as factors explaining why some paintings are more valuable than others, the financial manager must watch factors influencing interest rates in general, as well as factors explaining differentials among rates. To accomplish the former, the typical financial manager utilizes the loanable funds framework which brings together the supply and demand for loanable funds to determine the rate of interest. The financial manager should follow the components of supply and demand to isolate the potential influences on interest rates. For example, as the economy approaches full employment the business sector's demand for loanable funds rises in order to expand the output of goods and services. If government spending also increases and is financed by selling government securities, the demand for loanable funds will be even higher. Unless the supply of loanable funds increases, for example through an increase in the supply of money, interest rates will rise and the demand for loanable funds by the business sector will decline. The objective is for the financial manager to foresee such crowding-out conditions in order to improve the timing of his financing decision. If he does not, the firm will face either a higher cost of capital or external capital rationing.

Inflation must also be considered in the timing of financial decisions. In chapter 3 we discussed the positive correlation between inflation (more specifically, expectations about future changes in prices) and interest rates. Expectations about inflation, expressed through the cost of capital, can have a significant impact on investment and financing decisions. For example, the financial manager wants to secure long-term debt financing before interest rates reflect inflationary expectations. In addition, an inflationary economy may permit the firm to increase prices and thus earn a higher internal rate of return for the project. Timing is also important in deciding when to purchase new plant and equipment because cost increases lower the internal rate of return. Thus the financial manager must continually monitor current prices as well as anticipated changes in prices.

The job of the financial manager is still not complete. Factors such as maturity, risk, call provisions, taxes, and marketability are also important; they help explain why differentials occur among interest rates. At this point, however, we will defer considering these factors to avoid duplication of topics to be covered in part 3. Specifically, we now turn from viewing the firm as a financial manager to analyzing it as an investor.

QUESTIONS

1. In attempting to maximize wealth, the financial officers of the firm must make crucial decisions in investments, financing, and dividends. How are these decisions interrelated?

2. Why should the financial manager be knowledgeable about the state of the economy?

3. How do environmental regulations affect investment and financing decisions?

4. Why is timing such a critical element in making financial and investment decisions?

5. What factors influencing interest rates should the financial manager watch?

6. How does inflation also influence the decisions of the financial manager?

3 INVESTMENTS

11 The Securities Markets

A businessman asked his banker
for a loan of $50,000. "That's a great deal of money,"
said the banker. "I will have to have a statement
from you."
"Well, sir," said the applicant,
"you may quote me as saying that I am very optimistic."

The resale of securities by investors generally takes place in the **secondary securities market**, not to be confused with the **primary market** in which the original sale of securities takes place. While the secondary market is indispensable to the functioning of the primary market, it does not make new funds directly available to corporations. Rather it facilitates the transfer of ownership of securities issued at some earlier time.

The secondary market comprises two types of organizations: (1) the organized exchanges, including the New York Stock Exchange (NYSE), the American Stock Exchange (ASE), and regional exchanges such as the Midwest Stock Exchange and (2) the over-the-counter market. While the New York Stock Exchange is the investment structure most familiar to many Americans, the other institutions also play a crucial role in providing a continuous market for the trading of securities.

THE ORGANIZED EXCHANGES

The **organized exchanges** are privately owned institutions designed to facilitate the trading of securities among their members. Since only members are allowed to trade stocks and bonds on the floor of an exchange, and since different securities are traded on different exchanges, a member of one exchange may also belong to the other exchanges. For example, a major brokerage firm that operates on a national basis would probably obtain memberships (commonly called seats) on both major exchanges and a number of regional exchanges. Since the number of memberships on each exchange is generally fixed, a prospective member must purchase a seat from someone who wants to sell. Like the price of securities bought and sold in the secondary market, the price of a membership is subject to the law of supply and demand. As the profits to be made from trading stock on an exchange increase, the price of a membership rises. In recent years the price of a seat on the New York Stock Exchange has fluctuated between approximately $50,000 and $500,000.

Listing a company's securities on one of the major exchanges offers a number of advantages to both the firm and its shareholders. For the company, it helps public relations since the company's name should become better known. In addition, its stock will probably become more widely owned, so the firm will find it easier to sell new securities. Shareholders have a more liquid market in which to buy and sell their stock and may receive more complete financial information from the company. The stock may also sell at a higher price because of the increased visibility and improved liquidity.

The New York Stock Exchange

The New York Stock Exchange is the largest of the organized exchanges, trading the securities of over 1500 corporations. Among the companies whose stocks are listed on the NYSE are such giants as Westinghouse, General Motors, IBM, Xerox, and Exxon. To have its securities traded on the NYSE, a firm must not only desire listing and pay the appropriate fee; it must also meet a set of relatively stringent requirements. It must have at least 1 million shares outstanding, of which 800,000 must be publicly held; a minimum of 2000 stockholders each owning 100 or more shares; pretax earnings of at least $2.5 million; and net tangible assets of over $16 million. Once listed, the company must provide quarterly reports, annual financial data, and other information that may affect its security price. It must also solicit proxies from shareholders for annual meetings.

The NYSE currently has 1366 members. A majority of the members are representatives of brokerage houses that buy and sell stocks and bonds for their firm's customers or, possibly, their own account. The members perform a variety of functions.

COMMISSION BROKERS   **Commission brokers** are members of the exchange who are also partners or officers in brokerage firms. These members generally execute orders on the floor of the exchange for the customers of their firms. Approximately one half of the exchange's members are commission brokers.

FLOOR BROKERS   A **floor broker,** sometimes referred to as a broker's broker or a two-dollar broker, is a member who executes transactions for other members of the exchange when the latter are unable to transact the business themselves. For example, a floor broker may help a commission broker who has a number of orders to be executed in a short period of time. The floor broker, who does not belong to a brokerage firm, charges a fee for his services.

FLOOR TRADERS   **Floor traders,** also called registered traders, are independent exchange members who buy and sell securities for their own account. These members do not represent either the public or brokerage firms and are not required to pay commissions for the execution of their orders. While the floor trader may have a competitive advantage over the public, some argue that he adds liquidity to the market.

BOND DEALERS AND BROKERS   Transactions in bonds are physically separated from stock trading at the NYSE. Members who execute buy and sell orders for bonds may do so for their own accounts or as representatives of others.

ODD-LOT DEALERS   Since trading on the floor of the exchange is limited to round lots of 100 shares each, **odd-lot dealers** provide commission brokers with a market in which to execute orders for less than 100 shares. The dealers purchase odd lots until they accumulate a round lot and then sell it on the floor of the exchange. Conversely, if other members wish to purchase odd lots, the odd-lot dealer must either sell from his inventory or accumulate orders until he has the 100 shares necessary to purchase a round lot on the floor. Odd-lot firms employ "associate brokers," who are members of the exchange, to carry on their business.

SPECIALISTS   **Specialists** account for approximately one-fourth of the members of the NYSE. These members undertake the task of "making a market" (buying securities from and selling securities to other members of the exchange) in one or more securities assigned by the exchange. In so doing, they must act as both dealers and brokers. As brokers, they execute orders that other members have left with them. For example, if the customer of a brokerage firm orders 100 shares of General Tire common stock at a maximum price of $21 per share, and the stock is then trading at $22, the firm's commission broker leaves the order with the specialist in General Tire stock. Since the stock may not decline to $21 per share for some time, the commission broker does not have to wait at the post where the stock is traded for an undetermined length of time. As a dealer, the specialist buys and sells the securities to which he is assigned for his own account. Because the specialist's job is to keep a "fair and orderly" market in his assigned stocks, he must stand ready to buy and sell against the trend. For example, if public orders to sell outnumber orders to buy, the specialist is expected to accumulate shares. Conversely, if purchase orders predominate, he must sell from his own inventory. In each case, he maintains a continuous market and attempts to keep price changes between trades to a minimum. Since the job of the specialist, so necessary to the proper functioning of the market, could be quite easily abused for personal profit, this member is closely monitored by exchange officials.

The American Stock Exchange

The American Stock Exchange (sometimes abbreviated ASE or AMEX) is an evolutionary product of the New York Curb Agency, where trading took place on the curbs and streets of New York City. The exchange went through a number of reorganizations and name changes through the years and eventually moved indoors in the early 1920s. Although the AMEX functions in a manner very similar to the New York Stock Exchange, it has fewer members, lists fewer securities, trades fewer shares per day, and has less stringent requirements for listing. Companies listed on the American Stock Exchange tend to be smaller and more speculative than those trading on the NYSE. Many of the companies now trading on the NYSE were formerly traded on the AMEX. Some issues have recently begun trading on both exchanges at the same time. As is the case with the New York Stock Exchange, companies may lose their AMEX listing if they do not meet minimum standards.

The Chicago Board Options Exchange

The Chicago Board Options Exchange (CBOE) was established in 1973 as the initial attempt in organized options trading. An option is a privilege to buy or sell a specific item at a predetermined price for a given length of time. Only call options on listed common stocks are currently being traded on the CBOE. A call allows the buyer of the option to purchase 100 shares of a certain common stock from the seller at a specified price on or before a given date. While much of the investment community was skeptical of the CBOE's potential, its success seems to have surpassed even the most optimistic expectations. In 1975 trading in call options was initiated at the American Stock Exchange, and even the regional exchanges are experimenting in options trading on a smaller basis. While only a limited number of options is currently available on the organized exchanges, the list is gradually being expanded.

Regional Stock Exchanges

There are a number of regional stock exchanges, the largest of which are the Midwest Stock Exchange in Chicago, the Pacific Coast Stock Exchange in Los Angeles and San Francisco, and the Philadelphia-Baltimore-Washington (PBW) Stock Exchange. Other regional exchanges are located in Boston, Cincinnati, Detroit, Pittsburgh, Salt Lake City, and Spokane. Although the regional exchanges were originally organized to trade the securities of companies of interest in their respective geographical areas, they eventually generated a majority of their business by trading stocks already listed on either the NYSE or AMEX. In 1973 the regional exchanges accounted for slightly more than 11% of all shares traded on organized exchanges.

THE OVER-THE-COUNTER MARKET

Unlike the organized exchanges, which trade securities at one specific location (except the Pacific Coast Exchange which has two trading floors), the over-the-counter market (OTC) has numerous dealers throughout the country. The term *over the counter* was once an accurate description of this market because negotiations and ownership transfers took place over the counters of banking houses; today nearly all business is carried out over the telephone and through the mail. Trading outside the organized exchanges is carried on by dealers that make markets in one or a number of securities. In many instances, more than one dealer makes a market in a single stock or bond. These dealers may negotiate trades directly with the public, with other dealers, or with brokers interested in buying or selling securities for their own customers. Prices in this market, although negotiable, are quoted on a bid-asked basis; the bid price is the price at which dealers are willing to buy, and the asked price is the price at which they are willing to sell. There are two sets of prices for securities traded over the counter. The first is the wholesale, or inside, set of prices at which securities firms trade among themselves. The other is the retail, or outside, set of prices at which firms buy from and sell to the public. It is often possible to buy or sell between the bid and asked prices if a broker shops for the customer. This is especially true when discount brokers are used. The spread between the asked price and the bid price is determined by a number of factors, including the trading activity and price volatility of the security.

For many years it was necessary to telephone a dealer in a particular security or to refer to price sheets published daily by the National Daily Quotation Service in order to obtain the bid and asked prices on an over-the-counter stock or bond. Since prices fluctuated during the day following each publication, and since a single security might be marketed by numerous dealers around the country, it was difficult to ensure that investors were receiving the best possible prices. In 1971 the National Association of Securities Dealers (NASD) initiated use of a computerized quotations system for use in the over-the-counter market. This network, known as NASDAQ, allows brokers and dealers to obtain bid and asked prices on the thousands of OTC stocks simply by "calling up" the quotations on a television-like screen. The screen displays sets of prices for several dealers offering to trade in the stock, thus making it easier for the broker or dealer to purchase or sell at a competitive price than if he had to contact each market-maker separately.

While many people think primarily of the New York Stock Exchange or the organized exchanges when discussing the securities markets, the size of the over-the-counter market is surprisingly large. This is especially true for bond trading, for which only a relatively small proportion of activity occurs on the organized exchanges. Nearly all trading in government securities takes place in the over-the-counter market. While the issues of most banks, investment companies, and insurance companies are traded only over the counter, this market is of less importance in the general trading of common stocks. The OTC market actually trades in a greater number of corporate securities, but the trading activity in each individual stock is much greater on the organized exchanges. In addition, the average security price is higher on the organized exchanges, which results in a greater dollar volume of transactions. However, securities of nonfinancial companies traded over the counter are not just younger or smaller firms. Large and well-established companies such as Anheuser Busch, Kelly Services, Roadway Express, and Pabst have their common stock traded over the counter.

THE THIRD AND FOURTH MARKETS

Large-volume traders, such as investment companies, pension funds, and bank trust departments, became increasingly dissatisfied with trading arrangements on the New York Stock Exchange during the 1960s and 1970s. Two specific arrangements on the exchange seemed to account for most of the problem. Until December 1968, the New York Stock Exchange did not allow its members to give commission discounts on large-volume orders. A customer wishing to buy or sell 2000 shares of a company's stock was required to pay 20 times the brokerage commission of a customer trading only 100 shares of the same stock, even though the brokerage firm's cost of executing each order was approximately the same. An additional bottleneck in using the exchange was the performance of the specialist in executing trades. Many institutional investors felt that the specialist's ability to make large-volume trades was limited and that the system was primarily conducive to executing a large number of small orders.

Another reason for increased trading outside the organized exchanges was the desire of some institutions to keep their buy-and-sell decisions secret as long as possible. Since third-market transactions are not carried by the tickers at boardrooms around the country, trading in large blocks off the exchanges does not immediately stimulate other participants to deal in the same security.

These two problems were of sufficient importance to drive many large investors away from the exchange even though the NYSE eventually eliminated fixed commissions. One method of bypassing the exchanges was to develop a third market in which broker-dealers who were not members of the NYSE made a separate market in listed securities. Since dealers in the third market cannot always match buyers and sellers simultaneously, they must often hold securities until a buyer can be found. Conversely, they may be required to sell from their own inventory if no seller can be found on short notice. In other words, broker-dealers in the third market operate in a manner similar to—and compete directly with—specialists on the organized exchanges.

The fourth market is much like the third except that no dealer enters into the exchange. Under this informal arrangement large institutions initiate and complete the trades by contacting each other. In some cases an intermediary may facilitate the exchange for a fixed fee or a small commission. However, no firm or individual stands ready to make a market in a particular security.

THE MECHANICS OF INVESTING

Someone who wants to trade stocks or bonds must generally first establish a relationship with a brokerage firm and one of its representatives. These representatives, known as account executives, registered representatives, or brokers, can typically provide a variety of services, although these are sometimes limited by the representatives as well as by the policies and resources of the firms employing them. At the minimum, a broker should be able to provide relatively simple financial advice and facilitate an order to purchase or sell securities. Better ones can give more sophisticated recommendations and advice on such topics as specific stocks, taxes, and estate planning. In any case a broker should attempt to understand the resources and goals of a potential customer. Without this basic knowledge, any advice on financial planning and security trades should be suspect. An investor who feels that the relationship is unsatisfactory should change firms or change brokers within a firm.

Types of Transactions

Investors have several options when placing orders through their brokers. Most investors use market orders, but other possibilities are available and may prove more satisfactory under certain conditions.

MARKET ORDERS A **market order** is an instruction to the broker to purchase or sell a security at the best available price if the security is traded in one of the organized markets. The broker has the order transmitted to the firm's representative on the exchange floor. The representative then obtains the lowest price available for an order to buy and the highest price available for an order to sell. If there is any market in the security at all, the order is executed immediately although the price may be different from that at which the security last traded. The broker's representative may or may not use a specialist. If he can obtain a better price by trading with another broker, the specialist is bypassed. While a market order has the advantage of swift execution, the disadvantage of an uncertain price should not be overlooked, especially if the security is traded infrequently. For example, if you place a market order for an inactive security, there may be no current market other than that made by the security's specialist when the order reaches the exchange floor. Since the spread between the bid price and the asked price may be relatively wide on this type of security, the price at which your order is executed could well be less favorable than you had anticipated.

LIMIT ORDERS A **limit order** restricts the execution of a sell order to a minimum price and a purchase order to a maximum price. For example, if a security is currently quoted at $15 bid and $15½ asked, you might place a limit order to sell at $15½. If your broker's representative on the exchange floor cannot fill your order with another broker or with the specialist, he leaves it with the specialist who lists it on his order book. Should market conditions push the price of the security higher, your order to sell will be filled. However, even if the stock trades at $15½, your order may not be executed since limit orders are filled in chronological order and other orders may be ahead of yours. In addition, trades at your specified price may take place between floor brokers without use of the specialist. The danger of placing a limit order to sell (buy) is that your order may not be executed since the price might stay at or below (above) the price you specify.

With a limit order, the customer may specify not only the price but also the length of time the order is to be effective. The two most common time frames are "day only" and "good till canceled." Under the former, an order that cannot be filled during the day in which it is entered is canceled and dropped from the specialist's book. A customer who wants to extend the time limit must reenter the order. A good-till-canceled order, also called an open order, is not withdrawn until it is either executed or canceled by the customer.

STOP ORDERS   A **stop order** is generally designed to limit the size of a potential loss or protect a paper profit. For example, if a security you own is currently trading at a price of $20, you may enter a stop order to sell if the price drops to $18 or less. Whether you originally purchased the security at a price higher or lower than $18, you are protecting yourself against a future drop in price. There are two dangers inherent in a stop-sell order. One is that the investor may be sold out during a temporary price decline. The other is that, because of an absence of buy orders, the security may be sold not at $18 but at a considerably lower price. The latter is unusual and generally occurs only in a very rapidly declining market. A stop order to buy could be placed to limit a loss or protect a profit after a short sale (this concept will be covered later). In addition, stop orders to buy or sell are used to establish initial positions in securities by certain types of traders. (Some of these "technical" trading rules are discussed in a later chapter.) To summarize, a stop-sell order is a special type of limit order that places the specified sell price below rather than above the current market. Conversely, a stop-buy order places the purchase price above the current market price rather than below it, as is the case with a regular limit order.

MARGIN ORDERS   An investor is ordinarily required to pay the full cost of a purchase by the fifth business day following execution of the order. If the investor prefers, however, he may pay only part of the cost and borrow the remainder through a loan arranged by his broker. The portion of the cost that the investor pays is called the initial margin. The minimum percentage requirement is established by the Federal Reserve Board. The required margin is set by the Federal Reserve as it attempts to exert control over the nation's credit conditions, securities markets, and money supply. An investor is charged interest on the amount of money borrowed, and the interest rate is generally tied to the prime rate, which is the interest rate charged by banks on loans to their most credit worthy customers. Typically, the rate on margin accounts varies from .5% to 1.5% above prime, with the low end of the range applying to accounts owing more money.

The advantage (and sometimes disadvantage) of buying on margin is that more securities can be purchased for a given sum of money. For example, with a margin requirement of 50% an investor can purchase $10,000 of securities by putting up only $5000 in cash. Should the securities increase in value by 50% to $15,000, the investor can double his investment to $10,000. On the other hand, if the market value of the securities falls by 50%, the investor loses his entire position. In reality, the investor is required to deposit more funds or risk being sold out before his position falls to zero, because most brokerage firms require that the equity in an account (value of the securities less the amount owed) equal at least 25% of the value of the securities in the account. In addition, the New

York Stock Exchange requires a 25% maintenance margin on NYSE-listed stocks. In this example, the account would require more funds if the security value fell to $6667 since the investor's equity would then be $1667 ($1667/$6667 = .25). Should the value of the securities rise, the investor can borrow additional funds against the increased value and pyramid his position. In any case, with a **margin purchase** the investor's equity changes more rapidly than the value of the securities bought.

SHORT SALES   When an individual sells short, he is selling a security that is borrowed rather than one that is owned. Since the investor must later purchase the stock or bond in order to repay the lender and cover the short position, he undertakes this transaction with the expectation that prices will fall. For example, if a stock is currently trading at $30 per share, and you believe its price will decline in the near future, you could arrange for your broker to borrow the stock and sell it short. If the price later fell to $20 per share, you could purchase the stock, repay the lender, and clear $10 per share less commissions. Although no date is specified for the covering transaction, the shares must eventually be purchased and delivered to the lender to replace those that were borrowed. The New York Stock Exchange now stipulates that a **short sale** in a security can be made only when the last change in the price of that security was up (called an "up-tick"). In a rapidly falling market the investor might have some difficulty making this type of transaction. In addition, the broker must be able to borrow the shares. Usually he does so from the firm's own portfolio or from one of its margin accounts. However, if the security has only a small number of shares outstanding or if it is infrequently traded, finding a lender might be a problem. While the lender can call for the return of his securities at any time, the broker can usually borrow the same shares elsewhere.

Since the losses that might be incurred by a short seller are theoretically unlimited (just as the gains from purchasing securities are theoretically unlimited), the investor might wish to place a stop order to buy back the stock and cover the transaction if the security price rises to a given level. This way he can limit his loss to a specific dollar amount. Because of the large potential loss and the pessimism often associated with short selling (which of course it should be), most investors shy away from this type of trading.

In addition to establishing initial positions, investors may find other uses for selling short. For example, if an investor is holding stock in which he has a large gain and if he does not want to sell for tax reasons, he may sell the same security short if he expects the price to decline. If the stock price does fall, he can cover his short sale and incur a tax liability against only the gain on his short position. If the number of shares sold short equals the number held long, the gain on the short sale exactly offsets the loss on the shares already held. Such a transaction is called "selling against the box." Selling against the box can also be used to push gains from one taxable year to the next. It cannot, however, be used to change a short-term capital gain into a long-term capital gain, since the effective holding period is established on the date the security is sold short.

Commission Schedules

To cover the cost of executing the orders of investors, brokerage firms must charge a commission for their services. Before May 1975 the commission schedules were set by the New York Stock Exchange and approved by the Securities and Exchange Commission. However, for years the NYSE had come under increasing pressure to end the practice of fixing commissions. At the present there is no set commission schedule; in theory at least, these fees are negotiable between the customer and the brokerage firm. In practice, very little change occurred for the small investor since most firms continue to charge all except very large customers close to the minimum fee schedule that existed before "negotiated" commissions.

Table 11–1 shows that commissions can be important costs to the small investor. For example, an individual purchasing 100 shares of an $11 stock pays $12 + .013($1100) = $26.30 in commissions, approximately 2.4% of the amount invested. The price of the security would have to rise by one-half point to equal the buy and sell commissions. The commission on purchasing 100 shares of a $40 stock is $22 + .009($4000) = $58, or 1.5% of the amount invested.

Commission rates for trading in bonds vary from one brokerage firm to another. Some set a flat fee of from $5 to $10 per bond, while others have a minimum charge for a trade involving five or fewer bonds. Most

TABLE 11–1   Minimum Commission Schedule before May 1975

Single 100-Share Orders		Multiple 100-Share Orders	
Dollar Amount	Minimum Commission	Dollar Amount	Minimum Commission
Under $ 100	Negotiable	$ 100–$ 2,499	1.3% + $ 12.00
$ 100– 799	2% + $ 6.40	2,500– 19,999	.9% + 22.00
800–2,499	1.3% + 12.00	20,000– 29,999	.6% + 82.00
2,500–4,780	.9% + 22.00	30,000– 300,000	.4% + 142.00
Over $4,780	$65.00	Over $300,000	Negotiable

NOTE: On multiple 100-share orders, an additional charge of $6 per round lot is added on the first to tenth round lot, and $4 per lot on the eleventh round lot and over.

Effective September 1973, orders up to $5000 paid a commission of 15% more than these fees. For orders of $5000 to $300,000, the additional charge is 10%.

houses reduce the cost per bond on large orders, and some charge less on the purchase of bonds with maturities of less than six months.

In summary, although commission schedules are now theoretically negotiable, most investors have very little bargaining power, and rates generally vary only slightly between brokerage houses. A number of discount houses charge commissions between one-half to two-thirds of those of most other firms. These houses offer fewer auxiliary services such as investment advice. Their advertisements can usually be found in major financial publications such as the *Wall Street Journal*.

THE PRIMARY SECURITIES MARKETS

The primary securities markets make funds directly available to state and local governmental units and corporations. Governments use these markets to issue bonds, while corporations generally find it necessary to sell both bonds and stock. Companies planning to raise new capital usually employ the services of an investment banker. These firms may help a company sell its securities to the public or may assist in placing an issue with a large institutional buyer such as a pension fund or an insurance company. While underwriters serve a vital need in the functioning of our financial system, most people are unfamiliar not only with their workings, but also with their names. One exception is Merrill Lynch, Pierce, Fenner, and Smith; this firm is one of the country's largest investment bankers although it is much better known as a retail brokerage house. Contrary to popular opinion, commercial banks such as Bank of America, First National City Bank, and the Chase Manhattan Bank are not investment bankers.

An **investment banker** is more familiar with the financial markets than is the typical industrial company or utility, so it can offer valuable advice on financial needs and various methods of satisfying those needs. For example, a company requiring long-term capital may need advice on the terms of a new bond issue. The investment banker may suggest the timing of the issue, interest rate, call protection, and maturity date the bond should offer and the issue size the company should consider. In addition to advising the client, the investment banker also takes care of the administrative duties required in offering the issue. Because numerous regulations apply to a new issue, this involves a great amount of work.

One of the most important functions of the investment banker is assuming the risk when a corporation sells new securities. The investment banker acts as principal in the sale of new securities; it actually purchases the securities from the issuing firm for resale to the public. Should it misjudge the market, the underwriter stands to lose a great deal of money since the stock or bonds may have to be resold at a lower price than originally estimated. When the investment banker acts as agent in an issue, the risk is assumed by the issuing company. Here the investment banker is only an intermediary attending to the sale and thus does not actually purchase the issue for resale. Since the investment banking firm assumes greater risk when it acts as a principal, its charge is greater.

REGULATION OF SECURITY ISSUES

Before the collapse of security prices in 1929 and the early 1930s, few effective securities regulations existed. Although some states had passed so-called blue-sky laws (to protect potential investors from buying a piece of the blue sky), legislation was piecemeal and largely ineffective. Fraudulent practices on a massive scale milked investors and speculators of millions of dollars. These activities ranged from selling securities in companies with nonexistent assets to publishing fictitious information about a company in order to run its stock price up or down. However, with the personal bankruptcies and general public disenchantment that accompanied the Great Crash, more restrictive legislation and more active enforcement of the securities markets followed.

State Regulation

State regulation is designed to protect investors when securities are sold on an intrastate basis and federal laws are not applicable. State regulations are generally of three types: (1) registration of securities dealers and salespersons; (2) registration of certain securities; and (3) antifraud provisions. While these state regulations help eliminate some of the more obvious abuses in the securities markets, they are backed up with stricter federal regulations.

Federal Regulation

Today's federal regulation of the securities markets is based on two pieces of legislation passed during the depression—the Securities Act of 1933 and the Securities Exchange Act of 1934. The 1933 act requires that a company issuing securities to the public provide complete and truthful disclosure of all facts relevant to the company. A company must file a registration statement with the Securities and Exchange Commission 20 days before the securities are to be sold. The SEC does not pass on the merits of the securities, but rather on the completeness and accuracy of the statement. The issuing company must also provide buyers or prospective buyers with a prospectus. This document is a summation of the registration statement filed with the SEC.

The Securities Exchange Act of 1934 established the Securities and Exchange Commission to administer and enforce the 1933 act. This act attempted to end the manipulation of securities and gave control over margin requirements to the Federal Reserve Board.

Additional legislation has been passed since the early 1930s. The Maloney Act of 1936 established self-regulation for over-the-counter dealers; the Investment Company Act of 1940 set regulation for both open-end and closed-end investment companies; and the Securities Investor Act of 1970 established a federal agency to insure customer accounts in brokerage firms. Even though these additional safeguards have been enacted, the primary regulation of the securities markets remains the 1933 and 1934 legislation.

SUMMARY

The securities markets are located in many places and include varied methods of security trading. The markets include the organized exchanges such as the New York and the American Stock Exchanges, the over-the-counter market of dealers around the country, and the relatively new third and fourth markets. Each is involved in the trading of securities that have been issued in the past.

The primary securities markets make funds directly available to governmental units and corporations. Investment bankers specialize in helping to raise funds and charge a fee for their services. Both the primary markets and the secondary markets are heavily regulated by the Securities and Exchange Commission.

QUESTIONS

1. Explain the difference between the primary securities market and the secondary securities market.

2. How do the organized exchanges operate?

3. What are the advantages of listing a company's securities on one of the major exchanges?

4. Name the types of members of the NYSE and describe each of their functions.

5. Describe the over-the-counter market and how it works.

6. Why were the third and fourth markets developed?

7. Compare the differences between placing a market order and a limit order.

8. When might one place a stop order?

9. How does an investor stand to gain if he executes a margin order?

10. What services do investment bankers perform for a company?

11. How do the Securities Acts of 1933 and 1934 protect the public against fraudulent practices in the securities market?

SELECTED REFERENCES

AMLING, FREDERICK. *Investments*. Englewood Cliffs, N.J.: Prentice-Hall, 1974. Part 4.

COOKE, GILBERT W. *The Stock Markets*. Cambridge, Mass.: Schenkman Publishing Co., 1969.

EITEMAN, WILFORD J.; DICE, CHARLES A.; and EITEMAN, DAVID K. *The Stock Market*. New York: McGraw-Hill, 1966.

ENGEL, LOUIS. *How to Buy Stocks*. New York: Bantam Books, 1971.

FISCHER, DONALD E., and JORDAN, RONALD J. *Security Analysis and Portfolio Management*. Englewood Cliffs, N.J.: Prentice-Hall, 1975. Chs. 2, 3.

LOLL, LEO M., and BUCKLEY, JULIAN G. *The Over-the-Counter Securities Markets*. Englewood Cliffs, N.J.: Prentice-Hall, 1973.

MENDELSON, MORRIS, and ROBBINS, SIDNEY. *Investment Analysis and Securities Markets*. New York: Basic Books, 1976. Part 1.

VAUGHN, DONALD E. *Survey of Investments*. Hinsdale, Ill.: Dryden Press, 1974. Parts 2, 3.

WIDICUS, WILBUR W., and STITZEL, THOMAS E. *Personal Investing*. Homewood, Ill.: Richard D. Irwin, 1976. Chs. 3, 4.

12   Fundamentals of Security Analysis

Bonds and preferred stocks are commonly considered safer investment vehicles than common stocks. Exactly what type of safety is being referred to is important, however, since the statement is not necessarily true. For example, the debentures of a firm on the verge of failing can hardly be considered a safer investment than the common stock of a giant and profitable corporation such as General Motors. Even a comparison of fixed-income securities and common stock issued by the same corporation might provide some surprising conclusions depending on the types of risk we are considering. Before delving more deeply into an analysis of fixed-income securities, we must first discuss some factors common to fixed- and variable-income securities.

PRELIMINARY ISSUES OF SECURITY OWNERSHIP

A proper background in basic investment fundamentals is important in evaluating any type of security. In this section we will discuss the concepts of risk, yield, and taxes. Then we will turn our attention specifically to fixed-income securities.

Risk

One cannot evaluate a stock or bond without understanding the risks associated with holding the security. Some sources of risk are more important for one security than another. Unfortunately, no security is completely free of risk. Equally unfortunate, an investor must generally accept a lower rate of return to obtain a lower degree of risk. We discussed a methodology for calculating risk (standard deviation and coefficient of variation) in chapter 7. In this section we will engage in a more qualitative discussion of the subject. We will cover the two major categories of risk—systematic and unsystematic—and the sources of these risks—purchasing power risk, interest rate risk, business and financial risk, and market risk.

SYSTEMATIC AND UNSYSTEMATIC RISK   The total risk from holding a security can be segregated into two categories, systematic and unsystematic. The former is the result of variables that affect the returns on all securities. For example, a recession generally results in reduced sales and earnings (and possibly reduced dividends and stock prices) for nearly all types of business. The prices of some securities (for example, the common stock of companies producing capital goods) are susceptible to large fluctuations as a result of these changes. These securities are said to have a large amount of systematic risk. Unsystematic risk is the result of variables unique to a particular firm or industry. For example, gold mining companies are heavily influenced by factors such as strikes and political decisions that are peculiar to that industry. In fact, the gold mining industry's risk is nearly all unsystematic. We will discuss the differences between these types of risk in more detail when we discuss portfolio analysis in chapter 14. The discussion that follows includes some of the components of systematic and unsystematic risk.

PURCHASING POWER RISK   Purchasing power risk is the risk that the purchasing power of a dollar return (interest or dividends and principal) from a security will be reduced by a rise in the prices of goods and services. A security does not have to decline in price or stop paying income to have its holder suffer from purchasing power risk. If the price of an investment is expected to rise because of a general increase in consumer prices, then less purchasing power risk is present.

It is commonly believed that fixed-income securities are subject to the greatest purchasing power risk. This belief stems from the fact that bonds and preferred stocks specify the number of dollars an investor is to receive. Hence, during an inflationary period, the holder of these securities consistently loses purchasing power. A couple of caveats are in order at this point. First, an investor can purchase bonds of various maturities. Those with very short maturities subject the holders to minimal purchasing power risk. Second, the return on a fixed-income security includes a factor for anticipated inflation. Thus it is somewhat misleading to say that the investor suffers a loss of purchasing power, since inflation is already accounted for in the security's return.

Investment vehicles providing variable returns may offer some protection against purchasing power risk. For example, assets that are relatively fixed in quantity such as real estate, diamonds, and rare coins might well rise more rapidly in price than consumer prices in general. It is generally believed that common stocks provide some protection against purchasing power risk since their dividends and/or prices may rise during inflation. However, whether stock price increases actually outpace inflation is subject to some doubt.

INTEREST RATE RISK   Interest rate risk is the risk that an investor's return from holding securities will suffer because of a rise in interest rates. This risk is most commonly associated with fixed-income investments, although it applies to common stocks as well. For example, as the risk-free rate of interest increases, corporations and governmental units must offer higher rates to sell new bond issues. At the same time the prices of older issues must fall to offer investors yields that compete with new issues. In other words, the price of a bond with a 5% coupon issued at par a number of years ago will decline if new bonds with 7% coupons of similar risk and maturity are currently being sold at par. The rise in interest rates tends to reduce the prices of preferred stocks and debt instruments of all risk classes and maturity lengths. In addition, a rise in interest rates exerts a downward pressure on common stock prices since the return on alternate investments (bonds and preferred stock) is more favorable. This does not mean that the prices of common stocks must necessarily fall during a period of rising interest rates, since changes in other areas (improved earnings or reduced financial risk) may more than offset the effect of higher interest rates. On the other hand, increased interest rates may be accompanied by higher expected rates of inflation and greater required interest payments on corporate debt, which could result in a greater degree of financial risk. This intertwining of various types of risk might also obscure the relationship between rising interest rates and speculative debt issues. For example, the bonds of a company near bankruptcy might actually increase in price during a period of rising interest rates because of improved expectations about the firm's ability to repay its debt. The price would increase in spite of, not because of, the rise in interest rates.

BUSINESS AND FINANCIAL RISK   Business and financial risk refers to the possibility of a reduction in the issuer's ability to meet interest and dividend payments. This type of risk, discussed in chapters 7 and 8, varies greatly depending on the issuer and even the type of security of the same issuer. Although business and financial risk is minimal for holders of United States government securities, the same cannot be said for owners of securities of other governmental bodies. Governments are subject to revolution (for example, Chile) and to a simple inability to meet financial obligations (New York City). Corporate bonds generally carry more business and financial risk than government securities. If cash flows decline in relation to a firm's fixed expenses, bond prices may fall and eventually interest payments may stop. The reduction in cash flows relative to fixed expenses may be the result of a decline in cash flows, an increase in fixed payments, or both. Thus business and financial risk tends to be higher for bondholders of firms with volatile sales and high degrees of operating and financial leverage. The same reasoning applies to preferred and common stockholders. The possibility of lower stock prices and reduced cash dividends could reduce the return to these owners. In fact, the latter two events are more likely than reduced interest or principal payments to bondholders of the same company since these investors are creditors. Hence common stockholders face greater business and financial risks than bondholders of the same firm. On the other hand, stockholders of large, stable, and lightly leveraged firms might well incur less business and financial risk than the bondholders of companies with volatile sales and high degrees of leverage.

MARKET RISK Market risk applies to common stockholders and refers to the possibility of a decline in a security's price because of a general change in investor expectations. History has shown that the prices of common stocks fluctuate greatly, many times for no fundamental reason. For example, the assassination of President Kennedy in 1963 was followed by a massive selling of common stocks. This was, in turn, followed by an equally rapid buying splurge. This type of risk is not particularly relevant to the investor who would not have to sell common stocks during a period of low prices. On the other hand, market risk is very important to the individual who places temporary funds in common stocks. Since most common stocks generally move in tandem during periods of declining prices, it is virtually impossible for investors to completely protect themselves against market risk. Some degree of protection can be sought by investing in diverse industries. For example, shares in gold mining companies often move counter to industrial stocks. Market risk can also be reduced by placing a portion of investable funds in securities other than common stocks.

Yield

Bonds and preferred stocks are usually, but not always, purchased on the basis of the interest and dividend payments they provide investors. In contrast, common stocks, like a number of other investments (real estate and rare objects), may provide little or no current income and be purchased on the basis of expected price appreciation.

The return to an investor in the form of dividend or interest payments received from holding a security is called **current yield**. The current yield on a security is calculated by dividing the security's market price into the annual interest or dividends the investor is to receive:

$$\text{Current yield} = \frac{\text{Annual interest or dividend payment}}{\text{Market price}} \qquad 12\text{-}1$$

For example, if you purchase a preferred stock for $60 per share and it pays $6 in annual dividends, the current yield is $6/$60, or 10%. The current yield for bonds and common stocks is calculated in the same manner. If an investor is interested in calculating the current yield to be received from purchasing a security, any fee that must be paid to a broker to conduct the transaction should be deducted from the market price in the denominator. Commissions on bonds are typically $5 to $10 per bond, while those on preferred and common stocks average 2% to 3% of the amount invested. Since not all brokerage firms have the same commission schedules, it pays for the investor to shop around.

A more inclusive measure of yield incorporates both interest or dividend payments and any increase or decrease in a security's price that may occur during the investor's holding period. Unless an investor expects to receive the same net amount on selling a security as was expended on its purchase, this concept of yield presents a more accurate picture of total return than current yield. A change in the price of a security might be due to a number of variables, including changes in the financial risk of the issuer, the time remaining to maturity (for bonds), and the returns available on alternative investments.

We covered the concept of yield from a corporation's point of view at some length in chapter 7. We can apply this same analysis to yield from the individual investor's viewpoint. For example, we said that a firm's rate of return on an investment is the discount rate that equates net cash inflows with net cash outflows. We calculate an investor's rate of return in the same manner. Since investors in securities do not have to concern themselves with corporate expenses such as maintenance and labor, their cash outflows usually consist only of the original prices paid for securities (plus commission), and their cash inflows consist of dividends or interest and the proceeds derived from selling the securities. In equation form this is

$$P_0 = \frac{D_1}{(1+r)^1} + \frac{D_2}{(1+r)^2} + \frac{D_3}{(1+r)^3} + \cdots + \frac{D_n}{(1+r)^n}$$
$$+ \frac{P_n}{(1+r)^n} \qquad 12\text{-}2$$

where

$P_0 =$ original cost of the security

$D =$ annual dividend or interest payment

P_n = proceeds received from selling the security

r = annual rate of return

For example, suppose we purchase 100 shares of preferred stock at $98 per share and expect to resell the stock at $102 per share in four years. In addition, assume the stock pays an annual dividend of $8 per share and brokerage costs amount to $2 per share for each transaction. Our rate of return is then

$$\$10,000 = \frac{\$800}{(1+r)^1} + \frac{\$800}{(1+r)^2} + \frac{\$800}{(1+r)^3} + \frac{\$800}{(1+r)^4} + \frac{\$10,000}{(1+r)^4}$$

In this example, solving for r produces a rate of return of 8%. (The methodology of the solution was discussed in chapter 7.)

Purchasing a bond or preferred stock at a cost equal to the expected selling price produces a total yield that is the same as the current yield. In other words, if no depreciation or appreciation in the security's price is expected to take place during the holding period, the investor's total yield is derived only from interest or dividend payments. With no change in expected price, it is easier to compute the return using eq. 12–1.

When the expected selling price is different from an investor's cost, the current yield formula does not present an accurate picture of the rate of return. For example, if you purchase a newly issued 8%, $1000 par bond that is to mature in 20 years and you expect to sell it for $1100 in four years, the total yield would be

$$\$1000 = \frac{\$80}{(1+r)^1} + \frac{\$80}{(1+r)^2} + \frac{\$80}{(1+r)^3} + \frac{\$80}{(1+r)^4} + \frac{\$1100}{(1+r)^4}$$

Using the tools discussed in chapter 7, we find that the annual rate of return during the four-year holding period is slightly over 9%. As expected, this is higher than the current yield of 8% because the price of the bond, as well as annual interest payments, is expected to appreciate. When expected price changes are combined with dividend or interest payments in calculating total yield, the result is less certain than the calculation of current yield. While dividends (and especially interest income) can be projected with some accuracy, estimates of future security prices are highly subjective. One of the few times that a security price is relatively certain is when a bond is expected to be held until maturity.

Taxes

The division of total yield between interest or dividends and price changes may have important tax implications for the investor. Bonds and stocks are capital assets; therefore price changes that occur between the purchase and sale dates result in capital gains or capital losses. If the holding period is over one year, the gain or loss is classified as long-term and receives special tax treatment. Only half of a long-term gain or loss is taxable income. In some cases the portion of a gain not subject to ordinary taxation may require a minimum tax payment of 15%. An alternative tax computation allows the investor to pay a maximum rate of 25% on the first $50,000 of long-term gains and 35% on the excess. When the investor has a combination of capital gains and losses, both short-term and long-term, the calculation of the taxable amount is somewhat complicated.

Short-term capital gains and losses do not receive this special treatment. Short-term gains are taxed at the stockholder's marginal tax rate, while short-term losses can be subtracted in full from taxable income. The only limit to this rule is that net short-term losses taken in a single year cannot amount to over $3000. If losses of over $3000 are incurred, the excess must be carried forward at $3000 per year without any time limit. Since long-term losses must be divided in half when offsetting taxable income, a maximum of $6000 in these losses can be taken in a single year.

Unlike long-term capital items, dividends and interest do not receive preferential tax treatment. Nearly all dividend and interest payments must be declared as ordinary income in the year in which they are received. For this reason investors paying income taxes at high marginal rates may prefer that earnings be reinvested rather than paid out in the form of cash dividends. In addition, these individuals may prefer low-coupon bonds (with a relatively low current yield) that sell at a discount. There are exceptions to this dividend and interest rule. For example, interest payments on most bonds issued by state and local governments and United States possessions are not subject to federal income taxes, while interest on federal government obligations is not subject to state and local taxes. In relatively rare cases, a portion of the dividend on common stock may be classified as a return of capital, thus reducing the cost basis of the stock when it is sold. In such instances this part of the dividend is not taxable as ordinary income in the year it is received.

If an investor has a variety of gains and losses (both short-term and long-term) during a taxable year, the net amount reportable as taxable income (or loss) is calculated in the following manner. First, long-term gains and long-term losses are used to offset one another. Second, short-term gains and short-term losses offset one another. Third, the net long-term result is combined with the net short-term calculation. If these two variables are of opposite sign (one a loss and the other a gain), losses are used to offset gains, dollar for dollar. If the investor has net long-term gains and net short-term gains, or net long-term losses and net short-term losses, no combination is necessary and the gains or losses are taxed separately.

To get a better idea of how this seemingly complicated offsetting process works, let us examine an illustration. Suppose during the current tax year that you sold securities that resulted in the following gains and losses:

Security	Gain	Loss	Type
IBM Common		$8000	Long-term
General Tire Common	$4000		Short-term
Avon Common	1000		Short-term
Empire Gas Bonds		3000	Short-term
Zayre Bonds	2000		Long-term
TWA Bonds		2000	Long-term

Short-term gains on General Tire and Avon total $5000, while a short-term loss of $3000 was taken on the bonds of Empire Gas. Combining the two produces a net short-term gain of $2000. A net long-term loss of $8000 results from combining the long-term gain on Zayre bonds with the long-term losses from selling IBM common stock and TWA bonds. When the net long-term loss of $8000 is offset with the net short-term gain of $2000, we have a $6000 long-term capital loss which offsets $3000 of ordinary income.

Since short-term losses are more valuable than long-term losses (the former can be used to offset a greater amount of income) and long-term gains are more valuable than short-term gains (the former are taxed at a lower effective rate), the investor should plan trading strategies accordingly. For example, short-term losses should not be used to offset long-term gains if possible. On the other hand, it works to the investor's advantage (for tax purposes) to be able to offset short-term gains with long-term losses. Other strategies should also become evident once the methodology of combining capital gains and losses is understood.

ANALYZING FIXED-INCOME SECURITIES

Until now we have discussed topics applicable to both fixed-income securities and common stocks. A basic understanding of risk, yield, and taxes is necessary for analyzing any type of security. We will now investigate subjects that apply more specifically to bonds and preferred stocks. Bonds are different from preferred stocks in part because they are issued by the government as well as the corporate sector. However, since both securities have similar characteristics for investors, we will examine them together.

Both bonds and preferred stocks provide an investor with fixed annual dollar payments. In chapter 9 we described the detailed characteristics of each of these instruments from the issuing corporation's point of view. It may be helpful to review some of the major points. Bonds represent debt; thus both principal and interest are legal liabilities of the issuer. Borrowing is an attractive method of financing corporate expenditures because interest payments are a tax-deductible expense (payments of principal are not). Preferred stock, on the other hand, represents corporate ownership and has no maturity date. Preferred stock dividends are not a legal liability and must be declared by a firm's board of directors. However, nearly all issues contain a cumulative feature requiring that passed dividends be paid before any dividends can be paid on common stock. Unlike interest on debt, dividends on preferred stock are not a deductible expense for corporations. As a result, preferred stock is a relatively expensive form of financing and accounts for only a minor portion of most corporate capital structures.

Both bonds and preferred stocks are generally subject to repurchase by the issuer at a predetermined call price. The call price, specified at the time of issue, is set above par value (usually one year's interest). Investors nearly always have a grace period of three to ten years immediately following the original issue during which a call cannot be made. When this time has elapsed, however, the holder has no choice but to sell if a call is made. The result is that the call price tends to serve as a ceiling after the period of protection is over. Even during this period, the possibility of a later call limits price appreciation.

Trading Fixed-Income Securities

Bond and preferred stock issues are traded on both the organized exchanges and the over-the-counter market. Because many issues are inactive and trade only sporadically, specialists and dealers may quote wide differences between bid and asked prices.

Bonds are generally quoted in points and fractions of a point, with one point representing $10. For example, a U. S. Home 5¾s96 may be quoted at 60⅞. The identification means that the bond, issued by U. S. Home Corporation, has a coupon rate of 5¾% of par value and matures at $1000 in 1996. The coupon rate translates into annual interest payments of $57.50 per bond. The quoted price represents the percentage of par at which the bond is trading. In this example, the price is $608.75 per bond. Preferred stocks are quoted at their full price per share. For example, Uniroyal preferred 8's, quoted at 82½, pay $8 in dividends annually and sell at $82.50 per share.

Preferred stock is traded with the dividend included in its price until a cutoff date called the ex-dividend date. Investors who purchase stock on or after this date do not receive the next dividend. Since the dividend payment is not received by the buyer, the stock price theoretically declines by the amount of the dividend on the ex-dividend date. Unlike preferred stock, bonds are priced without accrued interest. In other words, the buyer of a bond must pay the quoted price plus commission plus interest that has accrued since the last date on which interest was paid. When an investor sells a bond, the proceeds include accrued interest in addition to the transaction price (less commissions).

Yields on Fixed-Income Securities

Bonds and preferred stocks are usually purchased on the basis of current interest or dividend payments. When the bondholder or stockholder anticipates a decline in interest rates and/or an improvement in the issuer's risk class, the calculation of the investor's total return should include price appreciation as well as interest or dividends. Price forecasts are subject to error for preferred stocks (which have no maturity) and bonds not expected to be held until maturity, so the total yield calculation is only an estimate. One of the few examples of a relatively certain future price occurs when a bond is expected to be held until maturity. On the maturity date the issuing firm remits to the investor the bond's principal (usually $1000). If the bond is purchased at a price above its maturity value (a premium), its price must gradually decline throughout its life. Conversely, if it is purchased at less than its maturity value (a discount), its price must gradually increase until it matures. The return to an investor from holding a bond until its maturity date is the **yield to maturity**, which is identical to total yield because it includes both annual interest payments and changes in the value of the bond. If the investor is planning to sell the bond before maturity, the investor's total yield may be greater or less than the annual **yield to maturity.**

Since bonds are typically sold to investors on the basis of their yields to maturity, there are some important aspects of this concept that we should discuss. Suppose you are considering the purchase of a discount bond that pays $57.50 in interest each year and matures in 14 years. The bond can be purchased for $575, and at its maturity you will be paid $1000. The current yield is $57.50/$575 or 10%. Solving eq. 12–2, using a bond table or a publication such as *Moody's Bond Record*, we find that the bond's yield to maturity is approximately 12%. An annual yield of 12% should make your investment amount to slightly over six times its original cost at the end of 14 years. In other words, the original outlay of $575 should amount to over $3450 at the time of the bond's maturity. However, if we calculate the total interest payments (14

$\times$ \$57.50 = \$805) and add this to the maturity value (\$1000), we find that we have considerably less than \$3450. The reason is that all the cash "thrown off" from the bond before its maturity (the interest payments) must, in turn, be reinvested at 12%. Only if each \$57.50 interest payment is immediately reinvested at 12% can the investor realize a terminal value of \$3450 on the bond's maturity date.

There is no reason to expect the price of the bond to increase evenly each year until it reaches maturity. In our example, an increase from \$575 to \$1000 over a 14-year period is an annual rate of growth of approximately 4%. In other words, an asset whose price increases from \$575 to \$1000 in 14 years is increasing at an annual compounded rate of 4%. Thus, if the average annual appreciation is 4% and the current yield from interest payments is 10%, how does the total sum to more than the yield to maturity (appreciation plus interest) of 12%? The answer is that yield to maturity takes into consideration the fact that the bond's price will increase throughout its life, thereby making the current yield less than 10% in later years. As a result, if the combined yield equals 12% in each year of the holding period, price appreciation will provide an ever-larger proportion and current yield an ever smaller proportion of the 12% as the bond approaches maturity. Of course, a change in other factors such as the issuer's risk class, interest rates, or the structure of the yield curve could alter the steady annual yield of 12%.

As we saw earlier, interest payments are taxed at ordinary income tax rates while price appreciation is taxed only when the bond is sold or matures and even then at a lower effective tax rate. As a result, an investor in a high marginal tax bracket may well prefer to purchase a low-coupon bond selling at a discount even if its total yield is below the yield that could be obtained on new issues selling at par. This same investor may find it disadvantageous to purchase high-coupon bonds selling above par since the eventual capital loss (at maturity) cannot be used to offset income on a dollar-for-dollar basis.

Interest Rates and Security Prices

We mentioned earlier in this chapter that investors in fixed-income securities are subject to the risk of rising interest rates. Since this is one of the major risks faced by owners of bonds and preferred stocks, it is important to understand how the prices of these securities are affected by changing interest rates.

The size of potential price changes of bonds and preferred stocks is directly related to the time remaining until maturity. The longer the time an issue has until maturity, the greater the fluctuations in price that will occur for a given change in interest rates. For preferred stock, which has no maturity date, the price fluctuations can be very large. Even for bonds with a maturity date 25 to 35 years in the future, the price changes can be large. On the other hand, the price of bonds approaching maturity fluctuates very little. Suppose we are examining an 8% preferred issue with a $100 par value. If yields for preferred stocks of the same risk class rise to 10%, the 8% stock will drop in price to

$$\text{Price} = \frac{\text{Annual dividend}}{\text{Current yield}} = \frac{\$8}{.10} = \$80 \qquad \qquad \text{12–3}$$

If the preferred falls to $80 per share, the current yield would be 10% ($8/$80), making the issue competitive with new issues. At the opposite end of the spectrum is an 8% coupon 20-year bond issued 19 years ago. If one-year bonds in the same risk class are yielding 10%, eq. 12–2 tells us our bond should sell for

$$\text{Price} = \frac{\$80}{(1 + .10)^1} + \frac{\$1000}{(1 + .10)^1} = \$981.72$$

In other words, a shorter period until maturity significantly reduces price fluctuations of a fixed-income security. The relationship among price, length of time until maturity, and changes in interest rates for an 8% coupon $1000 par bond are shown in fig. 12–1.

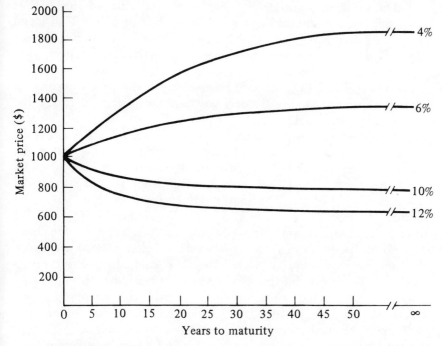

FIGURE 12–1 Market Price of an 8% Coupon, $1000-Par Bond at Various Maturity Lengths and Interest Rates

Figure 12–1 illustrates how the prices of bonds of different maturities fluctuate as interest rates change. Bonds with no maturity dates (or preferred stocks) show the greatest price fluctuation for a given change in interest rates. For example, 8% preferred stock will sell at approximately twice its par value if interest rates decline to 4%. If rates climb to 12%, the price of this same preferred issue will decline to two-thirds of its par value. At the opposite end of the scale, 8% bonds that mature in one year will sell at approximately $1039 if interest rates decline to 4%. At a 12% rate of interest, the bonds will sell for $964. The upper price potential will be limited if the bond can be called. Some investors in long-term high-coupon bonds issued during the early 1970s discovered the reasons for this price ceiling when issuers began calling their securities after the call protection had expired.

Measuring the Quality of Fixed-Income Securities

The concept of risk includes a number of adverse possibilities that can occur after a security is purchased. Inflation, higher interest rates, and a general market decline in security prices are three possibilities for the investor. Perhaps the primary concern of most investors in fixed-income securities, however, is financial or business risk.

The worst consequence of financial risk for preferred stockholders and bondholders is the bankruptcy of the issuer. Not only will dividend and interest payments be suspended, but the chance of recovering the par value of the security is remote. Since bondholders are creditors, they must be paid prior to owners. In other words, preferred stockholders assume more financial risk than do bondholders of the same company. In some cases, payments to bondholders may be resumed after a default if the firm can avoid bankruptcy.

An investor may use a number of evaluation techniques to assess the degree of financial risk. For fixed-income securities, coverage ratios are commonly used. Other things equal, the greater the number of times interest payments or fixed charges are covered, the less the chance that the issuing firm will default. The proper ratio depends on the stability of earnings. For example, a firm in a highly cyclical industry requires higher coverage ratios than a firm with very stable earnings. Typically, the coverage ratio on bonds is calculated using earnings before interest and taxes, while the coverage ratio on preferred stock is computed using earnings after taxes. The reason for this difference is that interest on bonds is paid with before-tax income, while dividends are paid with after-tax income. In each case an average earnings calculation for a period of five or more years should be used in the numerator. Considering only a single year may produce a misleading result since the firm could be suffering from abnormal business conditions. In addition, the trend of a coverage ratio must be considered. A ratio that appears adequate but has been showing a downward trend may indicate trouble.

When a firm has more than one class of bonds outstanding, analysts generally prefer to include interest charges on all debt in calculating interest coverage ratios. Some of these bonds may be secured while others are unsecured. However, since a default on any class of bonds may force the company into bankruptcy, senior bondholders are just as interested as junior bondholders in a firm's ability to meet all interest charges. If sinking-fund payments are to be included in the coverage, earnings prior to depreciation charges should be used.

Although coverage ratios are the most commonly used measures of the quality of fixed-income securities, other variables can be equally revealing. An issuer's debt-to-equity ratio is a measure of the proportion of assets financed by borrowing. A period of poor earnings and low coverage ratios may present a relatively small threat to the security of lenders if the firm has a large equity base to support a limited amount of debt. Off-balance-sheet debt such as leases should also be considered in evaluating the amount of debt.

A firm's liquidity position is important in evaluating its ability to service debt. For example, a firm may appear very profitable, have good growth, and possess a relatively low debt ratio and yet have trouble paying its bills on time. The latter may be the result of a credit policy that is too liberal (large receivables) or excessive inventory. Regardless of the cause, the firm may have trouble servicing its debt.

As we discussed in chapter 8, heavy reliance on short-term borrowing may increase a firm's profitability but lower its ability to meet debt repayments. Since short-term loans to support permanent capital must be periodically refinanced, tight money conditions might make refinancing extremely difficult.

In addition to these factors, other variables should be taken into consideration in evaluating the quality of a firm's debt. Among these are the quality and depth of management, the protective provisions in the indenture agreement, and the economic prospects of the firm and the industry.

All these factors are taken into consideration by bond rating companies such as Standard & Poor's and Moody's. For a fee from the issuer, these firms rate the investment quality of a fixed-income security. The rating grades for debt issues used by the two firms are similar. Table 12–1 illustrates that the ratings are approximately the same for both rating agencies through the grade of B. At this level a bond is paying interest but there is serious doubt that these payments will continue during adverse economic conditions. At gradings below a level of B, the two agencies differ somewhat in their ratings. Note that all bond issues within a single category do not have exactly the same investment characteristics. Some

TABLE 12–1   Interpretation of Standard & Poor's and Moody's Bond
Rating Grades

Standard & Poor's	Moody's	Interpretation
AAA	Aaa	Highest grade
AA	Aa	High grade
A	A	Upper-medium grade
BBB	Baa	Medium grade
BB	Ba	Lower-medium grade
B	B	Speculative
CCC–CC		Outright speculative
	Caa	Poor standing
C		Income bonds on which no interest is being paid
	Ca	Highly speculative
	C	Very poor prospects
DDD–D		In default, with rank indicating relative salvage value.

issues at the high end of a grouping may be candidates for upgrading while other issues may be of lower quality. As a result, all issues in a rating category do not carry the same yield. In addition to debt, Standard & Poor's also evaluates the investment quality of preferred stock issues. Grading categories for these issues are similar to those used for debt.

Presumably, a firm like Moody's or Standard & Poor's can conduct a more thorough investigation of a particular debt or preferred stock issue than can an individual investor. For example, to rate corporate debt issues, these firms not only inspect a company's financial statements, but also evaluate its market position and management. In the case of tax-exempt issues, the firms consider the value of a community's real estate valuation, per capita income, and the schedule at which debt is to be retired. While all this information is available to an individual, any meaningful evaluation is both difficult and time-consuming.

SUMMARY

Security owners are subject to a number of different risks. These include purchasing power risk, interest rate risk, business and financial risk, and market risk. The degree of each type of risk varies according to the type of security and according to the issuer. The tax consequences of owning various securities differ, and a stockholder must make this an important consideration in investment selection.

Fixed-income securities provide investors with constant annual dollar payments. As a result, bonds and preferred stocks are generally purchased on the basis of current interest and dividend payments. The price of a fixed-income security varies inversely with the market rate of interest.

QUESTIONS

1. What are some of the risks associated with holding a stock or bond?

2. The total risk from holding a security can be segregated into two categories, systematic and unsystematic. Give examples of each.

3. Why do fixed-income securities subject the investor to the greatest purchasing power risk, while securities that involve variable returns provide some protection against purchasing power risk?

4. Why do corporate bonds generally carry more financial risk than government securities?

5. How is the expected rate of return calculated on an investment?

6. Explain why short-term losses are more valuable than long-term losses and why long-term gains are more valuable than short-term gains.

7. Since bonds are usually sold to investors on the basis of their yields to maturity, what are some important aspects that the investor should consider?

8. How are potential price changes of bonds and preferred stocks directly related to the time remaining until maturity?

9. Why do preferred stockholders assume more financial risk than bondholders?

10. What techniques may one use to assess the degree of financial risk from holding a security?

11. What type of investigation does a firm like Moody's or Standard & Poor's conduct when they rate corporate debt issues for a company?

SELECTED REFERENCES

BADGER, RALPH E.; TORGERSON, HAROLD W.; and GUTHMANN, HARRY G. *Investment Principles and Practices.* Englewood Cliffs, N.J.: Prentice-Hall, 1969. Chs. 7, 8.

BELLEMORE, DOUGLAS H., and RITCHIE, JOHN C. *Investments: Principles, Practices, Analyses.* Cincinnati, Ohio: South-Western Publishing Co., 1974. Part 3.

D'AMBROSIO, CHARLES A. *Principles of Modern Investments.* Chicago: Science Research Associates, 1976. Chs. 10, 11, 12.

DARST, DAVID M. *The Complete Bond Book.* New York: McGraw-Hill, 1975.

FRANCIS, JACK CLARK. *Investments: Analysis and Management.* New York: McGraw-Hill, 1976. Part 2.

SPRECHER, C. RONALD. *An Introduction to Investment Management.* Boston: Houghton Mifflin, 1975. Part 3.

STEVENSON, RICHARD, and JENNINGS, EDWARD. *Fundamentals of Investments.* St. Paul, Minn.: West Publishing Co., 1976. Chs. 6, 12, 16, 17.

13 Analysis of Variable-Income Securities

A subscriber to an investment advisory service of dubious value and integrity wrote to them that he had followed their counsel exactly and now found himself cleaned out. "You have constantly told me," continued the letter, "to communicate with you if I got into trouble so that you could advise me how to act. Now that I am broke, how do I act? Please wire."

Two days later the man received a wire from the service. It read ACT BROKE.

While bonds and preferred stocks are generally bought for their current yields, common stocks and securities convertible into common stock may be purchased even though no current cash payments are being made. The owner of these securities expects the major portion of total return to accrue from price appreciation and/or future cash payments. Before investigating the methods of analyzing variable-income securities, we will review some of the fundamental concepts of common stocks, many of which we discussed in chapter 8.

FUNDAMENTALS OF COMMON STOCK

While bondholders are creditors of a corporation, common stockholders and preferred stockholders are owners. But the similarities between common stocks and preferred stocks are few. For example, nearly all common stockholders are permitted to elect candidates to the board of directors, while preferred stockholders are generally allowed to vote only under unusual circumstances. Since the firms are not legally required to declare dividends, stockholders are less certain of receiving dividends than bondholders are of receiving interest payments. However, preferred stockholders must be paid before common stockholders. If a firm liquidates, preferred stockholders have a prior claim on the distribution of proceeds from the sale of assets up to the par value of their securities. Hence common stockholders are less certain of both dividend payments and the recovery of their investment if the firm is liquidated. On the other hand, the return to bondholders and preferred stockholders is more certain but also more limited. Because common stockholders receive the cash flows that remain after all other obligations have been paid, these residual amounts may increase (or decrease). To a considerable degree, it is this possibility that causes the prices of common stocks to fluctuate so violently.

Dividends may be declared in the form of cash, property, or additional shares of stock. Generally they are in cash and are paid quarterly. There are four important dates in any dividend decision: the **declaration date**, the **ex-dividend date**, the **stock-of-record date**, and the **payment date**. The declaration date is the date on which a firm's directors declare a dividend; at that time they must set a stock-of-record date and the payment date. The record date is the date on which the corporation examines its books to see who owns the firm's stock and is to receive the dividend. The payment date, which usually follows the record date by approximately one month, is the date on which the firm sends the dividend to its owners. Because a company requires some time to determine exactly who owns its shares, the stock begins trading without the dividend four business days before the record date. This is the ex-dividend date. A person who purchases the stock five days before the record date receives the dividend, while a person making the purchase four days before the record date does not receive the dividend. On the other hand, stockholders who sell their shares on the ex-dividend date will receive the next dividend since they will be the shareholders of record on the record date. Because each share of stock is presumably worth less on the ex-dividend date than on the day immediately preceding it, the price will theoretically drop by the amount of the dividend. Hence the decision to purchase a stock on or before its ex-dividend date is determined mostly by an investor's tax status. Purchasing the stock before the ex-dividend date entitles the investor to the dividend, which is taxable as regular income (with a $100 exclusion per taxpayer). Purchasing it on or after the ex-dividend date results in a lower cost basis and a higher profit (or smaller loss) when the shares are eventually sold.

FUNDAMENTAL ANALYSIS

Most common stock analysis involves an attempt to establish an **intrinsic value** for a particular security. Intrinsic value has been defined as the "value justified by the facts" and is determined by variables such as management, earnings, dividends, and assets. The goal of fundamental analysis is to estimate a security's intrinsic value and compare the result with the market price. If the market price is less than the intrinsic value, the security is a candidate for purchase. If the market price is above the calculated intrinsic value, the security should be avoided or sold if it is already held. Since the variables that influence a security's intrinsic value are subject to change, the intrinsic value itself changes over time. However, the intrinsic value is less volatile than market price, thus presenting the investor with opportunities to profit from differences between the two.

In this section we will examine some of the variables used to establish the intrinsic value. We will also introduce the concept of efficient markets and explain why some students of the market consider it impossible for an investor to accurately differentiate between a security's intrinsic value and market price. In the next section we will introduce an entirely different method of evaluating a security—technical analysis.

Assets

The assets of a company provide one measure of a company's size (the other is sales). However, assets do not necessarily indicate either stability or profitability. A firm's assets may be in the form of nonliquid fixed assets or more liquid variable assets. A high ratio of fixed to variable assets could produce a volatile net operating income from one year to the next regardless of the amount of total assets. Perhaps more important is the type of financing used to obtain the assets. The major portion of assets may have been acquired through borrowing. In other words, a firm may control a large dollar amount of assets, but these assets may be financed by debt and therefore pledged to creditors.

A financial measurement that takes both assets and debt into account is **book value**. Book value is calculated by subtracting liabilities from assets. If preferred stock is included in a firm's capital structure, the par value of this stock must also be subtracted from assets. In most presentations, the result is divided by the number of common shares outstanding and stated as book value per share.

Book value per share theoretically indicates the liquidating value of a company's common stock. Hence this variable might be interpreted as a measure of the funds a common stockholder could expect to recover in the event of a bankruptcy. In actual practice this is true only if the firm can liquidate its assets at the book values shown on its balance sheet. In many cases the book value bears little relation to liquidation value because a firm may have to sell assets at distress prices. In other instances firms carry assets on their balance sheet at original cost even though they have appreciated significantly in value. Such a practice occurs especially with companies that own large amounts of natural resources such as land or minerals. Hence book value may give a poor indication of the market values, or even the liquidating values, of a firm's assets.

Many analysts also regard book value as a poor indicator of a firm's future earnings and dividends. Although **return on equity** (net profits divided by owners' equity) is a commonly used measure of corporate performance, the absolute size of book value per share provides little guidance in projecting future **earnings per share** or dividends per share. As we shall see, however, it can be useful when combined with return on equity.

In summary, book value per share (considered independently) generally provides little indication of a common stock's intrinsic value. In most cases it affords minimal guidance in determining liquidating value and little assistance in projecting earnings and dividends.

Earnings

While book value alone is not a reliable guide to intrinsic value, it can be combined with the rate of return on common equity to provide an important determinant of intrinsic value. Book value per share, multiplied by the rate of return on common stock equity, produces earnings per share (EPS). Many analysts believe EPS and the expected rate of growth in EPS are the two most important factors in common stock evaluation. For example, suppose a company has the balance sheet shown in table 13–1. Total book value is equal to $100,000 and book value per

TABLE 13–1   Sample Balance Sheet

Current Assets		$ 50,000
Fixed Assets	$300,000	
Less: Accumulated Depreciation	50,000	
Net Fixed Assets		250,000
Total Assets		$300,000
Current Liabilities		$ 70,000
Long-Term Debt		130,000
Common Stock (5000 shares)	$ 25,000	
Retained Earnings	75,000	
Owners' Equity		100,000
Total Liabilities and Net Worth		$300,000

share is $20 ($100,000/5000). If the company earns $15,000 in profits after taxes, its return on total assets is 5% ($15,000/$300,000), and return on common stock equity is 15% ($15,000/$100,000). Earnings per share, calculated by dividing the number of common shares outstanding into total earnings available for common, is equal to $3 ($15,000/5000). As you can see, the return on common equity and the amount of equity behind each common share (book value per share) determine the earnings per share of common stock outstanding.

If the rate of return on equity is projected to remain approximately the same throughout the near future, the growth in earnings per share depends on the proportion of earnings retained for reinvestment and the proportion paid in dividends. The larger the percentage of earnings reinvested in the business, the greater earnings per share will be in subsequent years. For example, if all earnings are reinvested in the firm, book value in the next year will climb 15% to $23 per share ($20 + $3). With the return on equity continuing at 15%, earnings per share in the next year will be $3.45. Under the same assumptions, earnings per share in the following year will be $3.97. If all earnings are paid out in dividends to shareholders, earnings per share will remain the same each year. Thus, if the entire $3 in earnings per share is paid out during the first year, book value will remain at $20 per share the next year. A continuing return on common equity of 15% will then produce an EPS of $3.

In addition to retaining a portion of earnings, a company can use other methods of increasing earnings per share. One obvious method is to increase the return on common equity, for example by improving the profit margin on sales by altering a firm's financial structure. The use of financial leverage is particularly important because the higher earnings are accompanied by increased risk.

Dividends

The only current income that a common stockholder receives is from dividend payments. Most investors also expect to earn a profit by selling the common stock at a price higher than its purchase price. If the holding period is a single year, the investor's rate of return is

$$r = \frac{P_{t+1} + D_{t+1} - P_t}{P_t} \qquad \text{13-1}$$

where

$r =$ investor's rate of return

$t =$ time period

$P =$ price of the security

$D =$ dividends received

To illustrate, if an investor purchases stock for $20 per share, receives a dividend of $1, and sells the stock one year later for $22 per share, the rate of return is

$$\frac{\$22 + \$1 - \$20}{\$20} = \frac{\$3}{\$20} = 15\%$$

If the stock is held for longer than one year, the rate of return must be calculated by using the more complicated eq. 12–2. In a compact form this equation is written as

$$P = \sum_{t=1}^{n} \frac{D_t}{(1+r)^t} + \frac{P_n}{(1+r)^n} \qquad\qquad 13\text{–}2$$

where

P = price of the security

t = time period

n = period when security is sold

D = dividend payments

r = investor's rate of return

As with eq. 12–2, the investor's rate of return is calculated using the discounting concepts developed in chapter 8.

Equation 13–2 illustrates that an investor's return consists of both the dividends received during the holding period and any change in price that occurs between the time the security is purchased and the time it is sold. If the investor does not expect to sell the stock, the return consists of dividends only. However, even if the security is sold, the next purchaser will decide on the basis of expected future dividends and selling price. This selling price, in turn, is calculated on the basis of the discounted value of expected future dividend payments and selling price. In other words, while an individual investor bases a decision to purchase a security on both dividends and expected selling price, the decision is actually determined solely by the discounted stream of dividends. In equation form this is

$$P_t = \sum_{t=1}^{\infty} \frac{D_t}{(1+r)^t} \qquad\qquad 13\text{–}3$$

Since few firms can be expected to last forever, the stream must realistically be considered to terminate with a liquidating dividend at some point in the future.

If the discounted stream of dividends is the most important variable in determining the value of a firm's common stock, why do the common stocks of many firms that pay no dividends enjoy such high price-earnings ratios? Most of these firms are expected to enjoy substantial increases in earnings and dividend-paying capacity in future years. As a result, investors are looking past the present period of no dividends and modest earnings (compared to the common stock price) toward a promising future of dividend payments and higher earnings. The firms are generally earning a relatively high rate of return on owners' equity, and earnings are needed for reinvestment in the business. To keep a proper amount of equity in the capital structure, the only alternative to retaining earnings (a low dividend payout ratio) is to sell additional common stock. Unless present owners purchase a sufficient number of the new shares, their equity positions in the firms will deteriorate because of the larger number of shares outstanding. However, as we saw in chapter 12, current tax laws penalize this type of financial transaction since cash dividend payments are taxed as regular income. In contrast, retained earnings (which should result in higher share prices) are not taxed until the shares are sold and even then the tax rate is reduced if the shares have been held more than one year.

Capitalization Rate

So far we have said that common stock valuation is a function of either the stream of earnings or dividends that accrue to investors. These expected flows must be discounted since returns on an investment are more valuable the earlier they are received. The rate at which the stream is discounted is called the **capitalization rate**. In other words, the expected stream of dividends or earnings, discounted at the appropriate rate of capitalization, determines the intrinsic value.

Unfortunately, an accurate determination of the proper capitalization rate is difficult to specify. It varies over time, for different industries, and even for different firms within the same industry. The rate of capitalization used in analyzing any type of security depends, in part, on the rate of return available on risk-free securities. The risk-free rate varies over time depending on factors such as the supply of and the demand for money (or loanable funds).

In addition to the rate of return on risk-free investments, the capitalization rate for variable-income securities must include a component for risk. In other words, the earnings or dividends that we capitalize are educated forecasts at best and therefore subject to error. Adding a risk factor to the risk-free discount rate results in a greater discount rate for capitalizing expected earnings or dividends and a relatively lower intrinsic value for a security. For example, a firm might increase the proportion of debt in its capital structure in an attempt to increase earnings per share by raising the return on owners' equity. If the attempt is successful, it should increase the projected earnings flow to stockholders. At the same time, however, it increases the variability of earnings and the risk to the owners. The result is that the higher projected earnings are discounted at a higher rate which may increase, lower, or leave the intrinsic value of the security unchanged. Suppose we let i be the risk-free rate of return, b the adjustment for risk, and k the sum of the two. The intrinsic value of a security based on projected future dividends is

$$\text{Intrinsic value} = \frac{D_1}{(1+i+b)^1} + \frac{D_2}{(1+i+b)^2} + \frac{D_3}{(1+i+b)^3}$$
$$+ \ldots + \frac{D_\infty}{(1+i+b)^\infty} \qquad \text{13-4}$$
$$= \sum_{t=1}^{\infty} \frac{D_t}{(1+i+b)^t} = \sum_{t=1}^{\infty} \frac{D_t}{(1+k)^t}$$

It is of course difficult to establish an exact value for b in eq. 13-4, but an understanding of the principle is important. Many investors seem to have a difficult time comprehending the relationship among stock prices, dividends, interest rates, and risk. Equation 13-4 attempts to tie these variables together. It illustrates why stock prices may decline when profits and dividends rise or increase when they fall. For example, stock prices may decline if expectations of higher inflation rates push interest rates higher even though the firm expects to be able to increase profits because of higher product prices. In addition, investors may fear government action, such as slowing the rate of growth in the money supply to curb the inflation, which would increase concern about a drying up of credit. These expectations, in turn, would increase the perceived degree of business or financial risk and result in a higher-risk premium. In other words, it is not the fear of inflation that results in lower intrinsic stock values, but rather expectations of economic conditions that may accompany an inflationary period.

The price-earnings ratio also involves capitalization. It is sometimes misunderstood, however, because it is stated in terms of current earnings rather than the present value of all projected earnings even though it is projected earnings rather than current earnings that determines a security's price. Thus a stock may be capitalized at only two or three times current earnings (a PE ratio of two or three) because investors project declining profits in future years. This situation existed for sugar refiners in 1975 when retail sugar prices were at very high levels. Investors expected the conditions that prevailed to be temporary and awarded low PE ratios to common stocks of companies in the industry. As sugar prices plummeted in subsequent years, the industry's profits declined even more rapidly and investors' expectations were validated.

Growth Models

Although investors cannot be expected to accurately project dividends over an infinite time horizon (eq. 13–4), they may be able to develop a rough estimate for the growth rate in dividends by projecting the past growth rate into the future. Or they may use sophisticated projections for the economy, the industry, and the firm. If a single annual growth rate in dividends is forecasted, we can formulate intrinsic value in the following equation:

$$\text{Intrinsic value} = \sum_{t=1}^{\infty} \frac{D_0 \, (1+g)^t}{(1+k)^t} \qquad \text{13–5}$$

where

D_0 = current dividend per share

g = constant growth rate in dividends

k = rate of discount

t = time periods

Equation 13–5 simply substitutes $D_0(1+g)^t$ for D_t in eq. 13–4. In other words, the dividend in any given period (t) in the future is equal to the dividend in the present period times one plus the growth rate in dividends to the power t. For example, a current dividend of \$1, projected to grow at a rate of 6%, equals \$1$(1+.06)^1$, or \$1.06, in the next period. This formulation works as long as the rate of discount (k) is greater than the projected rate of growth (g). Otherwise, the dividend stream adjusted for risk and the time value of money will grow larger and larger, resulting in an infinite intrinsic value. In simplified form eq. 13–5 can be shown as

$$\text{Intrinsic value} = \frac{D_0(1+g)}{k-g} \quad \text{or} \quad \frac{D_1}{k-g} \qquad \text{13–6}$$

For example, if a dividend of $3 per share is expected to grow indefinitely at an annual rate of 8% and the stream is discounted at 12% the intrinsic value is

$$\frac{\$3(1 + .08)}{(.12 - .08)} = \frac{\$3(1.08)}{.04} = \$81$$

A more valid assumption than continuous growth at a constant rate is periodic growth at different rates. Since even growth companies eventually approach maturity, it is unrealistic to project that dividends will grow at the same rate forever. It is more likely that they will begin a period of slower growth at some point. If g' is the slower growth rate expected to begin in some future year $(N + 1)$, eq. 13–5 becomes

$$\text{Intrinsic value} = \sum_{t=1}^{N} \frac{D_o(1 + g)^t}{(1 + k)^t} + \sum_{t=N+1}^{\infty} \frac{D_N (1 + g')^{t-N}}{(1 + k)^t} \qquad \text{13–7}$$

If growth is projected to stop $(g' = 0)$ in year $N + 1$, we simply discount the constant D_N in the numerator of the second portion of the equation in each year from $N + 1$ to infinity.

Equation 13–7 may be difficult for some readers to understand. To help illustrate its use, suppose we assume the $3 dividend is expected to grow by 8% annually for the first 10 years ($6.48 in year 10) and by only 3% thereafter. The security's intrinsic value is then

$$\sum_{t=1}^{10} \frac{\$3(1 + .08)^t}{(1 + .12)^t} + \sum_{t=11}^{\infty} \frac{\$6.48(1 + .03)^{t-10}}{(1 + .12)^t}$$

In the numerator of the second term, $6.48 represents D_N or $3(1 + .08)^{10}$.

Although projected dividends become less certain the further into the future they are to occur, they are discounted over a longer period of time. Thus future dividends play a progressively smaller part in determining a security's intrinsic value (if $k > g$). In addition, the investor may want to discount future dividends at a progressively higher rate to account for the greater risk.

TECHNICAL ANALYSIS

A second method for selecting common stocks is through **technical analysis**. Rather than concentrating on fundamental economic concepts such as interest rates, inflation, productivity, and gross national product and financial considerations such as income statements, balance sheets, and projected earnings per share, technical analysis relies on variables such as trading volume and past changes in stock prices. In fact, the "pure" technical trader does not want to clutter the decision making with any fundamental economic and financial variables. Technicians believe that fundamentals are just as likely to confuse as to help in buying and selling securities. One of the basic assumptions of most technical trading is that "smart money" (insiders and institutional investors) has already acquired or sold a security by the time fundamentals dictate a purchase or sale. According to technicians, however, it is possible to use trading volume and price changes of securities to become aware of what the smart money is doing.

Suppose a mining company announces it has discovered considerable gold reserves on land where it has mineral rights. Technicians believe it is possible to interpret security volume and price movements that indicate significant news before the actual announcement is made by the firm's directors. They also argue that by the time the discovery is officially announced, the stock price has adjusted to the news since enough people became aware of the discovery before the official announcement.

Technical analysis is generally used to determine the time to buy and sell specific securities, although in some cases it is also used to forecast target prices. The price and volume data are plotted on graphs or charts (technicians are also called chartists) so that they can be interpreted. The crucial assumption of this analysis is that price formations are repeated. The graphs simply make it easier to discover significant price formations. Heavy trading volume is generally interpreted as a reinforcement that a price formation is indicating a correct buy or sell signal.

Methods of Charting

There are two major methods used to record security price data. The first, bar charting, is probably the most familiar. The vertical axis of a bar chart measures a security's price and the horizontal axis represents time. With this graph, the technician draws a vertical line connecting the high and low price at which the security traded during the desired period (usually a day or week) and makes a small horizontal mark to indicate the closing price. A small portion on the lower part of the graph is used to record trading volume for the same time period used for prices.

A second method of recording security prices is the point-and-figure chart. This unusual chart is designed to measure only significant changes in price, so time is relatively unimportant. While bar charts require the chartist to move to the next column after each piece of data is recorded, each subsequent column of a point-and-figure chart is used only when a significant price reversal (change in the direction of price movement) is observed. The size of a reversal required to begin a new column depends on the price and volatility of the stock being charted. The technician may decide that a stock trading at over $50–$60 per share should reverse its direction of movement by at least $3 before a new column is used.

Security prices are entered on a point-and-figure chart by marking X's when price increases and O's when price declines. Since the chartist moves to a new column only when a price reverses, columns must alternate between X's and O's (X's and O's never appear in the same column). Now you can understand why time is not important on a point-and-figure chart. So long as a stock price continues to move in the same direction, or is reasonably stable, no new column is started. The greater the size of a price reversal the chartist defines as significant, the longer the period of time before a new column is started.

Figure 13–1 illustrates a bar chart and a point-and-figure chart for one security over the same period of time. Since horizontal movement (moving to another column) on the point-and-figure chart occurs less frequently than on the bar chart, the two graphs are not of the same width.

Interpreting Chart Formations

Bar charts and point-and-figure charts are used in approximately the same manner. The recorded price movements, viewed over time, reveal formations that allegedly can be used to determine upper and lower price boundaries and to project future price movements. While there is little disagreement about the construction of the charts, their interpretation is somewhat less precise. Figure 13–2 illustrates a few of the more popular formations.

Each graph depicted in fig. 13–2 indicates the probable direction of price movement. If the formations were inverted, the predicted price movements would be in the opposite direction. To ascertain whether a signal is true, chartists correlate trading volume with price movements. For example, an upside breakout (moving above the previous high price) of the triple-top formation would be suspect if it occurred on relatively low volume. On the other hand, a breakout on relatively heavy volume would give a strong signal to buy.

Most of the time a record of price changes does not develop into as clear-cut a formation as those illustrated in fig. 13–2. In these instances, the analyst must draw his or her own conclusions. Hence most price records are subject to individual interpretation.

Other Technical Indicators

In addition to graphs of trading volume and individual security prices, technical analysts use other data to forecast movements of the

Bar Chart

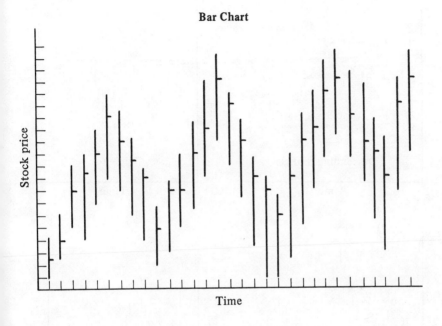

Point-and-Figure Chart

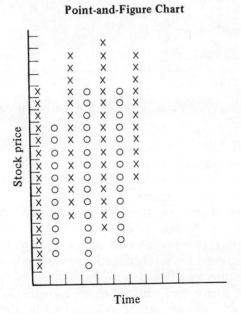

FIGURE 13-1 Examples of Stock Price Charts

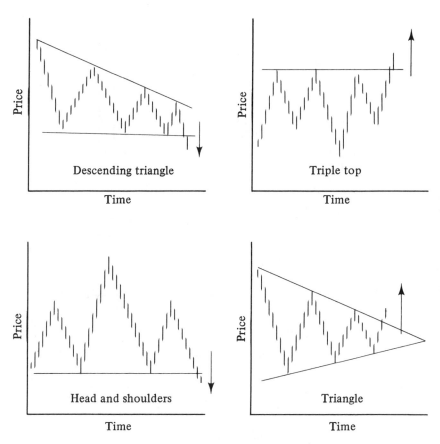

FIGURE 13–2   Price Formations Used in Technical Analysis

stock market. The best-known technical theory for projecting stock prices is the Dow Theory, which is based on price movements of the Dow Jones Industrial Average and the Dow Jones Transportation Average. The theory states that during a period when these two averages exhibit relatively minor fluctuations, stocks are either being accumulated (purchased) or distributed (sold) by market professionals. When a breakout above a former resistance level or below a former support level occurs, the direction of the breakout indicates the future direction of stock prices. Both averages must break out in the same direction to give a strong buy or sell signal.

A technique that is used with bar charts is the filter. This technique involves the purchase of a security if its price rises by a given percentage (the filter) or the sale of a security if its price falls by a given percentage. The size of the filter is set by the technician before trading begins and is the only rule necessary to implement this technique. As the filter is made smaller, trading increases, resulting in higher brokerage commissions. If a large filter is used, brokerage commissions are reduced but the chance of buying at peaks and selling at troughs increases.

The belief that small investors generally make erroneous decisions is the source of a number of technical rules. One is that the investor should observe how odd lotters (those buying and selling less than 100 shares) are trading and do the opposite. For example, if odd lotters are buying more shares than they are selling, this is a signal that the next major movement of the market will be downward. A similar rule is that the trend of odd-lot short sales (selling less than 100 shares of borrowed stock) indicates whether an investor should be selling or buying securities. If odd lotters are selling short heavily, the market should begin moving upward.

Technicians also use total short interest to provide guidance toward market movements. An increase in the ratio of daily short sales to daily volume is an indication of future market strength since shares sold short must eventually be covered with purchases. This is the case even though initial short positions are taken because investors anticipate a decline in stock prices.

Technical analysis uses numerous other tools including moving-average price lines, Barron's Confidence Index, and formulas to measure the relative strength of a particular security. In addition, technicians use chart formations other than the two we have discussed. While technical data supposedly indicate which securities should be traded and when, many market professionals consider technical analysis a waste of time. Others use it in conjunction with the fundamental analysis, and still others use technical analysis exclusively.

EFFICIENT MARKETS

A school of thought popularized by the academic community and becoming more widely accepted among investors contends that the security markets are efficient. This means that the price of a specific security incorporates all information relevant to valuing the security. Thus the security always sells at or near its intrinsic value, and attempting to find stocks and bonds that are undervalued or overvalued is useless. According to popular belief, if markets are efficient, an investor could randomly pick securities to buy and sell by throwing darts at the financial pages of a newspaper. On the contrary, investors must still consider important financial variables such as their tax status, liquidity position, and near-term and long-run goals.

Surprisingly, the conclusion of the efficient market hypothesis (that securities move randomly around their intrinsic values) is based on the assumption that investors effectively analyze securities. In other words, the buying and selling of securities on the basis of the best available data is the very factor that causes securities to sell at prices near their intrinsic values. Although securities may temporarily move away from their intrinsic values, the movements are random and impossible to forecast. As new information becomes available, a security's intrinsic value and market price changes. If the information had been expected, it would not be classified as new and would not have affected either intrinsic value or market price. For example, if a firm announces an increase in dividends that had already been anticipated by investors, there is no reason to expect an increase in the price of the firm's common stock. In fact, if the increase is less than had been expected, the price of the stock might actually decline. Thus an investor must not equate the announcement of information with new information.

The **efficient market hypothesis** is classified on three levels according to the degree of efficiency. The three classifications are termed the weak form, the semistrong form, and the strong form. The correctness of these classifications carries important implications for investors, and empirical studies of the three classifications have been undertaken to determine their validity.

The weak form of the hypothesis contends that historical security price and volume statistics cannot be used to earn an above-average rate of return. Thus an investor could expect to earn the same return by randomly selecting securities. In addition, a buy-and-hold strategy should produce the same return as frequent trading. In fact, because brokerage commissions are lower with longer holding periods, a buy-and-hold strategy should produce superior net returns because of lower costs. This classification of the efficient market hypothesis is commonly known as the random walk hypothesis because it argues that stocks move randomly about their intrinsic value. The weak form implies that the use of bar graphs and point-and-figure charts is useless in attempting to produce superior investment results. This does not mean that a person using technical analysis will never achieve superior results or "beat the averages." Better performance may result simply because of luck or because the securities selected by the technician involve more risk than the securities of a comparable portfolio.

Computer-assisted studies undertaken to test the validity of the weak form classification have included using various sizes of filters and running correlations to determine whether the direction of price changes is related to the previous direction of price changes (for example, can a stock that has increased in price be expected to continue to increase?). The results of nearly all these studies indicate that the weak form of the efficient market hypothesis is valid. That is, previous price and volume data cannot be used to improve investment performance.

The semistrong hypothesis states that current security prices incorporate all publicly available data. While the weak form of the efficient market hypothesis has important ramifications for the investor trading on the basis of technical analysis, the semistrong form is of interest to those using fundamental analysis. If security prices reflect all publicly available information, the investor cannot earn above-average returns by examining income statements and balance sheets, analyzing economic conditions, and estimating future earnings and dividends because security prices already incorporate all these data. If an investor has access to information not available to the public (for example, a member of the Department of Justice who knows an antitrust case will be filed against a company), the validity of the semistrong hypothesis does not rule out above-average profits.

The semistrong hypothesis is more difficult to test than the weak form. Not only does it require more evidence, but the extent of the evidence must be defined. In other words, we must define what is included in the term "public information" and decide when it is publicly available. Studies of the semistrong hypothesis have tested whether specific new information has already been incorporated into a firm's stock price by the time it becomes publicly available. For example, tests were run to determine whether security prices had already adjusted to news such as earnings, stock splits, and changes in the Federal Reserve discount rate. In nearly every instance the shares of those companies affected by the changes had discounted the news before it became publicly available. Although there is less support for the semistrong form than for the weak form, the evidence that has been gathered tends to support the semistrong form.

The strong form of the hypothesis contends that security prices reflect all information, even if it is not publicly available. In other words, an investor cannot expect to earn higher-than-normal returns by using all available public information nor can he expect to earn higher returns by having access to "inside" information. This hypothesis is even more difficult to verify than the semistrong form. But it does seem unlikely that the strong form is accurate in the purest sense. If one person or a very small group of individuals is privy to some very significant information, it is likely that they can use their knowledge to achieve significant profits. If we admit that corporate officers and stock exchange specialists (who have supply and demand data for securities) can earn above-average returns, what is the status of other groups that may have access to privileged information? If we assume that professional portfolio managers should be able to acquire a limited amount of information before it becomes public, we can use their performance as a guide to the validity of the strong-form hypothesis.

The performance of mutual funds has been studied over the years. The overwhelming preponderance of evidence suggests that when fund portfolios are adjusted for risk, there is no reason to expect a portfolio manager to achieve an above-average return. In fact, when high portfolio turnover (heavy trading of stocks by a fund) and management fees are taken into account, an individual investing in mutual funds can actually expect a below-average return.

The evidence on the strong form of the efficient market hypothesis shows mixed results. Excluding the hypothesis in its most stringent form, however, the accumulated evidence indicates that security markets are efficient and the adjustment of security prices to intrinsic values is very rapid. As a result, it is doubtful that individuals can expect to earn larger-than-normal returns by using either technical or fundamental analysis. This does not mean that all fundamental analysis is useless (although it does cast doubt on technical analysis). The fundamental concepts of risk, diversification, and taxability are still useful to both individuals and portfolio managers.

ALTERNATIVE INVESTMENTS

In addition to directly purchasing a variable-income security, an investor can often acquire the same security indirectly by purchasing other investment vehicles that are convertible into the primary security. These include options that allow the purchase of common stock at a predetermined price and convertible bonds that can be exchanged for a given number of shares. These securities must be evaluated, in whole or part, on the basis of their common stock equivalents.

Convertible Bonds

Convertible bonds carry the attributes of other forms of corporate debt but in addition are convertible into a predetermined number of shares of the issuing firm's common stock. The timing of the conversion is usually at the bondholder's option, and the privilege generally lasts until the bond's maturity (or until the bond is called by the issuer). The number of shares of stock that can be obtained for each bond generally remains the same until the bond's maturity. In some cases, however, the conversion ratio may change over time. Until the bonds are surrendered, the holder receives periodic interest payments, with the amount depending on the bond's coupon rate and principal value. If the bond is not converted before maturity (because the common shares that can be obtained have a lower market value than the bond), the holder receives the principal while the conversion privilege and all interest payments cease. If the bond is converted, the exchange is irrevocable and the investor cannot decide at some later date to convert the common stock for the bond.

The exchange rate for common stock is generally stated in terms of a conversion price of common shares. For example, if a $1000 bond states a conversion price of $25 per share, the holder could exchange the bond for 40 shares ($1000/$25) of stock. A lower conversion price yields a proportionately greater number of shares. At the time of issue, the coupon rate and conversion price are set so that the conversion price is 10% to 20% above the market price of the stock. The closer the conversion price to the common stock's market price, the lower the coupon rate the bond must carry in order to sell at par value. As the market price of the common stock increases, the market price of the bond also rises. In this example, if the price of the common increases to $40 per share, the bond will sell for at least $1600. In reality, it will probably sell for slightly more than $1600. If the common stock price falls, the bond price will also decline, but to a lesser extent. The reason is that even without the conversion privilege the bond is valuable for its interest and principal payments. If the common stock falls from $20 to $5 per share (a 75% decline), the bond may decline only 10% to 20%, depending on the relationship between its yield to maturity and the yields to maturity of bonds of equal maturity and risk class.

In summary, a convertible bond must be evaluated both for its value as common stock and straight debt. In most cases investors should not purchase a convertible bond unless they would also consider purchasing the same firm's common stock. Similarly, if the investor has decided to purchase common stock, the merits of convertible bonds of the same firm (if available) should be assessed. A limited number of issues of convertible preferred stocks are also available and should be analyzed in the same manner.

Options

Like convertible bonds, **options** allow holders to obtain shares of common stock at a fixed price. However, this is about all these two securities have in common. Options pay no current income, must be accompanied by payments to obtain the stock, and can expire without value. As you may gather, options generally entail considerably more risk than convertible bonds. However, the profit potential is also generally much greater.

Options come in a variety of forms including rights, warrants, employee stock options, and **calls**. In all cases, however, an option gives the owner the right to purchase a specified number of shares of stock at a predetermined price per share until a specified time. A very limited number of perpetual warrants (no expiration date) have been issued. With rights, warrants, and employee stock options, shares are purchased directly from the company and the funds are used to acquire productive assets. Rights are utilized in new stock offerings to existing owners, while warrants are generally issued as a part of a bond offering. Once the new bonds and warrants are originally issued as a package, the two can begin trading separately. Stock options issued to employees also provide a limited amount of funds to a corporation when the options are exercised (used to purchase stock), but they are designed primarily as employee incentives.

Calls are somewhat different from the other forms of options because they are not issued by a corporation to raise funds. Rather they are sold by investors to other investors. The purchase of a call allows the holder to buy 100 shares of a specific common stock from the seller at a predetermined price. Calls used to be sold only in the over-the-counter market. However, in 1973 trading began on the Chicago Board Options Exchange and later spread to other organized exchanges. Like other options, calls are considerably riskier than common stock. An investor should not purchase a call without evaluating the short-term prospects of a firm's common stock. The same caution is required before purchasing stock in order to sell calls.

SUMMARY

Common stock represents ownership in a corporation. Common stockholders are allowed to vote for a firm's directors and have a right to the cash flows that remain after all other obligations have been paid. The investment value of common stock is generally evaluated on the basis of fundamental analysis. This method attempts to establish an intrinsic value on the basis of variables such as management, earnings, dividends, and assets. A second method of selecting common stocks is through technical analysis. This relies on variables such as trading volume and past changes in stock prices.

An investment concept that has gained increasing acceptance contends that the security markets are efficient. In other words, a security price already incorporates all information relevant to its valuation. If this is true, attempts to find overvalued and undervalued securities are fruitless.

QUESTIONS

1. List the four important dates in any dividend decision and explain each.

2. What is intrinsic value? Explain how it is determined using fundamental analysis.

3. How is book value calculated, and what are its theoretical implications?

4. How is earnings per share calculated? What methods can be utilized to increase earnings per share?

5. Define capitalization rates and discuss their relationship to intrinsic value.

6. Discuss technical analysis and its relationship to fundamental security analysis.

7. There are two major methods used in technical analysis to record security price data. List them and discuss the usefulness of each.

8. What is a filter and how is it used?

9. Define the efficient market hypothesis and discuss its relevance to security analysis.

10. Define and briefly discuss (a) convertible bonds, (b) options, and (c) calls.

SELECTED REFERENCES

BELLEMORE, DOUGLAS H. and RITCHIE, JOHN C. *Investments: Principles, Practices, and Analyses.* Cincinnati, Ohio: South-Western Publishing Co., 1974. Part 4.

COHEN, JEROME B.; ZINBARG, EDWARD D.; and ZEIKEL, ARTHUR. *Investment Analysis and Portfolio Management.* Homewood, Ill.: Richard D. Irwin, 1977. Part 2.

GRAHAM, BENJAMIN; DODD, DAVID L.; and COTTLE, SIDNEY. *Security Analysis: Principles and Technique.* New York: McGraw-Hill, 1962. Part 4.

LORIE, JAMES H., and HAMILTON, MARY T. *The Stock Market: Theories and Evidence.* Homewood, Ill.: Richard D. Irwin, 1973. Sect. 2.

MALKIEL, BURTON G. *A Random Walk Down Wall Street.* New York: W. W. Norton, 1973.

SMITH, KEITH V., and EITEMAN, DAVID K. *Essentials of Investing.* Homewood, Ill.: Richard D. Irwin, 1974. Chs. 4, 6.

WIDCUS, WILBUR W., and STITZEL, THOMAS E. *Personal Investing.* Homewood, Ill.: Richard D. Irwin, 1976. Chs. 6, 10.

WILLIAMS, EDWARD E., and FINDLAY, M. CHAPMAN, III. *Investment Analysis.* Englewood Cliffs, N.J.: Prentice-Hall, 1974. Chs. 9–14.

14   Portfolio Analysis

*A shady stockbroker persuaded
a sucker to buy 5,000 shares of a phony uranium
stock and a week later phoned his victim,
"You're lucky! The stock doubled in price."
"Buy me another 5,000 shares,"
said the customer.
Several days later the broker
phoned again and said the stock had just hit
$3 per share.
"That's high enough for me,"
said the customer. "Sell all I've got."
"Sell?" asked the broker. "Sell
to whom?"*

In previous chapters we have looked at ways of analyzing fixed- and variable-income securities. We have discussed methods of calculating the expected return and risk of a security. However, individual investments cannot be considered in isolation; they must be evaluated on the basis of other investments already in the portfolio. A single security with a given risk and expected return may produce one result when incorporated into Mr. Woelfel's portfolio and an entirely different result when combined with the investments in Ms. Vernon's portfolio. **Portfolio theory** is concerned with evaluating the risk and expected return of investment combinations rather than individual investments. Through this analysis we can also observe the incremental effect of adding a single investment to an existing combination of investments.

Too often investors ignore the fundamental concepts of diversification and portfolio theory. Not only may they weight a portfolio too heavily with a single security, but they may also add a security based only on an evaluation of that particular security rather than on its overall effect on the entire portfolio. They may do so for a number of reasons. An investor may become enthralled with the risk-return trade-off of one particular security without even considering how it fits into the existing portfolio. On the other hand, a few securities may appreciate greatly in value and overwhelm the total value of other securities in the portfolio. In other words, while proper diversification may have once existed, the shifting values of individual securities require constant supervision of the portfolio. To observe how individual investments can be combined into an "efficient" combination, we will devote the remainder of this chapter to a discussion of portfolio analysis.

INVESTMENT OBJECTIVES

The first step in developing a portfolio is defining the objectives that are to be met. Many investors never take this step, and many of those who do select investments that are inconsistent with their stated objectives.

Factors Affecting Investment Objectives

If most individuals were asked to state their investment goals, they would probably say something like "the maximum possible return and preservation of capital." While the combination of these two goals is undoubtedly desirable, financial theory tells us that it is impossible to achieve both maximum return and minimum risk with the same investment. High expected rates of return go hand-in-hand with investments carrying high degrees of risk. We will cover the trade-off between expected return and safety in more detail later in this chapter, but investors must have a knowledge of the relationship before establishing their goals. High-risk securities might be appropriate for some investors, but not for others. On the other hand, nearly all investors want to earn high rates of return.

The objectives that an investor's portfolio is to meet depend on a number of variables. An individual's income, family status, risk preference, and job security are some of the more important factors affecting the objectives. For example, a single person with no dependents can accept greater risks in the pursuits of high rates of return than a married person with four young children. Likewise, a retired couple has different investment objectives from a middle-aged couple in a high marginal income tax bracket. In short, before constructing a portfolio, an investor must define the investment objectives appropriate for his or her circumstances.

The Investor's Life Cycle

Perhaps the most inclusive factor affecting portfolio objectives is an investor's stage in the life cycle. Income, expenditures, and financial needs vary for any family as the years pass. The variation of these factors, depending on an individual's stage in life, is known as life cycle variation.

The first stage in the life cycle begins on leaving school and pursuing a full-time career. During this period an individual may repay college debts, acquire durable goods such as an automobile and furniture, purchase life insurance, or incur a large mortgage by purchasing a home. Although every person does not necessarily undertake all these transactions, the main idea is that individuals in the early stages of life have a small amount of money to devote to an investment program. In fact, a young couple with children may have expenditures in excess of their income. If only a small amount of saving can take place, it should be kept in a highly liquid form, usually an investment offering a low rate of return such as a savings account.

A single individual in the early stage of the life cycle is in a somewhat different situation. With no dependents, this individual has fewer expenses and can approach an investment program with less concern about safety. Even this individual must first establish a highly liquid emergency fund. Subsequent investments can then give priority to higher-risk, higher-return possibilities.

As people move into middle age, their investment objectives change. During this period people generally have higher income and can devote a greater proportion of income to savings. Many debts acquired earlier in life (college, home) have been significantly reduced, and finally responsibilities are reasonably well provided for. Because their tax rate is relatively high and their need for current income reduced, this age group may be expected to concentrate its attention on investments that are expected to produce growth of principal or capital appreciation. They may choose real estate and growth or speculative securities, for example. The emphasis on growth reflects the investor's tax position and ability to absorb a greater degree of risk in seeking higher rates of return.

The latter stages of the life cycle concentrate on providing for retirement. An individual has probably repaid nearly all large debt commitments and is free of most family obligations. Both income and expenditures generally decline during the retirement period, and a need for growth of principal is replaced by the need to provide income to replace lost earnings. Thus individuals begin switching from speculative and growth investments to those providing high current income. Since retired individuals may be required to spend a portion of principal in addition to current income, they also seek greater liquidity. A major part of the decision making at this stage of life is strongly affected by the income tax consequences of earlier investment choices and the individual's goals for estate purposes. (Unfortunately, estate planning is so complicated that it is beyond the scope of this text.)

In summary, the objectives of an investment portfolio must be defined as a first step in approaching a proper risk-return relationship. Selecting securities at random by throwing darts at the financial page is a poor method of achieving the desired goals. The remaining portion of this chapter concentrates on estimating the two important variables risk and return. Using these ideas, investors should be able to select portfolios that meet their investment objectives.

EFFICIENT INVESTMENTS

In an earlier chapter we discussed the concepts of risk and return for a single investment. We will now evaluate these same concepts for multiple investments.

Two-Asset Analysis

While expected return is calculated in approximately the same manner in the two-asset case as in the single-asset case, the calculation of risk is somewhat more complicated because variations in one security may partially offset variations in another security. This difference is important because it means that diversification can be used to reduce risk. We mentioned earlier that the majority of investors are averse to risk. Thus an understanding of the relationship between diversification and risk reduction helps the investor in portfolio construction.

As an illustration of two-asset diversification, suppose we place equal amounts of money in each of two securities. If the prices of the two securities always move in the same direction by exactly the same proportion, we do not reduce the standard deviation (a measure of risk) of the return on our portfolio. In other words, the standard deviation of the return of our combined securities is the same as the standard deviation of the return of either of the two securities taken individually.

If we invest in two securities whose prices move in opposite directions by exactly the same proportion, we find that the variations of the two securities cancel each other and the standard deviation of our portfolio's return is zero. An increase in the price of one security exactly offsets a decline in the price of the other security. Each of these examples is illustrated in fig. 14–1.

The relationship between the price changes of the two securities is termed **covariance**. If the price movements are of similar proportion and direction (as in case 1), the two securities are said to have a high degree

Case I: Price Movements in Same Direction

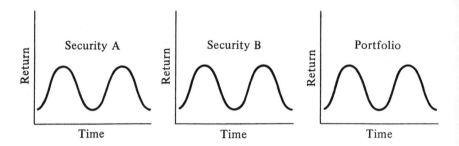

Case II: Price Movements in Opposite Directions

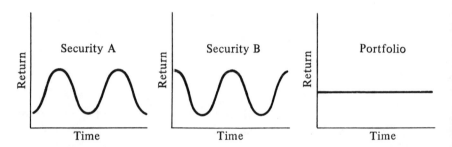

FIGURE 14–1 Variations in Portfolio Return as Compared to Variations in the Returns of Securities in the Portfolio

of positive covariance. If the price movements are of similar proportion but opposite direction (case 2), the securities have a high degree of negative covariance.

Although few if any securities change in price exactly as we have shown in fig. 14–1, the implications of covariance are important for understanding portfolio construction. If the investor selects two securities that do not have a high degree of positive covariance, the variation in the return of the portfolio is reduced. For example, if the common stocks of two steel companies make up the portfolio, the variations of the prices of the securities will be similar and variations of returns from the portfolio will be relatively large. On the other hand, if the common stock of a steel company is combined with the security of a household products company, variations of returns from the portfolio will be reduced.

The formula for calculating the risk (standard deviation) of a two-asset portfolio is somewhat complicated. For those who are mathematically inclined (and to show that it is possible), we include eq. 14–1.

$$\sigma_p = \sqrt{x_a\sigma_a + x_b\sigma_b + 2x_ax_b\sigma_{ab}} \qquad\qquad \textbf{14-1}$$

where

σ_p = standard deviation of expected portfolio returns

x_a, x_b = percent of funds invested in assets a and b

σ_a, σ_b = standard deviations of expected returns from assets a and b

σ_{ab} = covariance between the returns from assets a and b

In other words, the risk of a two-asset portfolio depends on the proportion of funds devoted to each asset, the variability of the returns of each asset, and the relationship between the price changes (covariance) of the two assets.

Calculating the expected return from a portfolio is relatively simple; the return from a portfolio depends on the expected return from each asset and the proportion of total funds devoted to each asset. The formula for the calculation is

$$E(r_p) = x_aE(r_a) + x_bE(r_b) \qquad\qquad \textbf{14-2}$$

where

$E(r_p)$ = expected return from the portfolio

x_a, x_b = proportion of funds devoted to assets a and b

$E(r_a), E(r_b)$ = expected returns from assets a and b

For example, if we devote 40% of our funds to an asset that is expected to return 10% annually and the remaining 60% of our funds to an asset that is expected to return 14% annually, our portfolio's expected return is $(.40)(.10) + (.60)(.14) = .124$, or 12.4%. Although we have computed the expected return for a two-asset portfolio, the expected return from a portfolio having any number of assets can be found using a similar calculation.

Choosing an Efficient Portfolio

The complexity of calculating the risk and expected return of a portfolio consisting of two predetermined assets can give you some insight into what occurs when individual assets number in the thousands and when combinations are increased to include any number of the individual assets. Even with these numerous possibilities, we must specify the proportion of funds to be allocated to each asset in each combination if we expect to choose the best possible combinations.

Assuming the expected return and risk have been calculated for each asset combination, we might plot the results on a graph such as that illustrated in fig. 14–2. Each point represents one portfolio as determined by its respective risk and return calculation. A portfolio's expected rate of return is measured on the vertical axis, and risk is scaled on the horizontal axis.

If investors are averse to risk, they will choose to maximize return at a given level of risk and minimize risk at a given rate of return. Applying these preferences to fig. 14–2, we find that portfolio C is more desirable than portfolio D (a higher return at the same level of risk) and portfolio A is more desirable than portfolio B (a lower level of risk with the same rate of return). We cannot definitely say that portfolio A is superior to portfolio C or that C is more desirable than A. Portfolio C promises a greater expected return, but it also involves a greater degree of risk. On the other hand, while portfolio A provides a lower level of risk it also promises a lower expected rate of return. We can say, however, that superior portfolios are located in the upper-left quadrant. In this quadrant we find portfolios that minimize risk at a given return and maximize return for a given level of risk. Even within the upper-left quadrant some portfolios are superior to others. Figure 14–3 illustrates a limited number of portfolios within the quadrant.

A superior or efficient portfolio is located on the perimeter of all portfolios within the quadrant. For this reason the perimeter is termed the efficient frontier. For example, portfolio A is superior to portfolio C because the former provides a lower level of risk at the same expected rate of return. Likewise, portfolio B is superior to portfolio C because B will give the investor a higher rate of return even though the variability of returns (risk) from holding each portfolio is the same. While this analysis compares only three portfolios within the quadrant, we could illustrate other portfolios that achieve the same result. In other words, portfolios located under the efficient frontier are inferior or less efficient than those that lie on the frontier.

Choosing between portfolios that lie on the frontier depends on the investor's risk preference. The individual unwilling to assume a high degree of risk in search of a higher expected return prefers portfolio A to portfolio B even though both are efficient. Conversely, for an investor willing to assume greater risk, portfolio B would be more desirable. Portfolio B is probably not highly diversified, which partially accounts for the high risk and high expected return.

This framework for contemporary portfolio theory was developed by Dr. Harry Markowitz in the 1950s. Two of Markowitz' main tenets—that

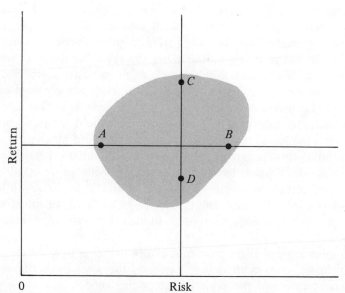

FIGURE 14-2   Risk and Return of Portfolio Opportunities

investors are averse to risk and that securities must be selected on the basis of those already in the investor's portfolio—are basic assumptions in the determination of the efficient frontier.

Critics of the Markowitz theoretical approach address themselves to

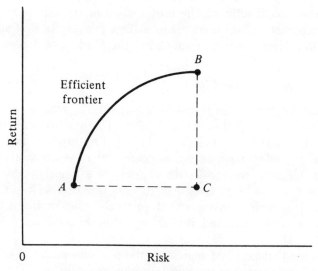

FIGURE 14-3   The Efficient Frontier

his concept of risk. They argue that a security's price volatility may not be an appropriate measure of risk for all investors. For example, an investor with a projected long holding period might consider the short-term volatility of returns relatively unimportant. On the other hand, an investor concerned with short-term holding periods might consider short-term volatility of returns as very important. Another criticism has centered on the assumption that investors are averse to the Markowitz definition of risk. Is it not possible, for example, that some investors would prefer a portfolio with a large variance of returns even though they could purchase a different portfolio of smaller variance that provided the same expected return? As an illustration, suppose two portfolios each provide an expected return of 12%. The returns of portfolio A vary from 2% to 20%, while the returns of portfolio B range from 10% to 14%. Some investors might prefer the chance for a 20% return even though they also risk an extremely low return.

To solve some of these problems, additional ideas were developed on portfolio theory. One methodology based on the work by Markowitz includes a concept called the capital asset pricing model.

CAPITAL ASSET PRICING THEORY

Using the Markowitz view of portfolio construction, an investor adjusts for risk preferences by moving along the efficient frontier. Moving clockwise leads to portfolios offering greater risk and greater expected return, and moving counterclockwise leads to portfolios with less variability and lower expected returns. The introduction of an additional variable—the risk-free asset—allows investors to make a different type of adjustment in order to achieve the same results as in the Markowitz framework.

The Capital Market Line

Since we have defined risk as a variance of returns, the risk-free asset must have negligible price variability. The asset typically used as a proxy for this variable is a Treasury bill. A Treasury bill fluctuates very little in price, and its repayment is as nearly certain as any available investment. In addition, trading in these assets is extremely active so that liquidity is not a problem. How does this risk-free asset fit into the capital asset pricing model? Suppose we return to the efficient frontier of portfolios. Figure 14–4 illustrates the efficient frontier combined with a risk-free asset.

Assume that point M represents the portfolio made up of all available securities weighted in proportion to the availabilities of the securities. In other words, it is the weighted average of all securities available in the

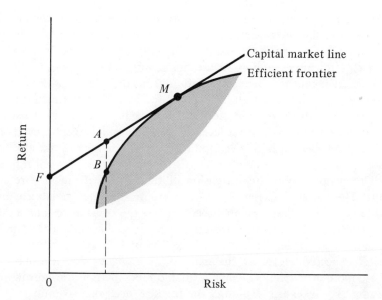

FIGURE 14-4 The Efficient Frontier and Capital Market Line

market. Although such a portfolio is not available, we can use securities represented by one of the popular averages such as the New York Stock Exchange Index or Standard & Poor's 500 stock average as a proxy. This portfolio represents the ultimate diversification. This does not mean that portfolio M is necessarily the optimal portfolio for all investors. The optimal combination of securities depends on an individual's risk preference.

The return on the risk-free asset is represented by point F on the graph. Once determined, this return can be combined with the return of a portfolio that lies on the efficient frontier to form a combination portfolio (a combination of the risk-free asset and the market portfolio). In fact, unless the investor prefers the risk and return level of portfolio M, he can improve his results by employing the combined portfolios represented by the capital market line. For example, by purchasing the risk-free asset and portfolio M in the proper proportions, the investor can achieve the risk-return represented by point A. This portfolio is superior to portfolio B on the efficient frontier since it provides a greater return at the same level of risk.

Movement along the capital market line is achieved by purchasing the portfolio represented by point M in combination with lending or borrowing at the risk-free rate. We have mentioned that the investor purchases both the risk-free asset and portfolio M in order to achieve the result indicated by point A. Since the risk-free asset has been defined as United States Treasury bills, the purchase is effectively the same as lending. Any combination to the right of portfolio M requires borrowing. In the latter case, the investor might purchase a portion of portfolio M on margin and pay cash for the remainder. Moving away from portfolio M to the left requires more lending, to the right more borrowing.

Introducing a risk-free asset into our analysis establishes a new efficient frontier. The new frontier, represented by the capital market line, is more efficient than the old frontier because it offers portfolios with higher expected returns at each level of risk. The only exception is portfolio M, which lies on both the capital market line and the old efficient frontier.

The advantages of this extension of the Markowitz model are significant. The investor no longer has to compute the price variability and expected return of every available security and the covariances among all these securities. The investor is required only to purchase the market portfolio and borrow or lend against it. Investors preferring a portfolio with a greater expected return at the expense of a higher risk level simply purchase more of portfolio M than available funds permit and borrow the remainder. To lower risk exposure, the investor need only commit a portion of funds to portfolio M and the remainder to Treasury bills.

Two problems might come to mind at this point. One is that while investors can lend at the risk-free rate, they cannot generally borrow at this same rate. Even buying securities on margin requires paying a rate above the prime interest rate. Another difficulty is that investors seldom have the funds to acquire a portfolio such as that represented by point M. In an earlier discussion we mentioned that an alternative to the market portfolio is a proxy such as one of the popular stock averages. The acquisition of one of these portfolios, however, would present an individual with practical difficulties. As we shall see later, this problem can be partially rectified.

Differences between the lending and borrowing rates can be accounted for by an adjustment to fig. 14–4. If investors must pay more for borrowed funds than they can obtain on funds that are loaned, we must use two risk-free rates in the analysis. Figure 14–5 illustrates the use of two capital market lines, each tangent to the efficient frontier.

The risk-free lending rate is represented by F_1, while the rate at which an investor may borrow funds is represented by F_b. The relevant alternatives for the investor lie on CPL_1 to the left of M and on CPL_b to the right of M'. Between M and M' the possible portfolios lie on the old efficient frontier.

While the introduction of different lending and borrowing rates complicates the analysis somewhat, it does not negate the theoretical foundation. Now we will see how the theory can be simplified and put into practical application.

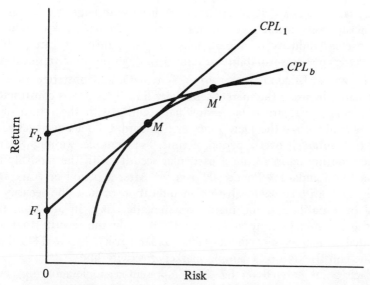

FIGURE 14–5 Efficient Portfolios with Different Lending and Borrowing Rates

Utilizing Capital Asset Pricing Theory

If we substitute a readily available stock price index for the market portfolio in the capital asset pricing model, we can compare individual securities by using a common benchmark. In other words, instead of comparing securities through covariances, we can compare individual securities by relating them to the average being utilized as a proxy for the market portfolio.

SYSTEMATIC AND UNSYSTEMATIC RISK We can compare risk among various securities by dividing total risk into two components, systematic and unsystematic risk. As we mentioned in chapter 12, systematic risk is the part of total risk caused by factors affecting all securities. For example, rising interest rates tend to drive down the prices of all securities. Thus all security holders face the possibility that interest rates will rise. Since systematic risk affects all securities to some extent, it is not possible to protect against it by diversifying the portfolio. That is, an investor purchasing a large number of different securities in various industries is still subject to a systematic variability of returns. Even though investors cannot eliminate systematic risk by diversifying, they can partially control the amount of this risk through proper portfolio selection.

Unsystematic risk is the remaining portion of total risk. The variability of returns attributable to unsystematic risk is due to factors unique to a specific asset. For example, the possibility of fluctuations in currency exchange rates is a risk that affects primarily firms with large asset holdings or product markets in foreign countries. Since unsystematic risk is peculiar to a particular industry or a particular company, investors can protect themselves against this variability of returns through proper diversification.

MEASURING MARKET SENSITIVITY   Systematic and unsystematic risk are calculated by using the **market-sensitivity line**. This line is constructed by comparing the return of an individual security with the return of a market portfolio (like the Dow Jones or Standard & Poor's averages) for various time intervals over a period of time. For example, we might compare the monthly returns from a particular security with the monthly returns on the Standard & Poor's 500 average. After a period of years, the monthly comparisons would give us an indication of how the security is affected by variations in the market (systematic risk). In addition, the comparisons would indicate variations of returns in the security that are not related to market movements (unsystematic risk). Figure 14–6 illustrates the construction of a sample market-sensitivity line.

Each point entered on fig. 14–6 represent a single monthly comparison of the return from holding the security with the return on the Standard & Poor's average. Once we have collected a sufficient number of monthly data points, we can begin to see a relationship between the two returns. If the returns are related in a positive manner (which is usually the case), the data points form a band running from the lower left to the upper right portion of the graph. The tighter the band, the closer the relationship between the two returns.

The market-sensitivity line is a least squares regression line drawn through the monthly data points. That is, it is a straight line drawn through the plotted points so that the sum of the squares of the vertical deviations from the line is minimized. Although this definition is somewhat cumbersome, actual construction of the line is not particularly difficult; the methodology can be found in any introductory statistics book. The idea to remember is that the line is drawn to minimize the total squared vertical distances between the line and the data points.

We are interested in three relationships illustrated by the market-sensitivity line: the slope, the intercept of the vertical axis, and the deviations of the plotted points from the line. Each of these variables has important implications for the investor.

BETA   The slope of the market-sensitivity line is a security's beta. The slope is the amount of vertical change for each unit of horizontal increase and thus shows the change in a security's return that can be expected from a given change in the market. The greater the slope of the line (beta), the larger the proportionate change in the price of a security for a given change in the market. For example, a slope or beta of 1.0 means that on average a given market change is accompanied by an equal proportionate change (in the same direction) in the price of the security.

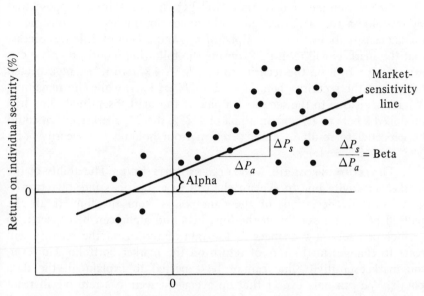

Return on Standard & Poor's Average (%)

Figure 14–6   The Market-Sensitivity Line

A beta of 2.0 indicates that a 10% change in the market return is accompanied on average by a 20% change in return from holding the security. Conversely, a less steep market-sensitivity line (beta less than one) indicates that the price of a security changes proportionately less than the market.

What this means is that a security with a high beta (greater than one) is a more aggressive asset than a security with a low beta (less than one). High-beta securities can be expected to exhibit greater proportionate price changes than low-beta securities. This does not mean they are necessarily superior since market declines are accompanied by even greater proportionate declines in the prices of high-beta securities. The high volatility of securities with betas greater than one may be desirable for some investors. On the other hand, more conservative investors may prefer portfolios composed mostly of low-beta securities.

ALPHA   Alpha is the point where the market-sensitivity line crosses the vertical axis. In other words, alpha is the return a security can be expected to earn, on average, when the market return is zero. Alpha may be positive, zero, or negative, depending on the security being examined. A security with a negative alpha would be expected to produce a return of less than zero during a period when the market return is zero. Although some securities may also possess negative betas (a downward sloping market-sensitivity line), these are very rare.

As an example of how alpha and beta are combined, suppose that we examine a security's past monthly price movements and construct a market-sensitivity line with an alpha of 3% and a beta of 2. If we forecast that the markets will return 2% during the following month, then we can expect the return on the security to be 7%. A 4% return can be expected because of the security's beta of 2 ($2 \times 2\% = 4\%$), while the remaining 3% return is due to the security's alpha. If the market-sensitivity line had produced a beta of 1.7 and an alpha of -2%, the 2% market return could be expected to result in a 1.4% return from holding the security [(1.7 $\times 2\%) - 2\% = 1.4\%$].

DEVIATIONS FROM THE MARKET-SENSITIVITY LINE   The ability of the market-sensitivity line to explain changes in a security's rate of return is determined by deviations of the data points from the line. If all the plotted points are exactly on the line, beta and alpha can be expected to predict precisely how changes in the rate of return on the security will react to changes in the rate of return on the market portfolio. However, the market-sensitivity line cannot be expected to explain all the data points. We can only expect that on average a security's return will react as the beta and alpha tell us it should react.

While the line explains changes in return induced by the market, deviations from the line are the result of factors unique to the firm or the industry. In other words, deviations from the market sensitivity line are a measure of unsystematic risk. If we analyzed the monthly returns from holding a security over a relatively long period of time and found they were perfectly correlated to returns from holding a market portfolio, there would be no deviations from the market-sensitivity line and thus no unsystematic risk. There is some debate as to whether alpha is a measure of unsystematic risk (in addition to deviations from the market-sensitivity line). In earlier formulations of the model, alpha was used to explain part of unsystematic risk, but this interpretation has been disputed by some students of the subject.

Risk and Portfolio Construction

This analysis of betas, alphas, market portfolios, and other variables may seem to offer little practical help in constructing an efficient portfolio. But things are not so bad as they might seem. The concepts are actually not difficult to put into practice.

Combining different securities in a portfolio tends to eliminate the unsystematic portion of total risk. Thus proper diversification can protect an investor from variations of returns unique to a particular firm or industry. Concentrating funds in a single industry, even though the portfolio includes securities in a number of different firms within the industry, cannot be expected to eliminate all unsystematic risk. For example, purchasing only securities issued by airlines or by electric utilities does not eliminate unsystematic risk, because each firm within the industries is subject to similar risks. Including securities issued by both industries in the same portfolio would improve diversification.

In addition to diversifying away the portion of risk attributable to deviations from the market-sensitivity line, the investor can also eliminate the effect of alphas. A diversified portfolio includes a sufficient number of assets that positive alphas of some securities are offset by negative alphas of other securities. The result is that the alpha of the entire portfolio tends to be eliminated.

If unsystematic risk is eliminated in a diversified portfolio, what happens to systematic risk? Even though systematic risk cannot be completely eliminated, it can be controlled through individual security selections. An individual desiring a volatile portfolio should purchase securities with high betas; a more conservative investor should concentrate on securities with low betas.

The market sensitivity of an entire portfolio is calculated by weighting the betas of each security by the proportion of funds committed to that security. Suppose that an investor purchases the seven securities listed in table 14–1. The weighted betas are calculated by multiplying each security's beta by the percentage of total funds invested in the respective security. The portfolio beta is the sum of the individual weighted betas.

The individual securities, when combined, result in a portfolio beta of .998. Thus we can expect the return on our portfolio to approximate the market's return. If the investor reallocated funds in the portfolio toward securities with high betas (A, D, or F), the portfolio beta would increase.

Computing betas of all the securities we might consider including in a portfolio would, in itself, be a formidable task. Fortunately, beta computations are available from a number of different sources including

TABLE 14–1   Security and Portfolio Betas

Security	Funds Invested	Percentage of Total Funds	Security Beta	Weighted Beta
A	$10,000	20	1.25	.200
B	6,000	12	.80	.096
C	12,000	24	1.00	.240
D	5,000	10	1.35	.135
E	5,000	10	.95	.095
F	4,000	8	1.10	.088
G	8,000	16	.90	.144
Total	$50,000	100		.998

the Value Line Investment Survey and Merrill Lynch, Pierce, Fenner, and Smith. These services do not all calculate betas in the same manner; thus different services may publish different betas for the same security.

SUMMARY

A security should be evaluated on the basis of other securities that are already owned. Combinations of stocks and bonds that provide superior investment results (risk and return) are said to be efficient portfolios, and which combination the investor chooses is determined by risk preference. As a general rule, an investor who is willing to accept a higher degree of risk can expect a greater return.

There are two broad categories of risk. Systematic risk is caused by factors that affect all securities, and unsystematic risk is due to variables unique to a specific asset. Systematic and unsystematic risk are calculated by using a market-sensitivity line.

QUESTIONS

1. Why must individual investments be evaluated on the basis of other investments already in the portfolio?

2. Discuss and explain the basic tenets of portfolio theory.

3. Is it possible to achieve both maximum return and minimum risk with the same investment? If not, why?

4. What are some of the factors that may affect investment objectives?

5. What is meant by an investor's life cycle, and how do investment objectives change over this life cycle?

6. How might diversification be used to reduce risk? Would this involve selection of securities with a high degree of positive or negative covariance?

7. What three factors affect the risk of a two-asset portfolio?

8. On what variables does the expected return from a portfolio depend?

9. In fig. 14–2 why are the superior portfolios located in the upper left quadrant?

10. What is meant by the efficient frontier, and what determines the choice between portfolios that lie on the frontier?

11. Why is the new frontier established by the capital market line more efficient than the old frontier?

12. What does the slope of the market-sensitivity line tell you about a proportionate change in the price of a security for a given change in the market?

SELECTED REFERENCES

COHEN, JEROME B.; ZINBARG, EDWARD D.; and ZEIKEL, ARTHUR. *Investment Analysis and Portfolio Management*. Homewood, Ill.: Richard D. Irwin, 1977. Part 4.

FISCHER, DONALD E., and JORDAN, RONALD J. *Security Analysis and Portfolio Management*. Englewood Cliffs, N.J.: Prentice-Hall, 1975. Part 6.

FRANCIS, JACK CLARK. *Investments: Analysis and Management*. New York: McGraw-Hill, 1976. Part 5.

LATANÉ, HENRY A.; TUTTLE, DONALD L.; and JONES, CHARLES P. *Security Analysis and Portfolio Management*. New York: Ronald Press, 1975. Part 4.

LORIE, JAMES H., and HAMILTON, MARY T. *The Stock Market: Theories and Evidence*. Homewood, Ill.: Richard D. Irwin, 1973. Sect. 3.

WILLIAMS, EDWARD E., and FINDLAY, M. CHAPMAN, III. *Investment Analysis*. Englewood Cliffs, N.J.: Prentice-Hall, 1974. Sect. 3.

15 Investments: Making Decisions Within the Financial and Economic Systems

The fellow who jumped to his death from the twentieth floor was a man who was always getting in on the ground floor.

THE INVESTOR: MAN ON THE OUTSIDE

The time is right in this final chapter to provide you with a total perspective so that we can tie all the preceding material together into a neat and understandable system. Our intent has been to avoid the idea that finance consists of the separate fields of financial markets and institutions, financial management, and investments. In attempting this, we have tried to demonstrate that the finance discipline should be viewed as a system in which interrelationships exist among these three fields.

In part 1 we demonstrated that the financial system and the economy cannot be considered separate entities. They interact to establish the environment in which financial managers and investors must make decisions. In chapters 6–9 we examined the decisions the chief financial officer of the firm must make and the tools used to make the decisions. Chapter 10 portrayed the financial manager as a man in the middle. That is, the financial manager operates in an environment established by the financial system and the economy. In addition, the financial manager must satisfy outsiders (creditors and owners). To do so, he must be aware of the factors these individuals utilize in evaluating the firm.

In part 3 we have thus far looked at the operations of the securities markets, the techniques commonly used in the analysis of fixed- and variable-income securities, and a system for constructing a portfolio. With this as a background, we can now see where the investor fits into the system.

Given the total perspective, the financial manager is in the middle. However, on an individual basis, the financial manager is on the inside and the investor is on the outside. As such, the investor is critically interested in how successful the financial manager is in making optimal investment, financing, and dividend policy decisions. But this is only part of the picture. Like the financial manager, the investor must operate in the environment established by the financial and economic systems. Corporate securities represent only one avenue for the investor. His options range from real estate to government securities to futures in scotch whiskey. Thus he must be knowledgeable about the available securities and the current status of the money and capital markets.

THE INVESTOR AND THE ECONOMIC AND FINANCIAL SYSTEMS

While the financial manager (as a representative of the firm) is a consumer of money, the investor is a consumer of securities. A series of steps should precede any decision by the investor to purchase securities. The investor's first step should be to determine his investible wealth. This process in itself may reduce the available alternatives. For example, if investible wealth is very small, some securities cannot be considered simply because they are sold in denominations that exceed the total investible wealth. Next the investor must establish the goals or objectives of his portfolio. In other words, how much return is required and how much risk is the investor willing to assume? (Note that the investor can choose to minimize risk or maximize return, but not both.)

The investor can now decide whether to invest at all (or whether to divest). This decision requires that the investor be knowledgeable about the economic and financial systems. Economic conditions are of great importance to the investor for obvious reasons. If the investor is contemplating the purchase of common stock, he should know that the stock market is generally considered a leading economic indicator. That is, stock prices may decline four to six months before the decline in economic activity. Therefore a decision to purchase common stock just prior to a recession might virtually ensure a loss. Similar reasoning applies to corporate bonds, since economic downturns typically diminish the capacity of businesses to repay their debt obligations. In essence, the investor has a vested interest in understanding economic goals and the way the economy functions to attain these goals.

The financial system is also critically important to the investor. In chapter 3, for example, we discussed the factors that determine interest rates. Understanding these factors through either the liquidity preference or loanable funds approach is important in forecasting future trends in interest rates. In chapter 12 we discussed interest rate risk; that is, an inverse relationship exists between interest rates and security prices. Therefore the investor who forecasts a decline in interest rates would be more confident of a decision to purchase securities.

The investor must go beyond understanding the economy and the financial system. He should also recognize that the two are interrelated. As illustrated in chapter 5, the financial and production sectors can be affected by a change in any one component in either sector. In essence, if the investor understands the material in part 1, the probability of making a correct decision will be increased. That decision is whether the investor should be holding securities at all. If no securities are held, should he be buying securities? An equally important part of that decision (and one which many investors and friendly stockbrokers tend to overlook) is whether the investor should be selling his investments if he already has a portfolio.

If the investor decides to invest, the next step is to isolate the types of securities that coincide with the portfolio objectives. Investors, like financial institutions, have different maturity requirements and different attitudes toward risk. Some are risk averters, some are indifferent to risk, and some are risk seekers. A parent with young children is probably a risk averter and thus requires a security with a very low probability of declining in value. The person with a high income might eliminate all the securities available to him except municipal bonds because of the tax-exempt status of the interest income. The elderly person facing retirement is interested in income and might prefer bonds, while a young person might prefer growth stocks that pay no dividends. In short, different investors have different needs. Thus many different types of securities must exist for the institutions seeking funds to compete effectively in the money and capital markets. Having identified his or her needs, the investor must know which options can satisfy those needs. Although our coverage did not include all available options, the investor must become familiar with the various securities such as those covered in chapter 4 on the money and capital markets.

For illustrative purposes, we will assume that our investor has eliminated all alternatives except common stocks. We will also assume that he or she follows the fundamental approach to security analysis. Next our investor should isolate industries that are going to perform favorably in the future. One way to do this is to examine the economic goals. If full employment is expected, how will this affect various industries? While attaining this goal is generally considered a positive factor for all industries, exceptions could exist. For example, if all people able and willing to work have found employment, labor shortages might exist in certain areas. If this occurs, the rate of growth of some industries might be slower than the growth that could have been attained without labor shortages simply because particular types of workers are unavailable. The investor also has an interest in examining the expected rate of economic growth. Other things equal, our investor will want to isolate industries that are going to outperform the economy in general. The individual who decided to invest in an industry with an expected growth rate of 6% might be making a poor decision if the economy is expected to grow at a rate of 9%.

Price stability as an economic goal is also important to the investor. Industries are affected in different ways during a period of inflation. With rising costs, the investor wants to isolate industries that can pass along the costs by increasing prices without eroding their competitive position. This analysis should not ignore the fourth economic goal, maintaining an acceptable balance-of-payments position. In other words, the goals of price stability and an acceptable balance-of-payments position may have to be considered simultaneously with an eye on both domestic and international economic activity. For example, simply increasing prices to cover higher costs may solve the inflation problem. However, the price increases may be so large that substitute products are developed. In addition, the competitive position of the industry relative to producers of the same product in other countries could erode. In either case, the result for the industry could be an absolute decline in revenues.

In addition to analyzing industries in terms of the economy (or production sector), we must also consider the financial sector. For example, the statement is often made that monetary policy discriminates against housing construction; that is, tight money and the accompanying high interest rates have a profound impact on residential construction. If we foresee a credit crunch, we may want to eliminate industries that supply materials for residential construction. In essence, like the decision of whether to invest at all, the choice of industry should be made with an understanding of the material in part 1 on the economic and financial systems.

THE INVESTOR AND THE FIRM

Having singled out industries that are expected to outperform the economy, the investor can isolate companies within each industry that should outperform their competitors. To do so, a substantial part of his or her analysis can be based on the approach taken in part 2. The financial manager and investor presumably share the common interest of maximizing the wealth of the owner through increases in the price of the firm's stock and dividend payments. If the managers of all firms are basically making the same types of decisions, then it is logical for the potential investor to evaluate firms by comparing the results of each decision on a company-by-company basis. As we will see, factors beyond these decisions (some qualitative) are always part of security analysis. However, an analysis of these basic decisions represents a reasonable starting point. As we discussed in part 2, these decisions include investment, financing, and dividend policy. We also indicated that these decisions cannot be made in isolation because they are interrelated. To be consistent, our analysis should reflect this relationship.

The investment decision involves the acquisition of assets, both short-term and long-term, that will presumably contribute to the profitability of the firm. Short-term assets, which include cash, marketable securities, accounts receivable, and inventories, are very important to the operation and profitability of the firm. For example, if the firm has excessive stocks of inventory, it faces high storage costs and the possibility of spoilage or obsolescence. More importantly, excessive inventory could represent an investment yielding a very low or no return. On the other hand, inadequate inventory stocks may result in lost sales and therefore low profitability. The investor has a vested interest in determining how well management is utilizing these assets. To examine this part of the investment decision quantitatively, the investor can employ the activity ratios discussed in chapter 6.

Long-term investments relate to the very heart of the operation of the firm. The firm is investing in plant and equipment that will play a direct part in the output of the firm's product. The process of making investment decisions involves the use of capital budgeting techniques, ranging from the payback method to the internal rate of return, to isolate proposed capital expenditures that will contribute to the profitability of the firm. The investor, in analyzing the types of products and profitability, must recognize that high potential profit is typically accompanied by high risk. He will want to consider the nature of the product in view of projected economic conditions. If the company produces a basic consumer durable, sales might vary considerably with swings in the economy. The investor might then ask whether other products sold by the firm can cushion profitability during downswings in the economy or whether they would intensify swings in profits (and losses). The investor may want to consider the firm's expenditures for pollution control. If the firm will have to spend substantial funds for this type of equipment, can it transform pollutants into marketable products? If not, can the firm pass along these costs in the form of higher prices without eroding its competitive position? These questions are representative of the types an investor should raise when analyzing a particular firm. To look at the past and current ability of the firm to generate a return, the investor can use profitability ratios such as the gross profit margin, net profit margin, and return on total assets. Ratios such as these indicate the past and present performance of the firm. However, the investor is interested in future profits since present and past owners of the firm have already benefited or lost from past operations. Therefore these ratios have value only if they can give the investor insight into the future. Profitability ratios are an indication of bottom line performance. As such, they reflect many decisions made within the firm. Nevertheless, proper investment decisions are critical to the firm's survival and profitability.

In part 2 we indicated that the financial manager is responsible for generating the funds to support the short-term and long-term investments. In general, current assets should be financed with short-term liabilities, while long-term assets should be financed with long-term liabilities. However, there are exceptions to this general rule. Some current assets may be permanent in nature, and prudent finance may very well prescribe long-term financing in this case. The investor should determine whether the firm is matching the life of the assets with the maturity of the financing. The investor is also interested in the amount of debt and more importantly the capacity of the firm to repay its obligations. For example, an obligation of $100 may be a much greater burden to an unemployed individual than $1000 is to one who holds a secure job. The investor is interested in this matching because the firm must service its debt obligations before any funds are available to shareholders. The level of indebtedness can be determined by utilizing ratios such as total debt to total assets or debt to equity. The times-interest-earned ratio provides an indication of the firm's capacity to repay the debt. Liquidity ratios (such as the current and quick ratios) indicate the firm's ability to meet its maturing obligations. An examination of the latter ratios is very important even though an investor, with the exception of periodic dividend payments, presumably has a longer-term financial relationship with the firm. For example, a firm that has a good product line and has made successful long-term investment decisions could still become insolvent because of poor management of its liquidity position.

Since dividends represent one part of the return accruing to the shareholder, the dividend policy of the firm must be examined by the investor. Part of this analysis entails looking at the past performance in terms of the level and stability of dividend payments. Some companies have a policy of paying no dividends and retaining all earnings to permit more rapid growth. A more typical policy is to maintain stable dividends and let the payout ratio (the percentage of earnings paid out in the form of dividends) vary. Because lowering dividends is unpopular, most firms increase dividends only if earnings have increased and are expected to stay at the higher level. Thus the investor would want to look for trends in earnings that indicate a likely increase in future dividends.

In examining the investment, financing, and dividend policy decisions of the firm, we have indicated the financial ratios from chapter 6 that could be utilized. Investors ordinarily investigate the ratios over a number of years to detect favorable or unfavorable trends. In addition, they should compare the ratios of one firm to those of competitors or to industry averages. However, we should emphasize again that the investor is interested in past performance of the firm only to the extent that the past provides some insight into the future.

In addition to the quantitative analysis of the firm, qualitative factors must also be considered. For example, the quality of management is a critical factor. The results indicated in our quantitative analysis provide some indication of the quality of management. However, poor management could produce good results simply because the industry is growing rapidly. At the same time, a high-quality management team could reverse poor financial results caused by poor management in the past. In addition to issues like these, the investor is also interested in questions like the depth of management. If the top officers of the firm are killed in a plane crash, are the other officers of the company capable of moving into the top positions without disrupting the operations of the firm? Does the firm have a research and development program? If it does, what results have accrued from such expenditures in the past and what can be expected in the future? Does the firm have a quality advertising program? If the firm has a history of diversifying, has it acquired other firms and fired high-quality management teams? If the company is regulated, as an electric utility is, what is the regulatory climate (the attitude and quality of the public service commission)?

These issues are intended only as a representative sample of the types of questions that the investor should consider. Many questions can be answered quantitatively by analyzing the financial statements. However, financial statements and other quantitative indicators can provide only so much information about a company. A thorough security analysis must include both a quantitative and qualitative assessment of the firm.

With this part of the analysis complete, the fundamentalist would proceed to employ the valuation techniques presented in part 3. The objective of this part of the process is to establish an intrinsic value for a particular security. In other words, on the basis of the facts that have been uncovered, the investor is attempting to determine a justified value for the security. One approach is to estimate the dividends to be paid over a specified interval of time and the expected price of the security of the end of the time interval. These cash flows are then discounted to the present using the investor's required rate of return to determine the present (intrinsic) value of the security. This value is then compared to the current market price of the security. If the market price is less than the intrinsic value, the security is a candidate for purchase. If the market price is above the intrinsic value, the security should be avoided.

Once the intrinsic values have been established and the securities whose market prices exceed the intrinsic values have been eliminated from consideration, the final step includes portfolio analysis and investment timing. On the basis of the methodology presented in chapter 14, the investor determines which securities should be purchased to maintain the desired risk-return relationship established in the portfolio objectives. At the same time, the investor uses the forecast of conditions in the economy and the financial markets, or technical analysis, to determine when the securities should be purchased. With these final steps, the process is complete.

To summarize, by drawing from the material presented in parts 1, 2, and 3, we have established a framework for making investment decisions. By considering the relationship between the economic and financial systems, analyzing individual firms (through financial statement analysis) from the point of view of decisions made from within the firm by the financial manager, and by employing valuation techniques and portfolio analysis, the investor can determine whether to invest at all, which types of investments to consider, which securities to buy, and when to buy.

THE IMPACT OF THE INVESTOR'S DECISIONS

Thus far in this chapter, our analysis has concentrated on investor decisions that are based on an analysis of the economy, the financial system, and decisions made within the firm by financial managers. We have stressed the interrelationship between the economic and financial sectors and how this interrelationship affects financial managers and investors. The decisions made by financial managers, as well as those made by investors, affect the economic and financial sectors. Within our framework of interrelationships, one void remains. The decisions made by the investor have an impact on all the other participants in the system.

If the investors conclude, for example, that the proper course of action at the current time is not to invest, the impact of their decisions is felt in the economy through alterations in the financial sector and the firm. As the investors (savers) become pessimistic and shy away from investing in securities, the financial sector first feels the impact through a decline in the supply of funds relative to demand. As a result of the interaction between supply and demand, interest rates are forced upward. As security prices decline (due to the pessimism of investors) and interest rates increase, the financial manager reacts because the cost of capital to the firm is now higher. Other things equal, an increase in the cost of capital forces the financial manager to reject some of the proposed capital expenditures that would otherwise have been undertaken. The resulting decline in business investment is reflected in the production (economic) sector by a decline in gross national product. Although our example depicts only one way investors can affect the other sectors, it is a representative sample. With the investor reacting to and having an impact on the other sectors, the system is complete.

QUESTIONS

1. The investor has been called the man on the outside while the financial manager was categorized as the man in the middle. Discuss.

2. Discuss the relationship between the investor and the economic and financial systems (how the investor makes decisions within these systems).

3. In view of your answer to question 2, explain how the fundamental security analyst determines which common stocks to add to a portfolio of securities.

4. Discuss the impact of investor decisions on financial managers and the economic and financial systems.

Appendix:
Present Value Tables

TABLE A Future Value of $1

Years	1%	2%	3%	4%	5%	6%	7%	8%	10%	12%	15%	20%	25%
1	1.0100	1.0200	1.0300	1.0400	1.0500	1.0600	1.0700	1.0800	1.1000	1.1200	1.1500	1.2000	1.2500
2	1.0201	1.0404	1.0609	1.0816	1.1025	1.1236	1.1449	1.1664	1.2100	1.2544	1.3225	1.4400	1.5625
3	1.0303	1.0612	1.0927	1.1249	1.1576	1.1910	1.2250	1.2597	1.3310	1.4049	1.5209	1.7280	1.9531
4	1.0406	1.0824	1.1255	1.1699	1.2155	1.2625	1.3108	1.3605	1.4641	1.5735	1.7490	2.0736	2.4414
5	1.0510	1.1041	1.1593	1.2167	1.2763	1.3382	1.4026	1.4693	1.6105	1.7623	2.0114	2.4883	3.0518
6	1.0615	1.1262	1.1941	1.2653	1.3401	1.4185	1.5007	1.5869	1.7716	1.9738	2.3131	2.9860	3.8147
7	1.0721	1.1487	1.2299	1.3159	1.4071	1.5036	1.6058	1.7138	1.9487	2.2107	2.6600	3.5832	4.7684
8	1.0829	1.1717	1.2668	1.3686	1.4775	1.5938	1.7182	1.8509	2.1436	2.4760	3.0590	4.2998	5.9605
9	1.0937	1.1951	1.3048	1.4233	1.5513	1.6895	1.8385	1.9990	2.3579	2.7731	3.5179	5.1598	7.4506
10	1.1046	1.2190	1.3439	1.4802	1.6289	1.7908	1.9672	2.1589	2.5937	3.1058	4.0456	6.1917	9.3132
11	1.1157	1.2434	1.3842	1.5395	1.7103	1.8983	2.1049	2.3316	2.8531	3.4785	4.6524	7.4301	11.6415
12	1.1268	1.2682	1.4258	1.6010	1.7959	2.0122	2.2522	2.5182	3.1384	3.8960	5.3503	8.9161	14.5519
13	1.1381	1.2936	1.4685	1.6651	1.8856	2.1329	2.4098	2.7196	3.4523	4.3635	6.1528	10.6993	18.1899
14	1.1495	1.3195	1.5126	1.7317	1.9800	2.2609	2.5785	2.9372	3.7975	4.8871	7.0757	12.8392	22.7374
15	1.1610	1.3459	1.5580	1.8009	2.0789	2.3966	2.7590	3.1722	4.1772	5.4736	8.1371	15.4070	28.4217
16	1.1726	1.3728	1.6047	1.8730	2.1829	2.5404	2.9522	3.4259	4.5950	6.1304	9.3576	18.4884	35.5271
17	1.1843	1.4002	1.6528	1.9479	2.2920	2.6928	3.1588	3.7000	5.0545	6.8660	10.7613	22.1861	44.4089
18	1.1961	1.4282	1.7024	2.0258	2.4066	2.8543	3.3799	3.9960	5.5599	7.6900	12.3755	26.6233	55.5112
19	1.2081	1.4568	1.7535	2.1068	2.5270	3.0256	3.6165	4.3157	6.1159	8.6128	14.2318	31.9480	69.3889
20	1.2202	1.4859	1.8061	2.1911	2.6533	3.2071	3.8697	4.6610	6.7275	9.6463	16.3665	38.3376	86.7362
21	1.2324	1.5157	1.8603	2.2788	2.7860	3.3996	4.1406	5.0338	7.4002	10.8038	18.8215	46.0051	108.4202
22	1.2447	1.5460	1.9161	2.3699	2.9253	3.6035	4.4304	5.4365	8.1403	12.1003	21.6447	55.2061	135.5253
23	1.2572	1.5769	1.9736	2.4647	3.0715	3.8197	4.7405	5.8715	8.9543	13.5523	24.8915	66.2474	169.4066
24	1.2697	1.6084	2.0328	2.5633	3.2251	4.0489	5.0724	6.3412	9.8497	15.1786	28.6252	79.4968	211.7582
25	1.2824	1.6406	2.0938	2.6658	3.3864	4.2919	5.4274	6.8485	10.8347	17.0001	32.9190	95.3962	264.6978
26	1.2953	1.6734	2.1566	2.7725	3.5557	4.5494	5.8074	7.3964	11.9182	19.0401	37.8568	114.4755	330.8722
27	1.3082	1.7069	2.2213	2.8834	3.7335	4.8223	6.2139	7.9881	13.1100	21.3249	43.5353	137.3706	413.5903
28	1.3213	1.7410	2.2879	2.9987	3.9201	5.1117	6.6488	8.6271	14.4210	23.8839	50.0656	164.8447	516.9879
29	1.3345	1.7758	2.3566	3.1187	4.1161	5.4184	7.1143	9.3173	15.8631	26.7499	57.5755	197.8136	646.2349
30	1.3478	1.8114	2.4273	3.2434	4.3219	5.7435	7.6123	10.0627	17.4494	29.9599	66.2118	237.3763	807.7936
31	1.3613	1.8476	2.5001	3.3731	4.5380	6.0881	8.1451	10.8677	19.1943	33.5551	76.1435	284.8516	1 009.7420
32	1.3749	1.8845	2.5751	3.5081	4.7649	6.4534	8.7153	11.7371	21.1138	37.5817	87.5651	341.8219	1 262.1774
33	1.3887	1.9222	2.6523	3.6484	5.0032	6.8406	9.3253	12.6760	23.2252	42.0915	100.6998	410.1863	1 577.7218
34	1.4026	1.9607	2.7319	3.7943	5.2533	7.2510	9.9781	13.6901	25.5477	47.1425	115.8048	492.2235	1 972.1523
35	1.4166	1.9999	2.8139	3.9461	5.5160	7.6861	10.6766	14.7853	28.1024	52.7996	133.1755	590.6682	2 465.1903
40	1.4889	2.2080	3.2620	4.8010	7.0400	10.2857	14.9745	21.7245	45.2593	93.0510	267.8635	1 469.7716	7 523.1638
45	1.5648	2.4379	3.7816	5.8412	8.9850	13.7646	21.0025	31.9204	72.8905	163.9876	538.7693	3 657.2620	22 958.8740
50	1.6446	2.6916	4.3839	7.1067	11.4674	18.4202	29.4570	46.9016	117.3909	289.0022	1 083.6574	9 100.4382	70 064.9232

TABLE B Future Value of a $1 Annuity

Years	1%	2%	3%	4%	5%	6%	7%	8%	10%	12%	15%	20%	25%
1	1.000	1.000	1.000	1.000	1.000	1.000	1.000	1.000	1.000	1.000	1.000	1.000	1.000
2	2.010	2.020	2.030	2.040	2.050	2.060	2.070	2.080	2.100	2.120	2.150	2.200	2.250
3	3.030	3.060	3.091	3.122	3.153	3.184	3.215	3.246	3.310	3.374	3.472	3.640	3.813
4	4.060	4.122	4.184	4.246	4.310	4.375	4.440	4.506	4.641	4.779	4.993	5.368	5.766
5	5.101	5.204	5.309	5.416	5.526	5.637	5.751	5.867	6.105	6.353	6.742	7.442	8.207
6	6.152	6.308	6.468	6.633	6.802	6.975	7.153	7.336	7.716	8.115	8.754	9.930	11.259
7	7.214	7.434	7.662	7.898	8.142	8.394	8.654	8.923	9.487	10.089	11.067	12.916	15.073
8	8.286	8.583	8.892	9.214	9.549	9.897	10.260	10.637	11.436	12.300	13.727	16.499	19.842
9	9.369	9.755	10.159	10.583	11.027	11.491	11.978	12.488	13.579	14.776	16.786	20.799	25.802
10	10.462	10.950	11.464	12.006	12.578	13.181	13.816	14.487	15.937	17.549	20.304	25.959	33.253
11	11.567	12.169	12.808	13.486	14.207	14.972	15.784	16.645	18.531	20.655	24.349	32.150	42.566
12	12.683	13.412	14.192	15.026	15.917	16.870	17.888	18.977	21.384	24.133	29.002	39.581	54.208
13	13.809	14.680	15.618	16.627	17.713	18.882	20.141	21.495	24.523	28.029	34.352	48.497	68.760
14	14.947	15.974	17.086	18.292	19.599	21.015	22.550	24.215	27.975	32.393	40.505	59.196	86.949
15	16.097	17.293	18.599	20.024	21.579	23.276	25.129	27.152	31.772	37.280	47.580	72.035	109.687
16	17.258	18.639	20.157	21.825	23.657	25.673	27.888	30.324	35.950	42.753	55.717	87.442	138.109
17	18.430	20.012	21.762	23.698	25.840	28.213	30.840	33.750	40.545	48.884	65.075	105.931	173.636
18	19.615	21.412	23.414	25.645	28.132	30.906	33.999	37.450	45.599	55.750	75.836	128.117	218.045
19	20.811	22.841	25.117	27.671	30.539	33.760	37.379	41.446	51.159	63.440	88.212	154.740	273.556
20	22.019	24.297	26.870	29.778	33.066	36.786	40.995	45.762	57.275	72.052	102.444	186.688	342.945
21	23.239	25.783	28.676	31.969	35.719	39.993	44.865	50.423	64.002	81.699	118.810	225.026	429.681
22	24.472	27.299	30.537	34.248	38.505	43.392	49.006	55.457	71.403	92.503	137.632	271.031	538.101
23	25.716	28.845	32.453	36.618	41.430	46.996	53.436	60.893	79.543	104.603	159.276	326.237	673.626
24	26.973	30.422	34.426	39.083	44.502	50.816	58.177	66.765	88.497	118.155	184.168	392.484	843.033
25	28.243	32.030	36.459	41.646	47.727	54.865	63.249	73.106	98.347	133.334	212.793	471.981	1054.791
26	29.526	33.671	38.553	44.312	51.113	59.156	68.676	79.954	109.182	150.334	245.712	567.377	1319.489
27	30.821	35.344	40.710	47.084	54.669	63.706	74.484	87.351	121.100	169.374	283.569	681.853	1650.361
28	32.129	37.051	42.931	49.968	58.403	68.528	80.698	95.339	134.210	190.699	327.104	819.223	2063.952
29	33.450	38.792	45.219	52.966	62.323	73.640	87.347	103.966	148.631	214.583	377.170	984.068	2580.939
30	34.785	40.568	47.575	56.085	66.439	79.058	94.461	113.283	164.494	241.333	434.745	1181.882	3227.174
31	36.133	42.379	50.003	59.328	70.761	84.802	102.073	123.346	181.943	271.292	500.957	1419.258	4034.968
32	37.494	44.227	52.503	62.701	75.299	90.890	110.218	134.214	201.138	304.847	577.100	1704.109	5044.710
33	38.869	46.112	55.078	66.210	80.064	97.343	118.933	145.951	222.252	342.429	664.666	2045.931	6306.887
34	40.258	48.034	57.730	69.858	85.067	104.184	128.259	158.627	245.477	384.520	765.365	2456.118	7884.609
35	41.660	49.994	60.462	73.652	90.320	111.435	138.237	172.317	271.024	431.663	881.170	2948.341	9856.761
40	48.886	60.402	75.401	95.026	120.800	154.762	199.635	259.057	442.593	767.091	1779.090	7343.858	30088.655
45	56.481	71.893	92.720	121.029	159.700	212.744	285.749	386.506	718.905	1358.230	3585.128	18281.310	91831.496
50	64.463	84.579	112.797	152.667	209.348	290.336	406.529	573.770	1163.909	2400.018	7217.716	45497.191	280255.693

TABLE C Present Value of $1

Years	1%	2%	3%	4%	5%	6%	7%	8%	10%	12%	15%	20%	25%
1	0.9901	0.9804	0.9709	0.9615	0.9524	0.9434	0.9346	0.9259	0.9091	0.8929	0.8696	0.8333	0.8000
2	0.9803	0.9612	0.9426	0.9246	0.9070	0.8900	0.8734	0.8573	0.8264	0.7972	0.7561	0.6944	0.6400
3	0.9706	0.9423	0.9151	0.8890	0.8638	0.8396	0.8163	0.7938	0.7513	0.7118	0.6575	0.5787	0.5120
4	0.9610	0.9238	0.8885	0.8548	0.8227	0.7921	0.7629	0.7350	0.6830	0.6355	0.5718	0.4823	0.4096
5	0.9515	0.9057	0.8626	0.8219	0.7835	0.7473	0.7130	0.6806	0.6209	0.5674	0.4972	0.4019	0.3277
6	0.9420	0.8880	0.8375	0.7903	0.7462	0.7050	0.6663	0.6302	0.5645	0.5066	0.4323	0.3349	0.2621
7	0.9327	0.8706	0.8131	0.7599	0.7107	0.6651	0.6227	0.5835	0.5132	0.4523	0.3759	0.2791	0.2097
8	0.9235	0.8535	0.7894	0.7307	0.6768	0.6274	0.5820	0.5403	0.4665	0.4039	0.3269	0.2326	0.1678
9	0.9143	0.8368	0.7664	0.7026	0.6446	0.5919	0.5439	0.5002	0.4241	0.3606	0.2843	0.1938	0.1342
10	0.9053	0.8203	0.7441	0.6756	0.6139	0.5584	0.5083	0.4632	0.3855	0.3220	0.2472	0.1615	0.1074
11	0.8963	0.8043	0.7224	0.6496	0.5847	0.5268	0.4751	0.4289	0.3505	0.2875	0.2149	0.1346	0.0859
12	0.8874	0.7885	0.7014	0.6246	0.5568	0.4970	0.4440	0.3971	0.3186	0.2567	0.1869	0.1122	0.0687
13	0.8787	0.7730	0.6810	0.6006	0.5303	0.4688	0.4150	0.3677	0.2897	0.2292	0.1625	0.0935	0.0550
14	0.8700	0.7579	0.6611	0.5775	0.5051	0.4423	0.3878	0.3405	0.2633	0.2046	0.1413	0.0779	0.0440
15	0.8613	0.7430	0.6419	0.5553	0.4810	0.4173	0.3624	0.3152	0.2394	0.1827	0.1229	0.0649	0.0352
16	0.8528	0.7284	0.6232	0.5339	0.4581	0.3936	0.3387	0.2919	0.2176	0.1631	0.1069	0.0541	0.0281
17	0.8444	0.7142	0.6050	0.5134	0.4363	0.3714	0.3166	0.2703	0.1978	0.1456	0.0929	0.0451	0.0225
18	0.8360	0.7002	0.5874	0.4936	0.4155	0.3503	0.2959	0.2502	0.1799	0.1300	0.0808	0.0376	0.0180
19	0.8277	0.6864	0.5703	0.4746	0.3957	0.3305	0.2765	0.2317	0.1635	0.1161	0.0703	0.0313	0.0144
20	0.8195	0.6730	0.5537	0.4564	0.3769	0.3118	0.2584	0.2145	0.1486	0.1037	0.0611	0.0261	0.0115
21	0.8114	0.6598	0.5375	0.4388	0.3589	0.2942	0.2415	0.1987	0.1351	0.0926	0.0531	0.0217	0.0092
22	0.8034	0.6468	0.5219	0.4220	0.3418	0.2775	0.2257	0.1839	0.1228	0.0826	0.0462	0.0181	0.0074
23	0.7954	0.6342	0.5067	0.4057	0.3256	0.2618	0.2109	0.1703	0.1117	0.0738	0.0402	0.0151	0.0059
24	0.7876	0.6217	0.4919	0.3901	0.3101	0.2470	0.1971	0.1577	0.1015	0.0659	0.0349	0.0126	0.0047
25	0.7798	0.6095	0.4776	0.3751	0.2953	0.2330	0.1842	0.1460	0.0923	0.0588	0.0304	0.0105	0.0038
26	0.7720	0.5976	0.4637	0.3607	0.2812	0.2198	0.1722	0.1352	0.0839	0.0525	0.0264	0.0087	0.0030
27	0.7644	0.5859	0.4502	0.3468	0.2678	0.2074	0.1609	0.1252	0.0763	0.0469	0.0230	0.0073	0.0024
28	0.7568	0.5744	0.4371	0.3335	0.2551	0.1956	0.1504	0.1159	0.0693	0.0419	0.0200	0.0061	0.0019
29	0.7493	0.5631	0.4243	0.3207	0.2429	0.1846	0.1406	0.1073	0.0630	0.0374	0.0174	0.0051	0.0015
30	0.7419	0.5521	0.4120	0.3083	0.2314	0.1741	0.1314	0.0994	0.0573	0.0334	0.0151	0.0042	0.0012
31	0.7346	0.5412	0.4000	0.2965	0.2204	0.1643	0.1228	0.0920	0.0521	0.0298	0.0131	0.0035	0.0010
32	0.7273	0.5306	0.3883	0.2851	0.2099	0.1550	0.1147	0.0852	0.0474	0.0266	0.0114	0.0029	0.0008
33	0.7201	0.5202	0.3770	0.2741	0.1999	0.1462	0.1072	0.0789	0.0431	0.0238	0.0099	0.0024	0.0006
34	0.7130	0.5100	0.3660	0.2636	0.1904	0.1379	0.1002	0.0730	0.0391	0.0212	0.0086	0.0020	0.0005
35	0.7059	0.5000	0.3554	0.2534	0.1813	0.1301	0.0937	0.0676	0.0356	0.0189	0.0075	0.0017	0.0004
40	0.6717	0.4529	0.3066	0.2083	0.1420	0.0972	0.0668	0.0460	0.0221	0.0107	0.0037	0.0007	0.0001
45	0.6391	0.4102	0.2644	0.1712	0.1113	0.0727	0.0476	0.0313	0.0137	0.0061	0.0019	0.0003	0.0001
50	0.6080	0.3715	0.2281	0.1407	0.0872	0.0543	0.0339	0.0213	0.0085	0.0035	0.0009	0.0001	0.0000

TABLE D Present Value of a $1 Annuity

Years	1%	2%	3%	4%	5%	6%	7%	8%	10%	12%	15%	20%	25%
1	0.990	0.980	0.971	0.962	0.952	0.943	0.935	0.926	0.909	0.893	0.870	0.833	0.800
2	1.970	1.942	1.913	1.886	1.859	1.833	1.808	1.783	1.736	1.690	1.626	1.528	1.440
3	2.941	2.884	2.829	2.775	2.723	2.673	2.624	2.577	2.487	2.402	2.283	2.106	1.952
4	3.902	3.808	3.717	3.630	3.546	3.465	3.387	3.312	3.170	3.037	2.855	2.589	2.362
5	4.853	4.713	4.580	4.452	4.329	4.212	4.100	3.993	3.791	3.605	3.352	2.991	2.689
6	5.795	5.601	5.417	5.242	5.076	4.917	4.767	4.623	4.355	4.111	3.784	3.326	2.951
7	6.728	6.472	6.230	6.002	5.786	5.582	5.389	5.206	4.868	4.564	4.160	3.605	3.161
8	7.652	7.325	7.020	6.733	6.463	6.210	5.971	5.747	5.335	4.968	4.487	3.837	3.329
9	8.566	8.162	7.786	7.435	7.108	6.802	6.515	6.247	5.759	5.328	4.772	4.031	3.463
10	9.471	8.983	8.530	8.111	7.722	7.360	7.024	6.710	6.144	5.650	5.019	4.192	3.571
11	10.368	9.787	9.253	8.760	8.306	7.887	7.499	7.139	6.495	5.938	5.234	4.327	3.656
12	11.255	10.575	9.954	9.385	8.863	8.384	7.943	7.536	6.814	6.194	5.421	4.439	3.725
13	12.134	11.348	10.635	9.986	9.394	8.853	8.358	7.904	7.103	6.424	5.583	4.533	3.780
14	13.004	12.106	11.296	10.563	9.899	9.295	8.745	8.244	7.367	6.628	5.724	4.611	3.824
15	13.865	12.849	11.938	11.118	10.380	9.712	9.108	8.559	7.606	6.811	5.847	4.675	3.859
16	14.718	13.578	12.561	11.652	10.838	10.106	9.447	8.851	7.824	6.974	5.954	4.730	3.887
17	15.562	14.292	13.166	12.166	11.274	10.477	9.763	9.122	8.022	7.120	6.047	4.775	3.910
18	16.398	14.992	13.754	12.659	11.690	10.828	10.059	9.372	8.201	7.250	6.128	4.812	3.928
19	17.226	15.678	14.324	13.134	12.085	11.158	10.336	9.604	8.365	7.366	6.198	4.844	3.942
20	18.046	16.351	14.877	13.590	12.462	11.470	10.594	9.818	8.514	7.469	6.259	4.870	3.954
21	18.857	17.011	15.415	14.029	12.821	11.764	10.836	10.017	8.649	7.562	6.312	4.891	3.963
22	19.660	17.658	15.937	14.451	13.163	12.042	11.061	10.201	8.772	7.645	6.359	4.909	3.970
23	20.456	18.292	16.444	14.857	13.489	12.303	11.272	10.371	8.883	7.718	6.399	4.925	3.976
24	21.243	18.914	16.936	15.247	13.799	12.550	11.469	10.529	8.985	7.784	6.434	4.937	3.981
25	22.023	19.523	17.413	15.622	14.094	12.783	11.654	10.675	9.077	7.843	6.464	4.948	3.985
26	22.795	20.121	17.877	15.983	14.375	13.003	11.826	10.810	9.161	7.896	6.491	4.956	3.988
27	23.560	20.707	18.327	16.330	14.643	13.211	11.987	10.935	9.237	7.943	6.514	4.964	3.990
28	24.316	21.281	18.764	16.663	14.898	13.406	12.137	11.051	9.307	7.984	6.534	4.970	3.992
29	25.066	21.844	19.188	16.984	15.141	13.591	12.278	11.158	9.370	8.022	6.551	4.975	3.994
30	25.808	22.396	19.600	17.292	15.372	13.765	12.409	11.258	9.427	8.055	6.566	4.979	3.995
31	26.542	22.938	20.000	17.588	15.593	13.929	12.532	11.350	9.479	8.085	6.579	4.982	3.996
32	27.270	23.468	20.389	17.874	15.803	14.084	12.647	11.435	9.526	8.112	6.591	4.985	3.997
33	27.990	23.989	20.766	18.148	16.003	14.230	12.754	11.514	9.569	8.135	6.600	4.988	3.997
34	28.703	24.499	21.132	18.411	16.193	14.368	12.854	11.587	9.609	8.157	6.609	4.990	3.998
35	29.409	24.999	21.487	18.665	16.374	14.498	12.948	11.655	9.644	8.176	6.617	4.992	3.998
40	32.835	27.355	23.115	19.793	17.159	15.046	13.332	11.925	9.779	8.244	6.642	4.997	3.999
45	36.095	29.490	24.519	20.720	17.774	15.456	13.606	12.108	9.863	8.283	6.654	4.999	4.000
50	39.196	31.424	25.730	21.482	18.256	15.762	13.801	12.233	9.915	8.305	6.661	4.999	4.000

Glossary

Accrued expenses Expenses of the firm that have been incurred but not paid.

Activity ratio A ratio that demonstrates how effectively the firm is utilizing its resources.

Balance of payments Transactions among countries that give rise to monetary payments.

Balance of trade The difference between the value of a country's imports and exports of goods and services for a specific period of time.

Balance sheet A financial statement taken at a particular point in time that illustrates a firm's assets, creditors' claims, and owners' equity.

Bankers' acceptance A negotiable time draft drawn on a bank by a drawer which orders the bank to pay to the drawer or another party a specified sum of money at a future date.

Book value Assets minus liabilities of the firm.

Break-even analysis An analysis for investigating the relationship among sales, fixed costs, variable costs, and profits.

Call An option that allows the holder to purchase 100 shares of a certain common stock at a specified price on or before a given date.

Call feature A feature that allows an issuer to repurchase its bonds or preferred stock before maturity at a stated price. The call price is set above face value and determined at the time of issue.

Capital budgeting The process that entails the calculation of the risk and rate of return on proposed long-term investment projects. The results are used to rank and select investments.

Capital market Financial markets that exist for the purpose of bringing together lenders and borrowers of long-term investment funds.

Capitalization rate The rate at which the expected flows on an investment must be discounted to determine its present value.

Certificate of deposit A bank receipt given in exchange for a deposit with the bank agreeing to return the amount of the deposit with interest to the receipt holder at a specified date in the future.

Commercial paper   Short-term unsecured promissory notes issued by large corporations.

Commission broker   An agent who executes orders for the purchase or sale of securities on the floor of an organized stock exchange.

Common stock   Securities that represent ownership in a corporation.

Cost of capital   The rate of return that must be earned on investment projects so that the market price of the firm's common stock remains unchanged.

Coupon rate   The stated rate of interest on the par value of a security. This rate is determined at the time of issue and does not change over the life of the security.

Covariance   Correlation between two variables.

Current assets   Assets that can readily be converted into cash or will be consumed within the current period.

Current yield   The return to an investor in the form of dividends or interest payments expressed in terms of the purchase price of the security. The yield is calculated by dividing the annual dividend or interest by the security's current price.

Cyclical unemployment   Unemployment resulting from a decline in the demand for goods and services.

Debenture   A long-term debt instrument backed by the borrower's promise of repayment but not by any specific property.

Declaration date   The date a firm's directors declare a dividend to be paid to the stockholders.

Depreciation   A cost allocation to account for the wear and tear of assets over a period of time.

Direct finance   The purchase of primary securities by savers from investors.

Earnings per share   Book value per share multiplied by the rate of return on common stock equity, or the total earnings available for common stock divided by the number of common shares outstanding.

Economic growth   An increase in a nation's capacity to produce goods and services. It is generally measured by per capita real gross national product.

Efficient market hypothesis   The theory that security prices incorporate all information that is relevant to their valuation.

Eurobond   Debt securities denominated in a currency different from the currency of the country in which the bonds are originally sold.

Eurocurrency   The general term used to denote deposits placed in banks located outside the United States which can be denominated in United States dollars or any other acceptable currency.

Ex ante saving   Planned or intended saving.

Ex-dividend date   The date on which a stock first trades without the right to receive the next dividend payment. This occurs four business days before the stock-of-record date.

Ex post saving   Actual saving.

Excess reserves The amount of funds held by a commercial bank in excess of the reserves required by the Federal Reserve System.

External financing Raising funds outside the corporation by selling securities or borrowing.

Federal funds The excess reserves one commercial bank has available to lend to another commercial bank for a very short period of time.

Financial leverage The proportion of total debt to total assets. Financial leverage involves the use of funds obtained at fixed rates.

Financial risk The risk that results from the use of debt as a source of financing.

First-In, First-Out (FIFO) An inventory costing method where the first goods acquired are also the first ones sold.

Fiscal policy The budgetary policy dealing with government spending, taxing, and borrowing.

Fixed assets Assets that will not be fully consumed within the current period.

Floor broker A member of an organized stock exchange who executes transactions for other members when they are unable to transact the business themselves.

Floor traders Independent stock exchange members who buy and sell securities for their own accounts.

Flotation costs The expense of preparing and selling a security issue.

Frictional unemployment Short-run unemployment that exists when people are either changing jobs or are seeking new jobs. This is caused by factors such as changing consumer demand.

Fundamental analysis A method of selecting securities based on economic concepts such as interest rates, inflation, productivity, and gross national product and on financial considerations such as income statements, balance sheets, and projected earnings per share.

Gross national product Total monetary output of goods and services in the economy during a year.

Income statement A financial statement that matches revenues and expenses over a period of time.

Indenture A contract between a bondholder and the borrowing company which specifies what is expected of the latter with respect to interest payments, repayment of principal, pledged property, and restrictions on dividends.

Indirect finance The channeling of funds from savers to investors by means of financial intermediaries.

Inflation A general increase in the level of prices.

Interest rate risk The risk that an investor's return from owning an asset will be reduced by a rise in interest rates.

Intermediate-term financing Financing with a source of funds in which the maturity ranges from one to ten years.

Internal financing Funds generated within the firm.

Internal rate of return Rate of return earned on an investment, or the discount rate that equates the present value of the stream of net cash inflows with the present value of net cash outflows.

Intrinsic value The value of a security that is justified by the facts and determined by variables such as management, earnings, dividends, and assets.

Investment banker The principal in the sale of new securities that purchases securities from the issuing firm for resale to the public.

Last-In, First-Out (LIFO) An inventory costing method where the last units purchased are the first ones sold.

Liabilities The claims of creditors.

Limit order An order for securities that restricts the execution of a sell order to a minimum price and a purchase order to a maximum price.

Liquidity The financial condition of a firm that enables it to convert its assets into cash very quickly with a minimum risk of loss. This provides an indication of the ability of the firm to meet its maturing obligations.

Long-term financing Funds provided by the sale of common stock, preferred stock, long-term debt, and the use of retained earnings.

Margin purchase The purchase of securities in which the investor pays only a part of the cost and borrows the remainder through a loan arranged by a broker.

Market order An order to purchase or sell a security at the best available price.

Market risk The uncertainty associated with the possible decline in the price of a security because of a general decline in security prices.

Market-sensitivity line The relationship between the return on an individual security and the return on the market.

Money market The market that exists for the purpose of bringing together lenders and borrowers of short-term funds.

Net investment The total monetary output of goods and services in the economy minus allowances for capital consumption and depreciation.

Net present value A method of ranking investment proposals. Calculated by subtracting the present value of the cost of the project from the present value of future cash inflows. If the proposal's NPV is greater than zero, the proposal is acceptable.

Odd-lot dealers Organized exchange members who provide commission brokers with a market in which to execute orders for less than 100 shares.

Odd lotters The term used to denote individuals who buy and sell less than 100 shares of a security.

Operating leverage A concept that indicates (because fixed costs are used in a firm's operation) the change in operating profit that is associated with a change in output.

Option A privilege to buy or sell a specific item at a predetermined price for a given length of time.

Organized exchanges Privately owned institutions designed to facilitate the trading of securities among their members.

Over-the-counter market A market for securities; it consists of dealers throughout the country in which nearly all business is handled over the telephone or through the mail.

Payback The time required for a project to return its investment outlay.

Payment date The date on which a firm sends dividend checks to its owners.

Portfolio theory The evaluation of the risk and expected return of investment combinations with the objective of attaining optimal portfolios.

Preemptive right The privilege of current stockholders to purchase additional new shares of common stock before they can be sold to outsiders.

Preferred stock A class of stock in which the stockholders have priority to dividends and assets over the owners of common stock. Dividends are generally fixed at the time of issue.

Primary securities market The market for the initial sale of securities.

Profitability ratio A ratio that measures profit in relation to either sales or investment.

Purchasing power risk The risk that the real return from owning an asset will be reduced by a rise in the prices of goods and services.

Repurchase agreement The sale of money market instruments with the stipulation that after a specific period of time the original seller will buy back the securities at a predetermined price.

Retained earnings After-tax earnings of a company that are not paid out in dividends.

Return on equity Net profits after taxes divided by owners' equity.

Salvage value The value of an asset at the end of its estimated life.

Saving The part of income not spent for consumption.

Secondary securities market A market that facilitates the transfer of ownership of securities issued at some earlier time.

Secured loans Loans that require the pledging of assets as collateral.

Service-life method of depreciation A method of depreciation based on either the probable operating hours or the units of production expected during an asset's lifetime.

Short sale The sale of a security not owned by the seller made in anticipation of a decline in a security's price.

Short-term financing Obtaining funds requiring repayment within one year.

Specialists Members of an organized securities exchange who undertake the task of making a market in one or more securities. They act as both dealers and brokers.

Standard deviation A measure of the dispersion of a probability distribution, also used as a measure of risk.

Statement of retained earnings A statement summarizing changes in retained earnings from the beginning to the end of a fiscal period.

Stock-of-record date The date on which the corporation examines its books to see who owns the firm's stock and is to receive the dividend.

Stop order An order to purchase a security at a price above or to sell at a price below the current market price.

Straight-line method of depreciation The allocation of an equal amount of depreciation during each year of an asset's life.

Structural unemployment Unemployment due to the lack of demand for labor resulting from changes in technology or changes in the demand for a particular type of product in a particular region.

Systematic risk The risk that is the result of variables affecting the return on all securities.

Tax-anticipation bill An obligation issued by the Treasury in order to attract funds that corporations accumulate for the payment of taxes at a future date. Thus corporations generate a return on their funds and provide the Treasury with a source of funds.

Technical analysis A method of selecting common stocks based on variables such as trading volume and past changes in stock prices.

Term loans An unsecured loan obtained from a financial institution which has a maturity greater than one year.

Trade credit Short-term credit extended by one firm to another resulting from the sale of goods.

Treasury bill A short-term obligation of the United States Treasury backed by the full faith and credit of the United States government, sold at auction at a discount from face value.

Unsecured loans Loans that do not require the pledging of assets as collateral.

Unsystematic risk The part of a security's risk that cannot be eliminated by diversification.

Vehicle currency A currency utilized by two countries to finance trade when the country issuing the currency is not involved in the trade.

Weighted-average cost of capital A weighted average of the components of a company's capital structure.

Yield to maturity The annual rate of return to an investor from holding a bond until its maturity date; it includes both interest payments and appreciation or depreciation in price.

Index